13.99

...ast Essex College
...END

...arvon Road, Southend on Sea. Essex SS2 6LS

PROBLEMS IN FOCUS SERIES

Each volume in the 'Problems in Focus' series is designed to make available to students important new work on key historical problems and periods that they encounter in their courses. Each volume is devoted to a central topic or theme, and the most important aspects of this are dealt with by specially commissioned essays from scholars in the relevant field. The editorial Introduction reviews the problem or period as a whole, and each essay provides an assessment of the particular aspect, pointing out the areas of development and controversy, and indicating where conclusions can be drawn or where further work is necessary. An annotated bibliography serves as a guide for further reading.

TITLES IN PRINT
The Wars of the Roses
   edited by A. J. Pollard
The Mid-Tudor Polity, c. 1540–1560
   edited by Jennifer Loach and Robert Tittler
Church and Society in England: Henry VIII to James I
   edited by Felicity Heal and Rosemary O'Day
The Reign of Elizabeth I
   edited by Christopher Haigh
The Early Stuart Church, 1603–1642
   edited by Kenneth Fincham
Culture and Politics in Early Stuart England
   edited by Kevin Sharpe and Peter Lake
The Origins of the English Civil War
   edited by Conrad Russell
Reactions to the English Civil War, 1642–1649
   edited by John Morrill
Absolutism in the Seventeenth Century
   edited by John Miller
Britain after the Glorious Revolution, 1689–1714
   edited by Geoffrey Holmes
Britain in the Age of Walpole
   edited by Jeremy Black
British Politics and Society from Walpole to Pitt, 1742–1789
   edited by Jeremy Black
Britain and the French Revolution
   edited by H. T. Dickinson
Enlightened Absolutism
   edited by H. M. Scott
Popular Movements, c. 1830–1850
   edited by J. T. Ward
British Imp...
   edited b...

South East Essex College
of Arts & Technology
Southend-on-Sea Essex SS2 6LS
Tel: (01702) 220400 Fax: (01702) 432320 Minicom: (01702) 220642

C/R   X
STL
942.04
WAR

KT-216-108

30130504255115

Later Victorian Britain, 1867–1900
edited by T. R. Gourvish and Alan O'Day
The Revolution in Ireland, 1879–1923
edited by D. G. Boyce
Britain since 1945
edited by T. R. Gourvish and Alan O'Day

FORTHCOMING TITLES
Henry VIII
edited by Diarmaid MacCulloch
The Fashioning of Britain
edited by John Morrill
The Restoration
edited by Lionel Glassey
Slavery and British Society, 1776–1846
edited by James Walvin
Europe's Balance of Power, 1815–1848
edited by Alan Sked

FURTHER TITLES ARE IN PREPARATION

Series Standing Order

If you would like to receive future titles in this series as they are published, you can make use of our standing order facility. To place a standing order please contact your bookseller or, in case of difficulty, write to us at the address below with your name and address and the name of the series. Please state with which title you wish to begin your standing order. (If you live outside the United Kingdom we may not have the rights for your area, in which case we will forward your order to the publisher concerned).

Customer Services Department, Macmillan Distribution Ltd, Houndmills, Basingstoke, Hampshire, RG21 2XS, England.

The Wars of the Roses

EDITED BY
A. J. POLLARD

Introduction and editorial matter © A. J. Pollard 1995
Individual chapters © M. A. Hicks, R. H. Britnell, Keith Dockray, Rosemary Horrox,
John L. Watts, Richard G. Davies, C. S. L. Davies, Colin Richmond 1995

All rights reserved. No reproduction, copy or transmission of
this publication may be made without written permission.

No paragraph of this publication may be reproduced, copied or
transmitted save with written permission or in accordance with
the provisions of the Copyright, Designs and Patents Act 1988,
or under the terms of any licence permitting limited copying
issued by the Copyright Licensing Agency, 90 Tottenham Court
Road, London W1P 9HE.

Any person who does any unauthorised act in relation to this
publication may be liable to criminal prosecution and civil
claims for damages.

First published 1995 by
MACMILLAN PRESS LTD
Houndmills, Basingstoke, Hampshire RG21 2XS
and London
Companies and representatives
throughout the world

ISBN 0–333–60165–3 hardcover
ISBN 0–333–60166–1 paperback

A catalogue record for this book is available
from the British Library

10   9   8   7   6   5   4   3   2   1
04   03   02   01   00   99   98   97   96   95

Printed in Malaysia

In memory of Charles Ross

Contents

viii   CONTENTS

1. Introduction: Society, Politics and the Wars of the Roses

A. J. POLLARD

In the grand sweep, or 'meta-narrative' as some would call it, of the Whig Interpretation of History dominant in the nineteenth century, the genius of the English was thought to lie in their skill in steering the middle course between the extremes of anarchy and tyranny which so bedevilled the histories of their inferior neighbours in continental Europe. Only occasionally had the English regrettably lapsed into either sin, and thankfully they had always been rescued by the innate moral rectitude of their natural rulers, the landed classes, before too much damage had been done. Royal tyranny had tended to be the greater danger, but in the fifteenth century the Wars of the Roses, that fearful era of 'Sackage, Carnage and Wreckage' had for a while reduced England to 'a very chaos'.[1] This shameful period of anarchy had, however, taught them a lesson that was never to be forgotten. The Wars of the Roses, even though they happened five hundred years ago, thus came to have a key place in 'Our Island Story'; and they still stand in our political vocabulary as a metaphor for the worst kind of anarchy imaginable.

Yet the overwhelming weight of twentieth-century scholarship has been to demythologise these wars. While modern historians still disagree about the precise length of active campaigning and fighting undertaken by the relatively small armies that fought the wars, the longest and most widely defined current estimate is that the wars occupied no more than two and a half years in a forty year period.[2] Whatever the calculation of the scale of the fighting, it is now generally agreed, as Dr Britnell confirms below, that the wars caused only minimal direct or indirect disruption of economy and society. The relatively prosperous lives of ordinary people were barely and only randomly touched by war. The fighting was largely restricted to struggles for power

1

within the landed elite and was only especially deadly for those with the misfortune to have royal blood coursing through their veins. The thirty years preceding the accession of Henry VII in 1485 were not years of continuous and all-consuming destructive anarchy.

A principal reason for the major revision undertaken in the last fifty years is the critical revaluation of the sources discussed by Professor Hicks in Chapter 2. The chronicle and narrative sources which shaped the traditional interpretation have been revealed to be inadequately informed, frequently inaccurate and often partisan, not only in their accounts of battles, but also in their general political commentary. In particular they are the repository of propaganda; and as Professor Hicks stresses, must be recognised as such. While narrative sources have been found wanting, record sources have been exploited on an unprecedented scale and these highlight the continuity of normal life throughout the period. As a result, it has even been suggested that since these wars were not the destructive struggles between the houses of Lancaster and York stressed by Tudor propaganda, and since anyway the idea that these houses were represented by red and white roses was invented for that purpose by Henry VII, the very phrase 'Wars of the Roses' should be abandoned.[3]

The phrase is still with us, for all its inappropriateness, because it sums up a period of repeated civil war in the second half of the fifteenth century. Yet the wars do not present a problem in military history. The questions of strategy, tactics, weaponry, size of armies are not greatly in dispute. Armies raised predominantly by levy and from tenants could not be kept in the field for any length of time. Campaigns were mounted to seek quick results; there were, with the exception of Carlisle in May/June 1461, no sustained sieges of towns or systematic conquests of territory.[4] Indeed these series of plots, murders, uprisings, rebellions, invasions and battles, most intense in 1459–64, 1469–71 and 1483–7, were arguably less 'total' than the upheavals of 1399–1406 which threatened the dismemberment of the realm of England. The problem in focus today concerns not the scale, disruptiveness or military dimension, but the political significance of these civil wars. What makes the Wars of the Roses distinctive is that they became in essence, if not necessarily in origin, dynastic.

There were in fact two Wars of the Roses; or to be more precise two sets of wars. It is difficult to be exact about the duration. The first wars came to focus on the dynastic struggle between the houses of Lancaster and York. They ended on 21 May 1471, the night that Henry VI was murdered in the Tower of London. That much is certain. Yet when they began and when they became truly dynastic are other matters. Some contemporary historians, as Keith Dockray points out below, would place the beginning as early as Cade's Revolt, in 1450, which fatally undermined the credibility of the regime; and others, the duke of York's armed demonstration against his exclusion from court in 1452. In these pages, Dr R. G. Davies offers 22 March 1454, the day death removed the restraining hand of the octogenarian Archbishop Kemp from the conduct of public affairs. Conventionally the wars are taken to have begun at the first Battle of St Albans, in 1455, when York actually used force for the first time to seize power. Yet St Albans might alternatively be interpreted as an isolated event which only became linked to sustained civil war when York and his allies rose in rebellion again, in September 1459. And the conflict only became openly dynastic twelve months later when York, returning from exile in Ireland, formally laid claim to the throne for the first time.[5] The decisive moment of the first wars came in March 1461 when York's son, Edward IV, having seized the throne, defeated the collected forces of the Lancastrians at Towton. Fighting continued sporadically for three years in the far north as Edward endeavoured to secure full control of his kingdom, but after the last significant Lancastrian resistance was crushed in 1464 the wars appeared to have ended. Yet since Edward, prince of Wales, the heir to Lancaster, was still at large, the issue was not finally resolved. The quarrel between Edward IV and Warwick, which came out into the open in 1469, paved the way for the renewal of civil war, and in 1470–1, the revival of the Lancastrian cause. The death of Edward of Lancaster on the field of Tewkesbury finally sealed the fate of his father and brought the first wars conclusively to an end in complete triumph for the house of York.

Had it not been for divisions within the house of York, that would have been that. However, the seizure of the throne by Richard III in the summer of 1483 launched a second phase of civil war, dynastic from the beginning. The second wars were between the dynasties of York and Tudor, Henry Tudor emerging as the rival claimant in the autumn of 1483. His victory at Bosworth on 22 August 1485 gained him the throne but did not secure his dynasty. Some would argue that his second victory, at Stoke in 1487, ended the wars, but the Warbeck conspiracy and the continued dissidence of the de la Pole family, descended of Edward IV, kept the cause of the White Rose alive. After the peaceful succession of Henry VIII in 1509 that cause was somewhat hopeful, but there is reason to suppose that Henry VIII himself did not believe that the threat had passed until, in 1525, he heard of the death of Richard de la Pole on the field of Pavia in the service of Francis I of France.[6]

It is important to remember that there were two separate sets of Wars of the Roses, one between Lancaster and York, which ended in 1471, and a second between York and Tudor, which began in 1483. And it is worth noting too that the first wars developed as a complex, drawn-out and deepening political crisis in the 1450s in which the dynastic issue, the outright struggle for possession of the throne between rival claimants, came only as the culmination of events, whereas the second wars began immediately as, and were never little more than, dynastic in character. This means that the explanations for them are not necessarily the same. The causes of these second wars, which were more straightforwardly political, whether one prefers to focus on the ambition of Richard III or the legacy of Edward IV, are less problematic.[7] It is the explanation of the complex crisis which enveloped England in the 1450s and out of which the wars developed that has always been and remains the central interpretive problem for historians.

As Keith Dockray points out, since the mid 1960s when McFarlane and Storey simultaneously offered opposing interpretations, there has been a continuing and still unresolved debate. Was the collapse of the Lancastrian dynasty in the 1450s solely the result of Henry VI's woeful inadequacies as a king or was it at least in part the consequence of deeper economic, social and political forces? McFarlane stated: 'Only an undermighty ruler had anything to fear from overmighty subjects; and if he were undermighty his personal lack of fitness was the cause, not the weakness of his office and its resources.'[8] Keith Dockray himself, in a concise summary of the tortuous events of a tumultuous decade, emphasises the personal inadequacies of Henry VI and thereby demonstrates the central importance of the fitness for office of the man who is king in an inherited monarchy. There can be no doubt that had England in the mid-fifteenth century been ruled by a man, as one would expect of a king, who at least showed some interest in the practice of government as well as a modicum of political sense, the Wars of the Roses would not have happened. But it is also arguable that even an able monarch would have faced serious difficulties. Dr Britnell suggests that the severe and complex recession of the mid-fifteenth century, in which an agrarian crisis, deeper in the north, was overtaken by a commercial crisis having greater impact in the south, had weakened the resources of the crown. On the one hand, because of loss of revenues it became difficult for royal government to meet all its obligation; and on the other, because the crown was expected to ensure the well-being of the community, dissatisfaction was intensified by its evident powerlessness. And this came on top of the crippling cost of sustaining an unwinnable war in France bequeathed to Henry VI by his megalomaniac father.

The problem, however, runs deeper than the question of the economic and financial state of the kingdom in mid-century. Were the Wars of the Roses in any sense a consequence of, or reflection of, long-term social change and a shift in the balance of power between crown and leading subject. It has long been argued that the reign of Edward III was something of a turning point in relationships between the monarchy and nobility. In its simplest and oldest form, this thesis focussed on the marriages of the king's sons to heiresses of the great earldoms and the creation of powerful noble families of the royal blood, who claimed the right to political pre-eminence and nursed potential claims to the throne; claims that became realities in the persons of Henry IV in 1399 and Edward IV in 1461. In a more subtle and more complex form it has been more recently suggested that by softening the law of treason, by withdrawing from the direct administration of justice in the provinces, by allowing the development of devices which enabled tenants in chief to escape the incidents of feudalism, and by making concessions to parliament in order to secure financial backing for his adventures in France, Edward III significantly weakened the office of the crown and thereby made the exercise of royal authority all the more dependent on personal attributes. This itself has been disputed: the argument being recently advanced that Edward neither made concessions nor weakened the crown: rather, he strengthened it by creating a partnership with the political elites for the common good.[9] Yet, whether one sees the changes brought about in the reign of Edward III as forced on the crown or encouraged by it, strengthening it or weakening it, it remains the case that England became a less centralised state during the later middle ages.[10] Thus greater dependence was placed on the king's own ability to regulate the affairs of his kingdom, and this increased the chance that things might fall apart under a king who was not up to the job. Nevertheless many historians would argue that medieval monarchy was always intensely and primarily personal and thus always in the last resort dependent on the personal ability of the king; and particularly point out that Henry V had no more difficulty in commanding the early fifteenth-century kingdom than Edward I the late thirteenth. Thus McFarlane's proposition concerning undermighty kings still lies at the heart of debate about the origins of the wars.

The preoccupation of twentieth-century historians with bastard feudalism, itself also traditionally associated with developments in the fourteenth century, is an aspect of this wider problem. The argument, in brief, is that the development of the system of indentured retaining allowed the great nobles to create powerful affinities which exercised local power at the expense of the crown, were used to prosecute private feuds and were in the last resort turned on the crown itself. Recent research and writings, however, have prompted a rethinking of bastard feudalism. The origins of retaining by indenture are traced far earlier in medieval society and it is suggested that it was not such a dramatic break with past practice as has conventionally been supposed. It is to be doubted, too, whether the creation of large indentured retinues was as commonplace as was once supposed. The largest and best documented of all, that of John of Gaunt, was created and maintained to support the international military ambitions of a great European prince and claimant to the throne of Castile; its effectiveness or indeed intention to control the English provinces has been questioned.[11]

It is of course always difficult to argue a general case from lack of evidence, but it is now conceivable that there was no such thing as a typical indentured retinue: Richard of York, like Gaunt, built up his retinue for and during war in France; the great northern magnates, the Nevilles (and Richard of Gloucester) and Percies, retained explicitly to create mobile reserves for the defence of the borders in their capacities as wardens of the west and east marches.[12] In all these cases the military function in defence of the realm or in prosecution of war abroad is indeed the *raison d'être.*

William, Lord Hastings, on the other hand, the best documented of late fifteenth-century retaining lords, as has been demonstrated recently, retained not for himself but on behalf of his king, Edward IV, in his offices as chamberlain of the household and steward of Tutbury. Lesser lords like Hastings, as the income tax returns of 1436 and occasional household accounts reveal, normally eschewed retaining.[13] Retaining by indenture, which much troubled late medieval legislators, was largely restricted to magnates who had significant military responsibilities.

'Bastard feudalism', however, is probably a phrase that is now of more hindrance than help.[14] It means different things to different scholars; in particular it both refers to the specific legal practice of retaining and is used loosely to describe the whole structure of late medieval political society. Several aspects of our understanding of that society that have an important bearing on our understanding of the Wars of the Roses, such as the reliability and loyalty of supporters or the level of aristocratic disorder, are more general and timeless than bastard feudalism. Retaining was but one legal device deployed in the much wider and less formal operation of 'good lordship'. Good lordship extended way beyond a narrow circle of people retained for military and political purposes. Good lordship, or good mastership if the superior were a knight or esquire rather than a peer, was the exercise of influence on the behalf of servants, tenants and 'well-wishers' in general. It derived from the expectation that those with wealth, authority and connections would use their influence for the benefit of others less well placed. It depended on an exchange of reciprocal obligations: favours done in return for services rendered. Good lordship knew no bounds; it was deployed in matters ecclesiastical, legal, economic and domestic as well as political. Upon the effective exercise of good lordship, as Dr Horrox emphasises, depended in part 'worship', or reputation. Politically the power of a lord depended on his perceived ability to deliver the goods. The more effective his lordship, the greater the number of well-willers and supporters he attracted. Thus access to court could be critical in satisfying the demands of those who looked to him. Conversely loss of influence could lead to loss of support, as clients turned to a more favourably placed rival. And at the apex was the king, dependent on good lordship properly exercised on his behalf in the provinces by his nobles, and himself ruling as the good lord of all good lords. If the Wars of the Roses were the failure of good lordship exercised in partnership for the common good by king and nobles, it is necessary to understand the precise nature of that failure.

Two aspects of this issue that have received recent attention are the relationship between the locality and the centre and the role of principle in politics. Recent research in fifteenth-century history has been dominated by the proliferation of local studies.[15] This is partly the result of a greater concentration on the family and private archives discussed below by Professor Hicks, which inevitably leads to a more local emphasis. But it is also in part a reflection of a growing awareness of the importance of locality in the politics of later medieval England. While one of the more centralised monarchies of Europe, late medieval England still remained in reality a confederation of locally based political associations under central rule. By any modern comparison, the executive was pitifully weak: there was no standing army (except for three border garrisons), no police, and no civil service in the provinces (except perhaps if one counts customs officials and clerks to the justices). As Dr Harriss has recently expressed it, the crown was,

> limited by local particularism, slow communications, and family and communal loyalties. It could not control society directly through its own agents, as does a modern government, but had to rely on local elites who often exercised and appropriated its authority.[16]

An important question hangs over the identification of those local elites: were they county communities or were they baronial affinities? Professor Coss has suggested that county communities were strong in some counties, and baronial affinities in others; that both perceptions are valid.[17] Many recent studies have focussed on county communities. The voice of the community of the shire was encouraged and given expression in parliament; evidence undoubtedly exists to show that contemporaries had a sense of the body of the shire,[18] and the shire in many instances provided a focal point of local landed society. Yet it is to be doubted whether a county community ever had the capacity or will to exercise independent collective political authority in the later middle ages. Moreover it would be a grave misunderstanding of the nature of late medieval local society to imagine that such sense of belonging to a county that did exist was restricted to the gentry. If the landed elite had such a sense of belonging then it incorporated all the landed elite, peers as well as gentry, and extended to the yeomanry and the forty shilling freeholders enfranchised in 1422. When it came to the exercise of political authority, however, the focus everywhere was on the baronial affinity: the exercise of good lordship by a local magnate. And the boundaries and influence of baronial affinities, which shrank and expanded over time, rose and fell with the fortunes of their heads, were not formed by county boundaries. Yet they were locally-based, focussed on the lordships, estates and offices held by the lords themselves. What historians have perceived as county communites politically assertive in the fifteenth century, as in Leicestershire and Nottinghamshire,[19] could well be illusions created by the absence of magnate domination, which left lesser lords and prominent gentry to exercise a much more localised domination over particular districts within a county.

The weight of current opinion is that fifteenth-century local politics was indeed, as it has generally been assumed to be, the politics of baronial affinities, especially the affinities of magnates – powerful dukes and earls who not only held extensive estates in the country but also wielded influence at court: the same mighty, potentially overmighty, subjects whose power might have been enhanced by trends since the mid-fourteenth century. By its very nature the precise map of local politics was constantly changing, as determined by the accidents of demography, personal ability and political fortune. It is possible, however, to plot something of the political geography of mid-fifteenth-century England; to draw certain strands together to show how local politics were particularly volatile and confrontational in the 1450s.

In some parts of England, once great affinities had collapsed and in the wake of their dissolution would-be successors were competing for domination. This is particularly true of the west midlands where the once great Beauchamp affinity had fragmented after the successive deaths of Richard earl of Warwick in 1439, and his son Henry in 1446. Similarly the fall in 1450 of William de la Pole, duke of Suffolk, who had bestrode East Anglia for a decade, was profoundly unsettling.[20] And in the west country in the early 1450s the Bonvilles challenged the disintegrating Courtenay affinity for domination. It is worth noting too that it was precisely from these regions at this time that K. B. McFarlane drew much of his evidence of the instability of bastard feudalism. Elsewhere there were to be found more stable and long-standing powerblocks; in the north, for instance, the Nevilles and Percies managed to maintain their dominance over their respective zones of influence for several generations, and despite major upheavals and vicissitudes.[21] Within these zones, good lordship could operate beneficially as was expected on behalf of the crown in ensuring order and the maintenance of the king's peace, often in the fifteenth century by the means of the unofficial, but popular, device of arbitration. In areas such as these, friction tended to occur more frequently on the perimeters of zones of influence. In Yorkshire the Percies took up arms in 1453 against the ever-increasing power of the Nevilles when it threatened to encroach on their own heartlands. Elsewhere at the same time other conflicts flared over disputed property claims, as between the Talbots and Berkeleys for possession of Berkeley in Gloucestershire, or Lord Cromwell and the duke of Exeter for control of the Fanhope inheritance in Bedfordshire.[22] Whether it arose out of the painful realignment of local politics in the wake of collapsing hegemonies, or the clash of titans, or disputes over property, it is indeed hard to find a peaceful and settled corner of England in the early 1450s.

Much of the responsibility for this, as Mr Dockray reaffirms, can be laid at the feet of Henry VI himself. Yet one aspect of his responsibility has not received the attention it warrants: this is the way in which Henry allowed the powerful interest of the crown and duchy of Lancaster throughout England to fall into other hands. An examination of the political geography of England fifty years earlier, during the reign of his grandfather Henry IV, shows how in almost every corner of the realm the king exercised indirect control through either lords in his service or his own household knights and esquires, based on his own estates and appointments to local office.[23] After 1422 this control was lost, partly as a consequence of an unavoidable fifteen-year minority, and partly thereafter because of Henry VI's own indifference (his personal lack of fitness to rule). Thus by 1450 local crown and duchy of Lancaster influence came to be exercised not in the interest of the crown but for the benefit and self-advancement of those lords who held the principal offices and succeeded to the leadership of the royal and Lancastrian affinities in the provinces. In East Anglia the duke of Suffolk's dominance was based on the exploitation of the duchy of Lancaster network; in the north the Nevilles, led by Richard Neville, earl of Salisbury, were allowed to establish a hegemony over a wide sweep of Yorkshire, Durham, Cumberland and Westmorland; in the south-west, however, Henry compounded folly by promoting both Bonville and Courtenay to overlapping office in the duchy of Cornwall, which was the immediate trigger for the conflict between them.[24]

The recent emphasis on local politics, therefore, leads one to find renewed force in Professor Storey's perception that there was, if not an escalation, then a coalescing of local conflicts, unchecked by the king, which helped to bring him down. Yet, while restated, the problem remains the same. Which was the more important element: the weakness of the monarchy as an institution or the incompetence (and then incapacity) of the king himself? Recently the argument has been moved in a new direction by consideration of the role of principle and ideals in mid-fifteenth-century politics. The geography of local politics explored above is an analysis of politics as the pursuit of power; lordship in action in the provinces. However, this emphasis on fifteenth-century politics, central as well as local, at court and in the country, as being no more than the pursuit and exercise of power has recently been challenged. 'Patronage', as the system of power-broking has been dubbed, has now been placed under the historical microscope. New questions are being asked. Did all political action really derive solely from the low calculation of self-advancement and self-interest? Was it never tempered by a higher minded commitment to ideals and principles? The issue is familiar; it is a matter of some interest to political analysts in and of all ages. It is not surprising, however, that in the twentieth century an emphasis has been placed on patronage. Influenced by the work of Sir Lewis Namier, cynical about politics and politicians, and sceptical of the objectivity of the main narrative sources, two generations of historians have been exploiting record sources by means of a prosopographical methodology which has revealed the minutiae of patronage in operation – the payment of annuities, the grants of offices, the rewarding and promotion of servants. In particular they have stressed the importance of the management by the crown of the patronage at its disposal to secure political loyalty in court and country. Emphasis has been on the effectiveness (or in the case of Henry VI, ineffectiveness) with which the crown's leading subjects were

managed. In other words a functional and structural view of
politics has usually been stressed in recent analysis of the Wars of
the Roses.

It was not always thus, and indeed, despite claims to the
contrary, it has never been completely so. It has always been
recognised that foreign policy was a matter that divided opinion
in the fifteenth century. In the early years of Henry VI's majority
passions ran high over whether or not war should be pursued to
the bitter end or an accommodation should be sought with
France – in more modern terms a dispute between hawks and
doves on the royal council.[25] And as C. S. L. Davies reminds us
below, one of the reasons, in the opinion of one contemporary
commentator the most important, for the quarrel between
Edward IV and Warwick was the direction of foreign policy. But
recently Dr Powell has argued that historians have neglected the
ideological and constitutional content of politics at their peril.[26]
The point has been taken up by Dr Carpenter who, having
castigated the premise that politics was wholly dominated by
patronage and an endless pursuit of self-advantage, has argued
that we need better to understand the *mentalité* of the landowning
class as a whole, and the fundamental beliefs and attitudes,
including their view of the constitution, that informed their
political actions. In particular she has stressed the importance of
this to our explanation of how and with what consequences
government came to break down in the middle of the fifteenth
century; in short, how we explain the Wars of the Roses.[27]

Let us be clear, the matter at issue is not that politics was driven
exclusively either by patronage or by principle, but that the
precise nature and influence of matters of principle in the politics
of the fifteenth century and their importance in comparison with
naked self-interest are ill defined. This issue is addressed in
several contributions to this volume. Dr Horrox stresses the
principles and values that underlay good lordship, that in a sense
lay within patronage itself, and which were fundamental to the
whole structure of politics. In a closed political world dominated
by a handful of closely related families and founded on personal
relationships, the exercise of good lordship itself, she argues,
involved a moral and ethical code of behaviour. It required
respect for the law and the principle of equity; it did not
countenance the perversion of the law for personal gain or the
promotion of clients at the expense of the public good; it

demanded loyalty from servants, and condemned treachery. Moreover, and Dr Watts reinforces this point, in late medieval England no distinction was drawn between private and public spheres; standards of private behaviour were also the standards of public behaviour. Thus good lordship was expected to work towards the overall goal of maintaining social harmony and peace: that 'love and amity' the restoration of which was the conventionally expressed aim of the arbitration awards through which good lords settled disputes. Politics founded on personal relationships, being perceived in terms of good or bad personal behaviour, were thus intensely moral. Of course, because mankind is not perfect, matters frequently went wrong; the law was often perverted; treachery, the most despicable of offences, all too frequently occurred; and order easily broke down. Social peace could quickly collapse into civil war. Yet, by the same token, peace could be quickly restored. Perhaps to the modern world, with its competing ideologies, this might seem to be all too superficial, but the modern observer should not fall into the error of assuming that it lacked principle. Personalities and principles were not opposites.

Dr Watts argues that behind this world of personal and individual values, there lay also a clearly articulated perception of the 'common weal'. As he points out, rebels habitually appealed to the common good to justify their actions. While the cynic customarily retorts: 'they would, wouldn't they', he suggests not only that the frequency of the appeal to the common good gives witness to the strength it must have had, but also that the question of the sincerity of the appellant does not affect the significance of the principles to which he gave expression. He proposes, therefore, that during the 1450s York responded to a widespread sense that Henry VI had failed to protect his subjects and provide for the common good. He sought to justify the use of force on these grounds. He found, however, an even more powerful principle ranged against him: the divine authority of a crowned king. This principle was articulated in the tract known as *Somnium Vigilantis*, probably presented to the Coventry Parliament of 1459, which proscribed York and his allies as traitors. It argued that only through obedience to the king could the common good be served. And its force, Watts suggests, led York to make his claim to the throne, which in effect finessed his opponents. Thus a significant constitutional issue was entwined with personal ambition in the conflicts of the 1450s. Indeed, it could be argued that the very nature of the office of the monarch was questioned.

There was another, related, ideological, dimension to the political *mentalité* of the age to which historians have also turned: the force of chivalric ideas and attitudes.[28] In an as yet unpublished paper, Dr M. K. Jones has suggested that contemporaries also sought a chivalric solution to the confusion surrounding them.[29] In particular he proposes that Edward IV, as king, endeavoured to achieve the restoration of social harmony and the protection of the common weal through the implementation of chivalric ideals. At first sight this seems to the modern mind to be somewhat bizarre, for chivalry was founded on a concept of honour which sanctioned, indeed glorified, the settlement of differences by violence. Yet also built into the chivalric code were the means of defusing tensions, resolving conflicts and restoring social peace. The elaborate code of practice concerning ransoms, the stress on worship, and the mechanisms for arbitration and reconciliation developed in the later middle ages all reflected a conscious and sincere belief that chivalry could control the worst abuses of chivalry. Thus, paradoxically, the shared aristocratic code of behaviour was both a source of violence and disorder and a means by which to contain its worst excesses. Even in the midst of civil war the participants believed that social harmony could be restored and the crisis resolved through chivalry.

The young, conventionally educated, aristocrat Edward IV, it can be argued, not only sponsored a revival of chivalric culture focussed on his own court, but also endeavoured to pursue a chivalric policy; a policy revealed in much publicised acts such as the reconciliation with the duke of Somerset in 1462 and the disgrace of the traitor Sir Ralph Grey in 1464;[30] in the attempted revival of the Hundred Years War in 1475; and even perhaps in his own form of personal rule through a band of trusted relations and companions, which has a decidedly Arthurian ring to it. If this is so, if Edward IV did indeed endeavour to solve the social and political crisis that he inherited by such conventional and conservative means, he failed. He failed to prevent the renewal of the wars both in 1469 and after his death. Indeed he himself might well soon have abandoned the attempt, as his increasingly ruthless and unchivalric treatment of his enemies, culminating in the execution of his brother George, duke of Clarence, suggests. Richard III also appealed to chivalry, with a degree of sincerity that cannot now be determined, but with no greater success.

The truth is that chivalry could not provide the means for a lasting political solution to England's problems. The challenge facing all medieval kings, triumphantly met by Henry V, was how to strike a balance between the preservation of the common good and the pursuit of chivalry; the crown being the guardian of one and the embodiment of the other. It is perhaps significant that Malory's *Morte D'Arthur*, completed in 1470, and drawing upon the author's experience and observation over the previous two decades, expressed a profound scepticism about the whole chivalric ethic and the possibility of there ever being another Henry V. It is after all about the *death* of Arthur, the failure of chivalry.[31] Malory perhaps saw what we see, and some perceptive contemporaries saw, that the restoration of effective social peace and political stability lay not through the further encouragement of aristocratic independence, but through the enforcement of royal control and authority.

Notwithstanding the commonly expressed ideal that the king ruled in partnership with and through the agency of his nobles, there was always an underlying tension in medieval society between royal authority and aristocratic independence. Normally that tension only came to a head in the arbitrary and despotic rule of a king riding rough-shod over considerations of the common good as articulated, or even defined, by the nobles; the 1450s witnessed the less frequent, more complex and harder to resolve conflict arising from the rule of an inept and, after 1453, physically incapable king. It is for these reasons that the Wars of the Roses can be said to have represented a profound crisis for the English monarchy, politics and society, the resolution of which ultimately lay in the Tudor emphasis on obedience to the monarch over and above consideration of the good of the community; and on royal control, over aristocratic independence. Paradoxically, successive usurpations of the throne in the name of superior titles, even though in their immediate impact they weakened the crown politically, may have reinforced the ideal and authority of monarchy, which itself was never questioned. This perhaps also helps to explain the ease and speed with which royal authority recovered and normal politics were restored both in the second reign of Edward IV and under Henry VII.

The related questions of the origins of the Wars of the Roses and the relationship between patronage and principle in mid-fifteenth-century politics present the principal problems in focus in this volume, just as they have also been the major topics of debate among historians in recent years. Yet there are other issues at stake. In addressing the question of principles and ideals in the politics of the mid-fifteenth century, the historian cannot ignore the Church; for after all the Church was the guardian of morality and ethics which guided the private and public lives of the laity, as well as being the second most powerful institution in the kingdom. Whilst Dr R. G. Davies points out that there was nothing fundamentally amiss with the mid-fifteenth-century Church in England, he draws attention to the insignificant role played by it in the wars. Churchmen, for the most part, offered no intellectual response to the crisis in the state: it was a common lawyer, Sir John Fortescue, who probably composed the *Somnium Vigilantis*. Perhaps one reason why the wars have appeared to historians to be so unprincipled is that the usual commentators were silent. While senior clergy participated in efforts to avoid war and make peace, they were on the whole unassertive, and even, as Davies suggests, in the case of Cardinal Archbishop Bourgchier cravenly subservient. Indeed, for the most part the bishops eschewed political entanglement; many of the most able, promoted by Henry VI, were scholars and pastors. This is not to deny the importance of other religious influences in politics, but these, as Dr Davies stresses, came from the cultural impact of beliefs in witchcraft, prophecy and the intercessory power of saints. An institution that was passive politically in the later fifteenth century, which allowed the privileges of sanctuary to be whittled away by successive kings, and was led by a papacy which, in contrast to its intervention in France earlier in the century, showed little interest in settling the dynastic dispute, later proved to be powerless in the face of Henry VIII's onslaught.

Consideration of the Church reminds us that England was part of a wider European community and that the Wars of the Roses should not be seen in isolation. Was the crisis in England part of a wider crisis in the British Isles and on the continent? Wales, Ireland and Calais were ruled by the kings of England. Because they could provide sanctuary for political exiles and the bases for invasion (Calais and Ireland in 1460, for instance), control of them was vital to successive governments. Wales and Ireland were both English colonies; albeit Wales was more fully integrated into the English dominion. In both colonies the wars led to factionalism. There was no overt revival of nationalism in Wales as a result of the civil wars: no repetition of Glyn Dwr's revolt. Henry VII may have made a special appeal to his own Welsh roots after 1485, but the wars in the principality and marches before he came to the throne amounted to little more than a struggle for control between English factions. Jasper Tudor, earl of Pembroke, Henry VI's half-brother, acted as the Lancastrian agent against York's associates from 1456. The tables were turned in 1461, but thereafter control of Wales was in effect contested by the houses of York and Tudor. Edward IV relied first on his old family retainer, Sir William Herbert, created earl of Pembroke to supplant Jasper Tudor; and secondly, in his second reign, on a council nominally advising his son the Prince of Wales and headed by his brother-in-law Earl Rivers. Henry VII restored Jasper Tudor in 1485 to the position he had been given by Henry VI and that he had recovered briefly in 1470–1.[32] The more distant Ireland, in which the crown and English colony only precariously controlled and dominated the local population, was never as politicised by the wars. However, Richard of York, who was lieutenant in the 1450s, cultivated the Fitzgerald earls of Kildare and Desmond as counterweights to the Lancastrian James Butler, earl of Ormond and Wiltshire. The Butlers were destroyed in 1461–3 and eventually Kildare emerged as Edward IV's deputy. After 1485, although Henry VII was anxious to extend the arrangement, Kildare opted to exploit Henry's weakness to his own advantage by backing the Simnel and Warbeck conspiracies. Only in Ireland, and then fleetingly at a late stage, did any hint of separatism and the disintegration of the English dominion in the British Isles emerge during the wars.[33]

Scotland, although sharing a land border with England, was a separate kingdom, and was therefore not only a part of the British Isles, but also a foreign power. Relationships with England's neighbours, considered by C. S. L. Davies, are of importance for two main reasons. First, there is the extent to which the wars were international. Disarray in England presented a golden opportunity to her traditional enemies. It is perhaps surprising that neither Scotland nor France were able to take greater advantage. This was partly, as Davies shows, a consequence of their own internal difficulties. Nevertheless intervention by the

French and Scots in English affairs was a major nuisance in 1461–4 and effectively extended civil war in the north for three years; the involvement of France and Burgundy in 1470–1 was intense; and French intervention in 1485 was decisive. Indeed, as Davies reveals, it could be argued that the Wars of the Roses became progressively internationalised. After 1485 they were continued more obsessively in the murky world of international conspiracy and diplomacy than they were at home. Indeed one could almost say that in the reign of Henry VII international relations became the pursuit of the Wars of the Roses by other means.[34]

Secondly, comparison with developments in France and the Netherlands allows us to consider the extent to which the Wars of the Roses were part of a wider European crisis. France too was in turmoil, but, like England, witnessed a restoration of stability at the end of the century. The nature of the turmoil, however, was different: in England political struggles were over control of central power; in France and the Netherlands the struggles were between the centre and separatist authorities. The later fifteenth century was, Davies suggests, a crucial period in the general history of European state formation. Both the English and French monarchies emerged strengthened and more unified from years of crisis: in the case of France, assisted by England's inability to intervene at decisive moments.

England during the Wars of the Roses was also an integral part of a European community because its nobility shared a common culture with the nobility of Europe, especially northern Europe. The influence of the court of Burgundy on English courtly culture is well established; and the quantity and range of the patronage of the arts in England throughout the later fifteenth century is readily apparent. Charles Ross expressed a consensus when he wrote in 1976 that 'England in the later fifteenth century was in fact the home of a rich, varied and vigorous civilization.'[35] Professor Richmond demonstrates that it was as vigorous and considerably more varied than is often supposed. While much visual art undoubtedly reflected a preoccupation with living hopefully and dying well, it would nevertheless be wrong to see the age as morbidly gloomy, let alone to imagine that such gloom might have been induced by the horrors of civil war. The arts of peace flourished, because society as a whole was for the most part untouched by the horrors of war. However, Richmond doubts whether this culture was as rich as we have come to believe. Most of it was English; and therein lies the catch. The English nobility, if they could afford it, went abroad to commission portraits or altar panels because the quality of English painting was so bad. For the most part, whether royal, noble or bourgeois, English taste was either vulgar (in the case of the royals) or lacking in imagination, derivative, shallow, complacent and undemanding. Professor Richmond's trenchant assessment, while confirming that the Wars of the Roses had little direct impact on cultural life, by emphasising the insular character of English visual culture reinstates the view that in the second half of the fifteenth century England still lay on the periphery of European civilisation.

It is perhaps salutary to take note that England was in the later fifteenth century an off-shore kingdom whose concerns were not of central importance to the well-being or future development of Europe. Confidence that English history, even the history of the Wars of the Roses, could teach our continental neighbours a thing or two, has evaporated since the nineteenth century. Even fifty years ago, perhaps especially fifty years ago, and before the United Kingdom entered the European Community, emphasis could still be placed on the manner in which, below the surface, the foundations were being laid for the surge of expansion and English greatness that were to follow.[36] But while the greatness of nations is ephemeral, the fundamental problems facing the historian of the Wars of the Roses remain the same. How profound were the causes, how profound the consequences? Were the motives of the participants no more elevated than the pursuit of base self-interest, or were important matters of principle at stake? And were the wars the reflection of a deeper crisis out of which the English monarchy emerged stronger and more autocratic? These are some of the questions explored in the chapters which follow.

2. The Sources

M. A. HICKS

The principal sources of the Wars of the Roses are the contemporary narratives and the records, which are more fully understood by each generation. Total recall and complete understanding inevitably elude us, even in the case of the best known events – the battles. The evidence for three campaigns is discussed in my opening section. Subsequent sections consider the chronicles, national records, and local records. Such categories, however, are not quite as obvious as they seem. The Wars of the Roses were both a series of events and a period of history; they resulted not merely from the actions and collision of individuals, but through the clash and interaction of communities, which in turn arise from deeper political, social, economic and even ideological origins. Since historians disagree on these root causes and their roles, so too they differ about the relevance of particular sources, especially local ones, and on their meaning. This chapter, therefore, addresses current historical concerns as well as the sources on which they draw.

I

The First Battle of St Albans lasted for four hours on the morning of Thursday, 22 May 1455. It was the first battle of the Wars of the Roses. Richard, duke of York (d. 1460) was victorious; his rival, Edmund, duke of Somerset, was killed and King Henry VI himself was captured. The battle, C. A. J. Armstrong observed, 'should be the best known of the Wars of the Roses'.[1] No other encounter was the subject of five surviving newsletters: one was completed even before the battle was over and another three within a fortnight. These are what Armstrong called the *Stow, Fastolf, Phillipps* and *Dijon Relations* and the *Letter to the Archbishop of Ravenna*. The reports of eyewitnesses, of course, make the best historical sources. On most issues our five are agreed. They complement and supplement one another, making it easy to

20

winkle out errors and to reconcile disagreements. *The Stow Relation*, for so long the basic source for the battle, has been corrected at many points.

Even so, it is no easy task to produce a definitive account of St Albans. Gaps remain: notably the size and composition of the armies. More important, all our eyewitnesses are biased. Three were Yorkists, none a Lancastrian. They blame the battle on the king's favourites, even though it was clearly York who first resorted to arms. We are therefore less certain about the Lancastrian point of view. Moreover the *Relations* are best on what they actually saw: on the day of the battle. For what went before and the reasons for it, there are more balanced and considered accounts by other chroniclers writing later, even though they too were predominantly Yorkist. Our narratives often disagree. To choose between two alternatives, we can resort to documents of the time that establish the precise situation at the moments when they were written. Thus we can reject the belief, apparently widespread in London, that the king was fleeing when he was intercepted by York at St Albans. It is instead obvious that he was on his way from London to his great council at Leicester and only slightly less certain that York's attack was long premeditated. What lay behind it all, contemporaries agreed, was the feud between York and Somerset. Only recently, however, have modern historians appreciated how and why this feud arose.[2] Twentieth-century historians can now explain the battle better than our five contemporary relators. As for the long-term significance of the battle, our *Relations* were too close to events for informed judgement. The destruction of Somerset did *not* avert civil war.

If First St Albans is illuminated by the testimony of five eyewitnesses, for the Barnet and Tewkesbury campaign of 1471 we have only one: *The Arrivall of Edward IV*. Its vivid and compelling narrative and lucid explanations are the inescapable basis of all modern narratives. Composed almost at once, initially for foreign consumption, from inside information on the Yorkist side, it too is biased towards the Yorkists: witness its description of the miracle of St Anne that occurred when Edward IV worshipped at Daventry; its approval for the removal from sanctuary and execution of defeated Lancastrians after the Battle of Tewkesbury; and, most notoriously of all, its attribution of Henry VI's timely death to 'pure displeasure and melancoly'. The full English version is the final, polished, composition: some details in the earlier, shorter, sometimes illustrated French versions, such as a skirmish near Leicester and the role of Lord Camoys, were edited out.[3] Other chronicles, unfortunately, provide only supplementary detail. *Warkworth's Chronicle*, for example, tells how the earl of Warwick's men at Barnet mistook the earl of Oxford's badge of a star with streams for the Yorkist sun in splendour. Fuller casualty lists for Tewkesbury are contained in the chronicles of Warkworth, John Benet, and Tewkesbury Abbey. Records, again, add to the picture, but contribute nothing to our overall interpretation. Named retainers, otherwise not known to have fallen at Barnet, were later commemorated by Richard, duke of Gloucester at Queens' College, Cambridge. Some Yorkist combatants were revealed when rewarded for their services, including Lord Grey of Codnor who was repaid his costs, and there are detailed accounts recording the fines extracted from the Bastard of Fauconberg's Kentish followers. A few more Lancastrians can be added from the 1475 act of attainder, from grants of their possessions and from the individual compositions that they made, like that between the Essex knight John Marney, who fought at Barnet, and Richard, duke of Gloucester. The returns of a judicial commission into the Battle of Barnet indicated sixty-eight of the defeated army: unfortunately they were mainly Oxford's Essex contingent and inhabitants of Warwick's properties at Ware and Bushey, who were better known to the local jurors.[4] Yet even with all this material, we probably know the identity of less than 5 per cent of those at either battle. We can check neither the numbers of the armies nor their constituent noble companies stated by the chronicles. There is no direct evidence, for instance, that Grey's retinue was included in the 3,000 men supposedly mobilised by Lord Hastings, his lord. Most serious of all, to a much greater extent than in First St Albans, we have no narrative of quality to balance *The Arrivall*. Not only are its assessments and explanations often unchallengeable – did King Edward *really* regard the earl of Northumberland's inactivity in Yorkshire as masterly? – but we are dependent on it not just for the strategy of Edward IV but for those of his opponents. Why *really* did the marquis Montagu let Edward IV march through Yorkshire, why did the duke of Exeter intercept him at Newark, why did Warwick refuse battle at Coventry and why did Clarence desert Henry VI for Edward IV? What was the objective of the Lancastrians prior to the Battle of Tewkesbury?

Were they heading for Chester? Where was Jasper Tudor, earl of Pembroke, what was his strength, and why did he take his nephew Henry Tudor with him when he fled abroad?

For Bosworth in 1485, the sources are less satisfactory than for either 1455 or 1471. We know the result but little else. Where was the battle? Even the site has changed, as the swamp has been drained,[5] and there is insufficient topographical precision in our best narrative, written thirty years later by the Italian Polydore Vergil. Why was Bosworth fought? Where was it that Henry VII was aiming for when he was brought to battle? We can be certain on neither point. And why was Richard III defeated and Henry VII victorious? Since Vergil's principal informants were those exiles who rose to high office in the new regime, it is hardly surprising that he attributes to them an honoured role and to the king's Stanley kinsfolk the decisive intervention. The contribution of the Stanleys and their men of Cheshire and Lancashire were celebrated also in the ballads of *Bosworth Field* and *Lady Bessy*. Vergil and the poets were writing late enough to be influenced by the improvements made in the story by the victors. It was they who presented Bosworth as decisive – the end of civil war – and downgraded subsequent problems with Lambert Simnel and Perkin Warbeck. Vergil's *Anglica Historica* and the ballads demand comparison with other contemporary accounts but there are none. That of Diego de Valera, which attributes a decisive role to Tamorlant – perhaps Northumberland? – seems more probably confused than accurate.[6] Whilst many of Henry's partisans were rewarded and many of Richard's were attainted, they comprise only a fraction of those named in the Stanley ballads. In the absence of other evidence, 'can we not simply take it they were not there at all?'[7] To do so, of course, makes it even harder to explain how either side raised an army, still less fought a major battle. The recent discovery that Henry Tudor was accompanied by 4,000 Frenchmen and Scots, a solid core of professional veterans,[8] fills gaps left by Vergil, identifies a pro-English bias to his narrative, and suggests a different reason for the result. It also casts doubt on conventional assessments of the relative popularity of Henry VII and Richard III.

Battles are the highpoints of any war. They cannot be ignored. 'Battles are the commonest subject matter for news-letters in the later middle ages.'[9] Chroniclers, heralds, diplomats, scribes, judges and accountants all amassed information for us to collect.

Battles are the best documented of events. For their study we can call on every source available to the political historian. Yet the results are uneven and much remains in doubt. If we know who fought and on what issues, the identity of the commanders and the principal casualties, and the results, both long and short-term – and let us not underestimate the extent or importance of such knowledge! – we are seldom clear about the strategy of both sides, about the tactics and total casualties, or about the size or composition of the armies. Much can be achieved with what we know, but we can never claim that our sources are sufficient to answer all the questions that we wish to ask.

II

Though fought five hundred years ago, such battles live on for historians, who find much that still awaits discovery and debate. Terrain and tactics, numbers, training and armaments, strategy and diplomacy can all be better understood. Yet such investigations always relate to what is known – the traditional narratives passed down to us, which we seek to amplify, clarify or correct. Admittedly imperfect, and the work, for the most part, of absentees lacking military experience and composed years later, these narratives remain the essential basis from which all accounts begin. Whenever we are tempted to reject them as incompatible with other evidence, such as the terrain, we risk moving beyond history into a fictional world where everything is possible and where anarchic imagination can reign.

So, too, with the politics of the Wars of the Roses. Historians are always prisoners of the past. The events that matter, the dates, locations, participants, causes and results, have been pre-selected for us by earlier writers. Ultimately these decisions and choices were made by those who witnessed the events themselves or wrote soon after from first-hand evidence that we do not possess. They supply us with our chronology, much of our detail, and even – to an extent much greater than we often admit – with our interpretations and explanations. We may not like what our sources say and may wish to extend or amend them – indeed, filling in the gaps is much of what professional historians do – but we cannot reject them wholesale in favour of our own preferences. Our efforts, for example, to extol the quality of the

government of Richard III has suffered from a crippling lack of
contemporary comment: we can substitute little but the most
insubstantial speculation.

These early histories are almost all chronicles or collections of
annals. They proceed year by year, collect events together under
the years to which they belong, and make little attempt at
rounded narratives or explanations of events. Historians value
many of them primarily as collections of miscellaneous
information: even the thinnest, such as Gairdner's *Brief Latin
Chronicle* or R. F. Green's *London Chronicle*, can contain a date of
birth or death found nowhere else. Each of the variants of the
London chronicles contains original information; so, too, the
different texts of the *Stow Relation* and *The Arrivall.* Fragments of
information from newly discovered or hitherto unappreciated
chronicles are constantly coming to light. Almost all these
chronicles take a national stance; the chronicles of particular
monasteries have all but passed away. Most of them, such as those
from the 1450s or from London, are short and cursory, little more
than bare annals, and seldom identify their sources. There is no
chronicle of the whole Wars of the Roses to compare with the
major monastic chronicles of earlier periods; not even one as full
throughout as the newsletters of First St Albans or *The Arrivall* that
we have already considered or the narratives of Richard III's
usurpation, by Dominic Mancini or Sir Thomas More. Mancini,
More and the Italian Polydore Vergil at the end of the period, in
the latter cases long afterwards, purveyed the new Renaissance
history and therefore sought to provide an overriding
interpretation of events; so too did the anonymous Crowland
Continuation of 1486, which deliberately corrects an earlier
monastic chronicle, and the *Memoires* of the Burgundian Philippe
de Commines, whose work has consequently carried much more
weight.

Chronicles cannot safely be regarded as mere repositories of
miscellaneous facts. That information comes from a chronicle is
no guarantee of veracity or objectivity. Chronicles can be
misinformed; they disagree, often on crucial points, and present
different versions of events. Historians need to recognise such
defects and discriminate between different accounts. It is easiest
to do this where there are several to compare, as in the 1450s: as
the Yorkist period proceeds, fewer annalists were at work and this
approach is less practicable. Much also can be learnt from

studying the texts themselves: indeed, with anonymous chronicles, this is all that can be done. Much, additionally, can be gleaned from the authorship or the circumstances of composition. Was the author an eyewitness, had he access to reliable information, when was he writing and from what point of view? If all history by definition is written after the event, it is crucial to know that the *Fastolf Relation* was written within hours and More's *Richard III* thirty years after the events described. In practice, few annals were written year by year. It was far more common, like the London chronicles, for whole decades to be written up at one sitting. Memory fades with time, perspectives change, particular events are located in sequences, and trivial episodes acquire a portentous significance. Chroniclers copied one another, sometimes resulting in the complex interrelationships defying analysis of which the families of London chronicles or of the Brut are striking examples. Much hangs on whether Polydore Vergil had read the Crowland Continuations.[10]

Such considerations can affect the validity of particular sources and hence the material they contain and the interpretations that are based on them. Thus much ink has been spilt discussing the Second Anonymous Crowland Continuation. If it is now accepted that it was written in 1486 in eleven days, it is not clear who was the author: Bishop Russell, Dr Henry Sharp, Dr Richard Lavender, or someone else?[11] We know what kind of man he was – a learned ecclesiastic and diplomat – but it still matters who he was, when he held office and when he left it, and when therefore he was best informed. Does the brevity of his observations arise always from his natural taciturnity or sometimes from straightforward ignorance about the facts? Whilst Dominic Mancini was undoubtedly present in London during Richard III's usurpation, he spoke no English: his narrative thus carries weight only if he moved in well-informed circles that spoke Latin. Almost certainly he did.[12] We accord Vergil the status of a primary authority for the Yorkist period because he deliberately consulted notables surviving from that time.[13] What we can accept from William Gregory, a well-informed London alderman, cannot be transferred unquestioningly to those sections of his chronicle added after his death; indeed, since he died in 1467 and there appears to be a single author from 1450–70, the last twenty years are the work of an unknown hand. It was not therefore Gregory himself who condemned the duke of Somerset's activities in

1462–4. Two independent versions of the trials of Sir Thomas
Cook in 1468–71 become only one if the Londoner Robert
Fabyan, undoubted author of *Fabyan's Chronicle*, also composed
The Great Chronicle of London.[14] The treatment of Edward IV's
brother Clarence in the chronicles of Tewkesbury Abbey and
John Warkworth can only be fully appreciated when it is realised
that the former was written before and the latter after his fall in
1478. Richard III himself was notoriously better treated in the
version of the Rous' Roll written during his reign than in that
rewritten after his death.[15] Some historians see, in this, grounds
for rejecting all Rous' work, but actually our improved
understanding enables us to make more of what is original from
each of his books. In much the same way, Henry VI's chaplain
John Blacman and his *Collectarium*, so long dismissed as a
hagiographic collection of apocryphal anecdotes, can be made to
yield first-hand information about the king and a valid alternative
interpretation of his career.[16]

In all these instances, our interpretation of the narrative of
events is coloured by our understanding of the chronicler. All
chronicles demand this scrutiny and the best modern editions
provide it. Regrettably, however, only a handful of them have
received it: most chronicles exist only in ancient editions with
inadequate introductions and scanty notes and it is only the
major ones that have been fully discussed by such experts as
C. L. Kingsford, Alison Hanham and Antonia Gransden. Such
supplementary material is never recorded in the modern
collections that juxtapose accounts from different chronicles or
silently provide a single preferred narrative.

Chronicles vary not only in accuracy, but in interpretation.
They were all written for a purpose, from a particular point of
view, and with a particular audience in mind. Too often this is
unknown; often, perhaps, it is immaterial, for we need not
understand the criteria for selection to see that selection has
occurred. Sometimes the bias is all too obvious. It is not
infrequent to discover bias where none was hitherto suspected.
We owe it to K. B. McFarlane that we no longer attribute the
'Annales Rerum Anglicarum' to William Worcestre, and to
Professor Lander that the traditional account of the Woodville
marriages is now recognised to be biased in favour of the earl of
Warwick.[17] It is a major achievement of postwar scholarship that
so many distortions have been identified. Those studying Richard

III deserve most credit. They have demonstrated that the
traditional orthodoxy from William Shakespeare to James
Gairdner derived from Sir Thomas More was hopelessly biased
towards the Tudors, perhaps even Tudor propaganda, and
'should not, indeed must not, be used by historians'.[18] They
identified the southern, London-based bias of the Crowland
Continuation and postulated an alternative northern pro-
Ricardian tradition that is not represented in any chronicle. It is
the version of the victors, we have learnt, that always
predominates: it is only recently that we have recognised the
Lancastrian myth – pro-Lancastrian propaganda – and the Yorkist
myth represented by the half-forgotten poems, the genealogies,
and the rolls of arms that were submerged by the triumphant and
enduring propaganda of the Tudors.

   This Tudor propaganda was written after victory at Bosworth:
the blind poet Bernard André and the official historiographer
Polydore Vergil were conscious propagandists; anyone else was at
best an unconscious propagandist, affected by hindsight and
exposed to the official government version promoted by Tudor
governments. Equally propagandist are earlier official versions of
events: the Lancastrian account of the deposition of Richard II is
a famous example. The various Relations of the First Battle of St
Albans, *The Arrivall*, and the *Chronicle of the Lincolnshire Rebellion*
(1470) are other examples. Full and accurate though these are,
vividly and convincingly written, they are nevertheless designed
to present a particular point of view, to win, convince, persuade,
and dissuade. The *Lincolnshire Rebellion* demonstrates, inter alia,
the infidelity of Warwick and Clarence, absolves the king of any
blame for the rift, and shows their defeat to be decisive.[19] Short
French versions of *The Arrivall* were mass-produced and
circulated to reassure Edward IV's allies and warn off potential
foes. Heraldic descriptions of the coronation of Edward IV's
queen (1465), the tournament of Lord Scales and the Bastard of
Burgundy (1467), the re-interment of Richard, duke of York
(1476), the marriage of Edward's second son (1478), and the
coronation of Richard III (1483) served similar purposes. Such
narratives were, moreover, only the longest versions of such work.
Many proclamations, acts of succession and attainder, newsletters,
and rebel manifestoes sought to present a particular message,
guiding or misleading public opinion. Often these contained a
historical element and indeed became part of history: Richard III's

systematic reinterpretation of Edward IV's regime misled contemporaries and deceives many historians still; Henry VII forged for himself a Celtic and Arthurian ancestry; and Tudor propaganda began before the usurpation of Henry VII.[20] Even when not assimilated into the historical tradition, such effusions are still evidence of what people believed or wanted to be believed at the time.

Propaganda or not, such material is also strictly contemporary, specific to particular times and places. It tells us of the situation at particular moments, before the sequence of events was complete, before it was re-arranged in logical order, and before explanations were rationalised into neat and coherent packages of cause and effect. Chronicles are seldom so precise. Written years in arrears, they often err in dates and details, generalise too much in their chronology, and seek constantly to improve on their data. They require the context of contemporary records. Most of this basic chronological work was done long ago, by long forgotten and unsung antiquaries, who established the dates of reigns, battles and parliaments, identified and dated the lords, bishops and officeholders whose particulars are so baldly stated in our standard guides. Very few significant events remain open to dispute and then usually because whole interpretations hang on them. This was true of the lively debate about the death of Lord Hastings in the 1970s. Knowing that Hastings' death was a stage in Richard's usurpation and believing this always to be obvious, most chroniclers had deduced that his death followed the removal from sanctuary of Prince Richard on 16 June: Hastings therefore died on Friday 20 June. Their assumptions were mistaken and so too was their date: actually he died on 13 June. This date has now been confirmed by an amazing range of evidence relating to his estates, appointments, salaries and works on Kirby Muxloe Castle from many government and private records.[21] Similarly the dated reports of the Milanese ambassador to France have been used to date precisely the negotiations between Warwick and Margaret of Anjou that was deliberately misrepresented in Warwick's manifesto *The Manner and Guiding of the Earl of Warwick at Angers.* Royal records enable us to chart the course of the Warwick inheritance dispute between Edward IV's brothers Clarence and Gloucester in the 1470s. John Stodeley's newsletter in 1454 and the Stallworth letters in 1483 pin down stages of narrative to particular days.[22] Even when inaccurate, such sources record what

the situation was thought to be, which often mattered as much as
the truth in determining contemporary responses.

III

Records produced at the time give precision to our narratives; on
occasion, they can correct them. By collating chronicles with
records, historians uncover inaccuracies and expose matter that is
perverse, contentious, or deliberately misleading. But records
offer much more than this. They enable us to amplify the
narratives – adding, as we have seen, names to those killed at
Barnet; to fill in gaps in the story; and even to cover topics that
the chronicles did not discuss. All records were composed for a
particular purpose, by a particular administrative process, and to a
standard format or diplomatic. They are most useful for that
purpose – as records of the actions of a particular official, for
example – and when that objective, procedure and diplomatic is
recalled. Thus historians have acquired a profound knowledge of
the routine operation of the great departments of state and the
central law courts. Yet such records are commonly used for other
purposes: to identify those trusted by the king and those he
mistrusted, to chart the operation of royal patronage, to uncover
the origins of royal policy, and to assess how effectively it was
implemented.

By far the largest collection of such records, containing most of
the more important, is the archive of central government
preserved in the Public Record Office in London. Year by year
the great departments of state – chancery, exchequer and the
central law-courts – composed enormous rolls in many different
series, each underpinned by subsidiary files of warrants, writs,
deeds and miscellanea. The more formal records of the king's
secretariat, the patent, close and the fine rolls of chancery, have
been calendared (published in shortened form) in dozens of
volumes; the rest remains in manuscript, generally in Latin, much
of it only recently or not yet sorted. Over the past fifty years
successive generations of historians have familiarised themselves
with ever more classes of documents and have exploited them
ever more fully for political history. These royal archives record
the enormous number of contacts between the crown and its
subjects. At times such material has seemed not merely to

supplement the chronicles, but to supplant them and to offer all the answers. Everything, it sometimes seems, boiled down to patronage: the politically-competent king used the selfish acquisitiveness of the political nation as his main instrument of political control and considerately recorded the relevant data for us on his patent rolls.

Pride of place among all this material, perhaps, belongs to the records of Parliament: that irregular event, when the king met all his most powerful subjects to make political decisions of the first magnitude, to legislate, and to publish the results. The legislation and formal proceedings are recorded in the parliament rolls, which survive for every parliament except that of the Readeption of Henry VI, and which were published long ago; in many cases there are also original acts, though others are occasionally discovered; and we have most of the election returns for members of the House of Commons. We find overt statements of policy and principle: by the king – in 1467, for example, Edward IV declared his intention to 'live upon mine own but in great and urgent causes';[23] by his nominee the speaker; and by his chancellor, who preached an introductory sermon to every parliament. Much has been made of the draft sermons of Chancellor Russell for the abortive parliaments of 1483.[24] We find acts declaring the title of new kings and acts of attainder that proscribe defeated traitors. These identify many lesser Lancastrians and Yorkists: reversals of attainder register when those proscribed submitted and made their peace. Often such acts declare a government's version of history – like those at the parliament of 1484 that declared Richard's title (*Titulus Regius*) and condemned Buckingham's rebels of 1483.

All such data has long been assimilated and analysed and is constantly recycled in new histories. Yet the evidence of Parliament is also rather disappointing. We have no records of parliamentary debates or votes. Whilst we know for the most part who was entitled to attend, we seldom know whether they did: only a few days of the House of Lord's Journal for 1461 survive in the Fane Fragment;[25] nothing for the Commons. Many historians have studied the composition of the House of Commons and sought to understand its significance; however, it will be many years before the History of Parliament Trust publishes its planned new volumes covering the Wars of the Roses. We can also extend our understanding of our evidence, the circumstances and

intentions of the legislators, by studying particular acts in context
or with reference to the original acts. Professor Lander made this
a very fruitful approach. Particularly striking instances are his
consideration of the 1474 act of resumption and the 1475 act of
attainder in the light of the Warwick inheritance dispute. Only
thirteen people were attainted, Lander showed, because the chief
culprits, Warwick and Montagu, could not be attainted without
disinheriting the duchesses of the king's two brothers Clarence
and Gloucester, which was politically impossible.[26] It was the 1473
act of resumption that compelled Clarence himself to agree to the
division of the Warwick inheritance set out in two acts of 1474–5.
The 1468 statute of livery, Edward IV's taxation of 1472–5, the
attainders of the Mountford family, Henry, duke of Somerset (d.
1464) and Clarence (d. 1478), and the parliamentary grant of
Cumberland to Gloucester have all received detailed scrutiny in
recent years.[27] Since attainders took account of the existing
situation, were resisted and were matters of negotiation, the
situation was often much less simple than the straightforward
decisions recorded on the parliament roll. A flood of light was cast
on the political divisions of the Wars of the Roses, their longevity,
the political settlements, and how successive kings maintained
control, by Lander's analysis of the attainders, by B. P. Wolffe's
assessment of acts of resumption, and the present author's
consideration of their interaction.[28] Such detailed work, however,
is decidedly patchy: undoubtedly there is more to be done.

Important though Parliament was, often it merely formalised
decisions made elsewhere. Parliament did as it was told: it resisted
or delayed taxation but indulged in no major constitutional
conflicts. In 1485, albeit reluctantly,[29] Henry VII's Parliament duly
attainted the king's defeated enemies just as its predecessors had
done in 1459, 1461, 1475 and 1484. Parliament was summoned
by successful usurpers to legitimate revolutions that had already
taken place. Executive actions presumed subsequent parliamentary confirmation. Thus pardons and partial restorations
preceded reversals of attainder, sometimes by several years, and
both the partition of the Warwick inheritance and Clarence's
execution were anticipated by grants legitimised only in
parliamentary sessions yet to come. To understand attainder or
resumption in full, recourse is needed to the chancery rolls, the
chancery inquisitions post mortem, and exchequer land
administration. Most important legislation was probably initiated

by the crown; usually it was the king's administration that implemented it; and it is certainly among his records that explanatory material has first to be sought.

The patent rolls register royal commissions, appointments and grants within England that illuminate government routine on royal patronage and coercion, the administration of justice, the maintenance of order, implementation of policy, and action in emergencies. Other rolls record relations with Scotland (the published Scotch Rolls) or France (the unpublished Treaty Rolls). There are pardons emanating from the royal prerogative of mercy, though many more are contained on the unpublished pardon rolls. To pardon usually called for a specific decision by the king. Sometimes there were wholesale amnesties, perhaps following particular crises as in 1468 and 1470, and sometimes after submissive rebels had been fined, as in 1471 and 1497. Not all those who took out pardons were necessarily rebels and some were specifically excluded, like Sir Thomas Malory of *Morte D'Arthur* fame. The published close and fine rolls and unpublished exchequer archive are more concerned with financial administration – customs, sheriffs' farms, feudal incidents, estate management – and with internal instructions, memoranda and audit. Such material, as always, makes better sense in context, illuminated by an appreciation of government economic policy, the patronage of a particular treasurer, Yorkist and early Tudor chamber finance, the elaborate system for prioritising payments at the exchequer, and the meaning of entries on the Exchequer of Receipt rolls.[30] The records of chancery or exchequer were not made for easy reference. Income, liabilities, balances and budgets were not readily available and have to be calculated with endless labour by modern historians.

Like the rolls of parliament, those of chancery and exchequer are highly formal. They seldom record the background decisions because decisions were made elsewhere: the great departments of state mainly implemented the initiatives of others – king and council – and often indeed merely issued verbatim copies of their own instructions. Behind each letter patent lies a warrant and behind each warrant is usually a petition, which (if written and surviving, not oral and lost) may record details subsequently omitted: why a grant was made and at whose instance. Thousands of warrants and petitions survive. Many circumstances, technical and formal, determined the dating of a patent, almost always later than the warrant and hence the original decision. Sometimes with significant results: apparently disconnected patents prove to have a single origin; grants of Clarence's lands prove not to be made after his execution, but before it or even prior to his trial.[31] Recipients thus presumed, conspired in and gambled on his fall.

Such decision-making occurred at two levels: the king and his council. Much was undertaken by the royal council, a fluid assembly of councillors, many of them officials, who met several times a week with or without the king and authorised action under the king's privy seal. Their decisions were copied into registers, which are lost and are duplicated by a mere handful of memoranda surviving as warrants directing action elsewhere. This is a major loss. Copies of lost minutes of 1454 found in an American library reveal how the nobility constituted a council of national unity to support the duke of York as Protector while Henry VI was insane.[32] Though seldom mentioned, the council clearly initiated many known acts. How often was the council behind privy seal letters authorising appointments and payments, interfering with trials at common law, or directing the conduct of town councils? We have also lost the privy seal archives and with them much of the informal correspondence of crown and subject. The handful of letters kept by recipients – mainly towns – or copied in their registers are thus especially valuable.

The Privy Seal Office was fixed at Westminster, whereas the king – the source of most decisions – was often elsewhere. With him in his household he took his own secretariat – the signet office, headed by his secretary, the custodian of his signet seal – and his own treasury of the chamber. Both secretary and signet were relatively inactive under Henry VI, a king of few and ill-considered initiatives, but bulked much larger under his adult successors, who directed government and politics in person. Many appointments, grants and payments were commanded by letters under the signet or that they had signed. The signet office of Edward V and Richard III produced the four massive registers of British Library Harleian Manuscript 433, which summarise appointments and grants, commands and commissions; list royal officials and feed men; and contain memoranda on oaths of office, defence, justice, finance and much else. A Longleat manuscript contains financial data from the spring of 1483.[33] Together these contain the working papers necessary to the king for informed decisions and policy-making. Whilst they survive best for Richard's reign, similar material existed earlier and later: B. P. Wolffe catalogued Edward IV's endless commands to the exchequer to leave the administration of the crown lands to the chamber's network of receivers and to accept his certificates of chamber accounts. In 1467 and 1473, when Parliament resumed royal grants, the king interviewed in person those seeking exemptions, reviewed records of their holdings in the signet office, and decided what they could retain and what they must surrender. No wonder he is recorded to have known all the gentry in person. Henry VII, notoriously, checked all the chamber accounts himself. Whilst systematic survival of state papers begins only with Henry VIII, clearly governments during the Wars of the Roses were much better informed than the records of chancery and exchequer suggest. Except under Richard III, our voluminous surviving records are not those on which governments based their decisions and are indeed inferior to them.

IV

Historians disagree whether late medieval England was a federation of noble spheres of influence or a federation of county communities, but all agree that national politics was profoundly influenced by local affairs. These, in turn, were shaped by national events. Consequently there is much miscellaneous material existing locally of direct relevance to the wars themselves. For Buckingham's rebellion in 1483, surviving indictments are preserved locally – one at Barnstaple records the recognition of a new (unnamed) king on 2 November at Bodmin – and the movements of the rebel bishop of Salisbury are itemised in his register.[34] Cathedral records of 1471 show Clarence at Salisbury and Somerset breaking the bishop's gaol at Wells. The most valuable and systematic of local records for national history are the urban archives and the collections of private letters.

Many important towns have records that have been inadequately exploited. When important events happen locally, urban archives can make substantial contributions: because so much happened in London, the city's records, like the London chronicles, deserve a special place. Most corporations kept accounts which record gifts to local notables, payments for emissaries passing to and fro, and the costs of urban contingents to campaigns. Many such accounts were summarised in the Victorian and early twentieth-century reports of the Historic Manuscript Commission, a few like Salisbury, Hull and Barnstaple have been extracted elsewhere, but only a handful (like York and Newcastle) have been properly edited. Urban archives, like all other records, yield less out of context and more when their local and archival contexts are understood. Most such resources deserve further attention. They have been especially helpful for dating summonses to Parliament and parliamentary sessions. Less numerous, but much more valuable, are books of minutes. Those of Coventry and York are justly celebrated and long in print; those of Dunwich and Sandwich are less well known; most undeservedly neglected are the journals of the City of London. There are, besides volumes of registered memoranda and the actual memoranda themselves, which often include royal letters ordering mobilisation or forbidding retaining, as at York and Southampton. Finally, ancillary or subsidiary records, such as the Salisbury churchwardens' accounts and those of London livery companies,[35] can amplify or supplement those of the corporation itself. Such records have a major place in the history of the town, but seldom add more than chronological or geographical precision to national history.

Letters were commonly exchanged among both rural and urban elites, but were not usually considered worthy of preservation. The Pastons, Stonors, Plumptons and Celys were unusual not in writing, but in keeping their letters. There are now good modern editions of all but the Plumpton correspondence. Among over two thousand papers, some inevitably bear directly on national politics: the dynastic revolution of 1483 is illuminated by two letters of Simon Stallworth to Sir William Stonor, by another from the warden of Tattershall College to Bishop Waynflete, and by a cryptic Cely memorandum.[36] In the last Stonor letter Viscount Lovell urged Sir William Stonor not to join Buckingham's Rebellion: unavailingly, so the whole collection was confiscated and this survives among the public records. Each collection is a family archive of everyday concerns and a prime source for social history as H. S. Bennett long ago so triumphantly showed in his *Pastons and Their England*. Yet much more can be made of these uniquely rich sources, as Mrs Hanham, Mrs Kirby, and Professor Richmond have shown.[37] Richmond in particular is making sense of much that was obscure about the Pastons and is illuminating facets of aristocratic life that Bennett neglected or scarcely touched. From a fuller understanding of these families, their local societies and their political systems, we can appreciate better their contribution to national politics and the Wars of the Roses. The Pastons' East Anglia was dominated and disputed by the dukes of Suffolk and Norfolk and the earl of Oxford. The advantage shifted with changes at the centre and itself contributed to such alterations. Local manpower was mobilised by Norfolk for the Yorkists in 1461, by Oxford in 1471 and 1487–9, and by another Norfolk for Richard III's Bosworth campaign. There is material in the *Paston Letters* on all these topics.

The localities were fundamentally important as the basis of the power that shaped national politics. National history is the sum of many local histories. As historians have realised these truths, so the potential subject matter of the Wars of the Roses has been extended and sources hitherto spurned have become relevant. It is now almost sixty years since it was first realised that a full understanding of political leaders – all members of the nobility – demanded a knowledge of their estates, income, expenditure and retainers. Such information presupposes the study of their archives: their title deeds and cartularies; their estate accounts; and household accounts, like those of John Howard that have been recently republished.[38] Now that the gentry are also regarded as independently important, historians are investigating the accounts and deeds of much smaller estates. Whilst some such materials are deposited in every local record office, the largest quantity by far are public records; thousands of deeds are known only from copies registered on the close and plea rolls and thousands more remain unsorted or merely listed. Ultimately the value of such materials depends on the interpretation attached to them. Whether lists of witnesses are crucial political sources or politically valueless depends on our assessments of who counted politically and how local politics worked: matters on which historians are not yet agreed.

Modern historians devote much attention to the operation of local politics. The objective of such politics, it is usually assumed, was control of local government; at the very least the personnel of local government reflected the realities of local power. But hardly any records of local government survive: virtually none locally. The main sources are those of central government, especially the

rolls of chancery and the courts of common law. From the
chancery rolls can be composed lists of the names and terms of
office – but hardly ever the reasons for appointment – of sheriffs,
escheators, justices of the peace and commissioners, estate and
customs officials. Their political significance can be deduced from
known familial and social contacts or by correlating the dates of
appointment and dismissal with political events. So, too, with the
Members of Parliament, whose elections are recorded, but seldom
the circumstances. Analyses of parliamentary representation, for
example of northern counties and boroughs, can illuminate the
political complexion of whole areas. Where contested elections
were reported in letters, provoked lawsuits, or were investigated
subsequently, the political divisions of county communities can be
exposed with extraordinary detail. In 1460, for example, the poll
of the Nottinghamshire electorate reveals the decisive
mobilisation of the men of the northern wapentake of Bassetlaw
behind John Stanhope and Sir Robert Strelley.[39] Such records are
rare, this one apparently unique, probably because contests were
rare, and co-operation rather than conflict was the norm.

Apparently more straightforward are the voluminous records
of the central courts. If one nobleman sues another, it is surely
evidence of friction. If one assaults another, besieges him in his
castle or fights a private battle against him, is this not the
strongest possible evidence of hostility? Such serious conflict had
substantial causes, often arising from disputes over inheritance
or the dominance of particular localities that could not be
compromised. They could have grave consequences. The parties
in one dispute could coalesce with those in others and divide a
whole county or even the whole country: thus the Nevilles joined
York against their enemies the Percies and Beauforts, who
became Lancastrians. 'The Wars of the Roses were thus the
outcome of the escalation of private feuds.' Professor Storey has
based his celebrated dictum on his pioneering analysis of the
records of major judicial commissions in the 1450s.[40] Others have
applied it to other feuds then or later. Local communities,
historians have deduced, were riven by litigation and feuding and
were chaotically lawless. Levels of lawlessness in turn are used as
indices of the effectiveness of government. Local disorder was
directly contributory to further outbreaks of civil war.
Unfortunately little of such evidence is in print and none in
English. It is not wholly unambiguous. Few civil actions ended

with verdicts and few feuds resulted in convictions. Those suing their rivals or indicting (charging) them with crimes were partisans, inclined to exaggerate their ills and to present the best side of their case. Relatively peaceful disputes were expressed in the warlike and violent terms needed to qualify for particular types of legal action. Often suitors initiated legal action to force their opponents to compromise: most civil suits, it has been suggested, ended peacefully out of court and many an inheritance dispute was settled by arbitration. Formerly neglected, arbitration awards are now a much more appreciated political source. Violence was actually unusual.[41] Thus legal action may often be evidence not of the breakdown of social control and public order but that differences were being resolved in an orderly and peaceful manner. Probably Storey was too ready to accept the truth of the indictments in his feuds, but his conclusions about their importance and significance were nevertheless correct.

V

The first four centuries after the Wars of the Roses witnessed uncritical reliance on the chronicles. How was More's *Richard III* ever regarded as objective? For the last half century historians have been dissatisfied with chronicles and have searched ever more widely for additional material treating the wider range of issues they have wished to discuss. This has been the age of the record. Ever more rolls and files at the Public Record Office have been ransacked and highly original uses have been devised for much apparently of little value. Elaborate narratives have been deduced from records alone: blow by blow accounts, for example, of the power struggles in one midland county.[42] Moreover, as we have advanced our understanding of the procedurer and diplomatic of the records, so we have undermined some of our confident conclusions. The most straightforward records have become nuanced and opaque. The value of such material too often rests on the interpretations that are placed upon it. Records seldom offer overt avowals of motives: their significance is not always or often beyond dispute. Even the perusal of vast quantities of second-rate material can add relatively little to what is already known. Our attempt to answer the major questions by oblique

approaches and with reference to an ever wider range of sources
has seldom borne the direct fruits that were once hoped.

That does not mean, of course, that we must abandon hope of
knowing any more. Crucial new information does turn up, such as
Earl Rivers' appointment of Duke Richard of Gloucester as arbiter
in March 1483.[43] Even new chronicles are not unheard of, though
we should not expect them. Yet the main sources are those that
we have known for a long time. Much more can be made of them
by better editions, by more detailed textual and contextual study
and by refinements in our interpretations. We can interpret them
better: even More's *Richard III* has much to offer us! Pride of
place, as always, rests with the contemporary narratives, but the
best opportunities, perhaps, rest with the propaganda and the
manifestoes. Documents such as the rebel manifesto of 1469 and
the *Manner and Guiding of the Earl of Warwick at Angers* (1470) have
been too readily rejected as self-serving deception by cynical
and materialistic historians. They too deserve critical modern
editions. What was the message, where was its appeal, and who
was the intended audience? Thanks to our preoccupation with
records, we now know both the period and the primary sources
much better, but there is much that remains to be done.

3. The Economic Context

R. H. BRITNELL

England in the mid-fifteenth century was rich in resources of land, minerals, communications and occupational skills. The country's inhabitants, perhaps numbering about 2,500,000, normally enjoyed standards of living that were high by international standards. An anonymous note on England's foreign trade dating from about this time observes that 'the common people of this land are the best fed, and also the best clad, of any nation Christian or heathen', and during the 1470s Sir John Fortescue, the former Chief Justice of Henry VI, observed that England was blessed with such good government that its inhabitants were wealthier than those of France, and amply provided with all they needed.[1] In comparison with earlier and later periods, 1430–85 was one of exceptionally high wages. Ordinary farm workers were able to obtain a wholesome and varied diet of wheaten bread, barley ale, meat and fish, supplemented by vegetables from their gardens.[2] Opportunities for paid work were generally good. Though there were inevitably fluctuations of employment in some occupations, especially those dependent upon overseas markets, involuntary idleness was not normally a problem.

Most people depended to some extent upon trade both to gain their livelihood and to meet their social obligations. The most easily identifiable markets for agricultural produce were the towns. London, with a population between 40,000 and 70,000, was England's largest city, and drew grain over long distances by water.[3] Even Colchester (Essex), with perhaps between 5,000 and 8,000 inhabitants, regularly engaged in coastal trade for its supplies of malt.[4] Most inland market towns, whose populations rarely exceeded 3,000 people, drew their supplies over only ten miles or so. Many of these had shrunk, so that their streets were lined with the sites of abandoned houses and shops. Yet few villages were beyond an easy day's journey of some sort of urban centre. Nor was trade confined to transactions between town and country. Villages, too, had significant numbers of industrial

41

workers, especially in parts of the country where the manufacture of woollen cloth had become a regional specialisation. In the valleys of the Stroud and its tributaries in Gloucestershire, the availability of sites for fulling mills had encouraged the industrial development of Stroud, Bisley, Chalford and neighbouring villages, and agrarian incomes were partly dependent on the prosperity of the cloth industry in large parts of Wiltshire by 1450. Demand for foodstuffs in some other regions of the country depended in part on other industries, such as tin-mining in Cornwall, lead-mining in Derbyshire, and coal-mining along the Tyne.[5]

Patterns of agriculture differed markedly from region to region, depending on local resources and market conditions. Though wheat was grown commercially almost everywhere, the patterns of crop rotation in which it was included varied greatly. In some places farmers grew large quantities of barley, especially for brewing, or oats, especially for horses.[6] Pasture farming was also locally specialised. Animals could travel long distances on foot, so that cattle breeders in north Wales were supplying markets in the west midlands (notably Birmingham and Coventry) and the south-east.[7] Wool was produced in most parts of England both for the domestic cloth industry and for export, but there were many different recognised qualities. A list of English wools drawn up in 1451 lists 51 varieties ranging from March wool at £9 6s. 8d. a sack to Sussex wool at £2 10s. 0d. a sack.[8] There were other local specialties. The warrens of East Anglia, for example, were a major source of rabbits for the London market: John Hopton's warren at Blythburgh in eastern Suffolk supplied 500 rabbits to a London poulterer in 1465–6 and a further 724 the following year.[9]

There were still opportunities for families to improve their lot by migration. However, this was less marked a feature of the period 1435–85 than it had been earlier. By the mid-fifteenth century fewer people were drawn towards town life than in the early decades of the century. Urban renewal was becoming more dependent than in the past on the reproductive powers of townspeople themselves. In part this was because of the increasing enforcement of guild regulations to protect some urban craft skills, but the major reason for fewer townward migrants was widespread stagnation of urban economies and deterioration of employment opportunities. Rural families were more likely in this period to migrate in order to take up land on better terms elsewhere.[10]

In law the capacity of villagers to benefit from such agrarian opportunities was restricted by the unfree status of many village families. By manorial custom, villeins were supposed to remain on their hereditary land and to pay the customary dues to their landlord in labour services, money or produce. In reality, there was little hope of holding them against their will if landlords elsewhere were anxious to recruit new tenants on favourable terms. This was often the case in the mid-fifteenth century, when the economic implications of earlier depopulation were still being worked out. England's population had fallen steeply between the Black Death of 1348–9 and 1430, and this was the period of most rapid adjustment in land values.[11] However, the land market was slow to absorb all the implications of this change because of the non-contractual nature of most rents. The continuing trickle of migration away from less desirable to more desirable niches in the economy caused many landlords to suffer continuing losses of rent, as from the abbot of Westminster's manor of Islip, between the 1430s and the 1460s.[12]

Though standards of living were high by the standards of earlier centuries, the mid-fifteenth century, from about 1430 to about 1465, and in some places longer, can be considered an age of economic recession. There is no self-contradiction here; recession, and sometimes prolonged recession, has been a recurrent feature of the world's richest economies in the twentieth century. It is nevertheless misleading to speak of mid-fifteenth-century recession as if it were a single phenomenon, or as if its chronology were everywhere the same. Two quite distinct causes can be isolated. One was the impact of epidemic diseases, which could be very disruptive if they reduced the number of tenants and the number of wage-earners by more than a few per cent. The second was the impact of crises in foreign trade, arising when sales abroad were adversely affected by war, trade embargoes or contracting demand in foreign markets. These two causes, the demographic and the commercial, need to be analysed separately. The demographic crises of this period varied greatly from one part of the country to another, so that many of the economic effects were regionally specific. The effects of disrupted overseas trade affected the whole country, but they were felt most in regions whose employment depended heavily on exports.

Though the chief phase of late medieval demographic contraction was past, the mid-fifteenth century was an unhealthy time. Total numbers were at best stationary, and in some places still slowly falling, between 1430 and 1485.[13] In the monastic communities of Canterbury and Westminster, the period 1430–85 was one when expectation of life fell, for reasons which must correspond to higher mortality rates in the outside world. Recurring crises, often caused by plague epidemics, are recorded throughout these decades. Some epidemics affected much of the kingdom, as in 1433–5, 1438–9, 1463–4, 1467, 1471, 1473 and 1479–80. At Westminster Abbey there were crises in 1433–4, 1457–8, 1463–4 and 1478–9. Evidence from the monastic community of Christ Church, Canterbury, records major epidemics in 1457, 1471 and 1487.[14] Occasionally these epidemics had sufficient impact to cause regional or local economic crises. The best example of this yet identified is the severe northern crisis of 1438–40 caused by a 'great pestilence' combined with poor harvests and famine.[15] The epidemic of 1462–5, coming on top of a period of acute political unrest, and coinciding with a sharp drop in cloth exports, contributed to the disruption of economic activity in much of southern and eastern England, though its importance has still to be determined.[16]

The effects of population losses were compounded by commercial difficulties. The forties, fifties and early sixties are known to have been a period of widespread economic contraction in Europe associated with declining internal trade, an outflow of precious metals to Asia, declining activity in the mints, a reduction of currency in circulation, and falling prices.[17] England could not be isolated from the consequences of a major continental recession since exports of wool, cloth and grain were a significant source of revenue for landlords and merchants, and maintained employment in numerous towns and villages. Having reached an all-time high in the early 1440s, cloth exports slumped to almost half that level in the early 1460s (Table 1). The worst year for exports, 1464–5, corresponds to the worst period of recession on the continent. In 1463 unrest amongst artisans in London and other cities provoked the introduction of wide-ranging bullionist and protectionist legislation. The crisis of the early 1460s provoked Edward IV into a debasement of the coinage in 1464–5, the first significant alteration in the quality of English currency since 1411.[18]

TABLE 1: *Annual exports of English woolsacks and cloth and an index of cloth prices (five-year averages)*

	woolsacks	cloths	cloth prices (1430–4 = 100)
1425–9	13,255	41,510	81
1430–4	7,508	40,860	**100**
1435–9	3,236	42,898	110
1440–4	9,759	56,944	93
1445–9	6,592	49,448	110
1450–4	7,769	37,380	82
1455–9	7,266	37,542	83
1460–4	5,315	30,934	89
1465–9	7,944	35,130	75
1470–4	7,575	35,725	85
1475–9	7,950	45,115	96
1480–4	7,160	55,184	110

SOURCE   J. H. Munro, 'Monetary Contraction and Industrial Change in the Late-Medieval Low Countries, 1335–1500', in N. J. Mayhew (ed.), *Coinage in the Low Countries (880–1500)* (BAR International Series, 54, Oxford, 1979), pp. 151, 155.

Though most of the problems in England's overseas trade were a direct consequence of this more general crisis, they were compounded by some failures of English policy. An act of piracy against German shipping, committed in 1449 by Robert Winnington, a naval commissioner of the English crown, was openly condoned by Henry VI's Council. The Hanseatic League took reprisals against English merchants and the Danes closed off the Oresund to English shipping. Yet though this interrupted the English trade to the Baltic, until an agreement was patched up in 1456, Hanseatic ships were actively trading through London and other east-coast ports, so only a minor part of the history of declining cloth exports can be explained as the consequence of these hostilities.[19] Meanwhile, there were other political causes of commercial dislocation. One was the retaliation of Philip the Good, duke of Burgundy, against English bullionist legislation. In 1447 he intensified measures to exclude English cloth from Burgundian markets, with considerable success. A petitioner to the Commons in the parliament of 1449 alleged that this ban was causing distress and unemployment in England. The ban was temporarily removed in 1452.[20] Meanwhile trade with France was disrupted following the reopening of war in 1449. The subsequent loss of England's French possessions was a serious problem for English trade and its effects were more prolonged since favourable conditions for trade between the two kingdoms were not restored until the Treaty of Picquigny in 1476. Government failure here undoubtedly contributed something to loss of exports after 1449, and subsequently affected the pace of recovery.[21] Some increase in the volume of English exports in the later 1460s accompanied the gradual revival of demand on the continent of Europe but full recovery was very slow, and not till the end of Edward IV's second reign did cloth exports compare with the level of the early 1440s.

Compared with the demographic and commercial sources of economic adversity, civil war played very little part in the economic misfortunes of the mid-fifteenth century. The evidence of the Early Chancery Proceedings and Ancient Indictments in the Public Record Office suggests that such plundering as there was was very localised, and that the livelihoods of the great majority of people were little affected.[22] In part this was because military activity was of such brief duration. In part, too, it was because indiscriminate destruction was in no one's interests. Perhaps the most brutal phase of the war was the last years of the Lancastrian regime in 1460–1. The Yorkshire estates of the duke of York and the earl of Salisbury were looted by Percy supporters in 1460. In the early weeks of 1461 Margaret of Anjou's army, moving southwards towards London after the Battle of Wakefield, was said to have created havoc on the way, though the prior of Crowland's report stresses thefts of valuables from churches rather than the destruction of productive assets.[23] These episodes seem to have been magnified by report. As a rule, even the zone where fighting was taking place suffered little adverse effect. In 1450, the wardens of Rochester Bridge lost £5 because the Tilbury ferry service across the Thames was discontinued during the time of Cade's Rebellion, but this is the only indication of any disturbance in their accounts. It would be impossible to guess from the accounts of Durham Priory's cells of Jarrow and Holy Island that Northumberland was the centre of Lancastrian resistance between 1461 and 1464, or that the Tyne was a military frontier. An account from the cell on Farne Island in 1464–5

shows that 5s. 0d. could not be collected for the rents of two acres
of land on the mainland recently damaged in the wars, but this
sum represents a temporary loss of less than 2 per cent of the
cell's total receipts, and the rents were collected the following
year. With the exception of Carlise in 1461, not a single English
town of any significance suffered a sustained siege or looting.[24]

The main determinant of profit levels in this period was
fluctuations in demand, for the demographic and commercial
reasons that have already been explained. Generally speaking the
extent to which prices were depressed in the mid-fifteenth
century varied according to differing degrees of direct and
indirect dependence upon exports. Table 2 compares changes in
the prices of four commodities over this period, taking an average
of the five years 1430–4 as a basis for comparison. It shows that
wool prices, which were established in an international context,
were more adversely affected than the prices of grain, which
entered significantly less into international trade. By the late
1450s wool prices were only 62 per cent of what they had been in
the early 1430s, while wheat prices were much the same as they
had been. Grain, in turn, was more adversely affected than the
price of oxen, which were not traded abroad. Ox hides were
exported from English ports, but these were side products of beef
production and did little to determine the market price of oxen.
Indeed, in the later 1450s the price of oxen was generally higher
than it had been in the early 1430s. These comparisons,
incidentally, suggest that the movement of commodity prices can
have had little to do with changing supply conditions in this
period, since sheep and oxen required similar resources of land
and were also similar in being relatively insensitive to changing
labour costs.

The first column of Table 2 shows that sheep-farming was a
significant source of instability in agriculture. Wool prices
declined gently during the 1440s but then moved sharply
downwards in the 1450s. This was a serious matter for many
farmers, since the keeping of sheep was a very widespread source
of cash in village economies. Landlords were finding, even in the
late forties, that they could not sell wool on acceptable terms, so
that it was accumulating on their manors. In the 1450s they were
reducing their investment in sheep-farming and some, like the
bishop of Worcester and the abbess of Syon, were giving up the
commercial production of wool altogether.[25] This recession was

TABLE 2: *Price indices of principal agricultural commodities (five year-averages)*

| | wool | (1430–4 = 100) | | |
		wheat	barley	oxen
1430–4	**100**	**100**	**100**	**100**
1435–9	95	148	125	106
1440–4	90	73	77	95
1445–9	89	94	83	95
1450–4	68	93	89	96
1455–9	62	97	86	109
1460–4	87	95	105	102
1465–9	94	95	94	112
1470–4	62	91	94	112
1475–9	64	105	83	109
1480–4	110	126	118	113

SOURCE   D. L. Farmer, 'Prices and Wages, 1350–1500', in E. Miller (ed.), *The Agrarian History of England and Wales, III: 1350–1500* (Cambridge, 1991), pp. 504–5, 510–11, 514–15.

particularly serious in regions like the High Peak of Derbyshire, where wool production was exceptionally important. At Hathersage, where tenants paid their manorial lord 'agistment' for pasturing their animals on his land, the evidence from the 1450s shows clearly the severity of the crisis in sheep-farming (Table 3). The severity of this drop in wool prices is undoubtedly related to the decline in exports of English wool and cloth during this same period.

The steep drop in grain prices between the later thirties and the earlier forties represents a very disturbed period when three years of exceptionally high prices (following the harvests of 1437, 1438 and 1439) were followed by three years when prices were exceptionally low (following the harvests of 1440, 1441 and 1442). But on the whole, the mid-century recession did not affect cereals prices very greatly. The early forties ushered in a long phase of somewhat lower grain prices from the forties to the mid-sixties, but in itself this was not enough to have any very profound effect upon the profits of cereals husbandry. In conjunction with higher working costs or marketing costs it could cause trouble, and Table 4 shows that though the wages fell slightly during the 1440s and

TABLE 3: *Agistment at Hathersage (Derbyshire), 1454–60*

| Year | ploughbeasts (averi) | | sheep | horses |
	winter	summer		
1454		178	260	–
1456	102	68	120	6
1460	70	75	60	12

SOURCE I. S. W. Blanchard, 'Economic Change in Derbyshire in the Late Middle Ages, 1272–1540' (University of London Ph.D. thesis, 1967), p. 217.

TABLE 4: *Changes in the wages of agricultural and building workers (five-year averages)*

| | 1430–4 = 100 | |
	agricultural	building
1430–4	**100**	**100**
1435–9	113	114
1440–4	113	110
1445–9	108	112
1450–4	107	117
1455–9	114	113
1460–4	117	109

SOURCE D. L. Farmer, 'Prices and Wages, 1350–1500', in Miller, *Agrarian History,* 522–3.

(for farm workers) during the 1450s, there was upward pressure during the 1430s and again from the later 1450s. This pressure is likely to have reduced the profitability of some arable farming.

Some arable farming, too, was affected by changes in demand either in continental markets or in those English towns whose employment depended on foreign trade. Table 5 records the changing output of grain on the arable of a highly commercialised demesne at Ormesby St Margaret (Norfolk), where some of the most intensive techniques known to medieval

TABLE 5: *Acreages of crops sown on the demesne at Ormesby St Margaret, Norfolk, 1431–58*

year	wheat ac.	barley ac.	peas and beans ac.	oats ac.	total ac.
1430–1	$91\frac{1}{2}$	$121\frac{5}{8}$	$52\frac{3}{4}$	$12\frac{3}{4}$	$278\frac{5}{8}$
1432–3	$67\frac{1}{2}$	128	$48\frac{1}{2}$	11	255
1434–5	70	127	60	20	277
1435–6	$74\frac{1}{4}$*	$128\frac{1}{2}$*	$51\frac{3}{4}$*	?	?
1436–7	71	$120\frac{1}{2}$	$55\frac{1}{2}$	18	265
1437–8	72	120	$47\frac{3}{4}$	17	$256\frac{3}{4}$
1438–9	44	$108\frac{3}{4}$	$53\frac{1}{2}$	27	$233\frac{1}{4}$
1439–40	54	$102\frac{1}{8}$	$45\frac{1}{2}$	27	$228\frac{5}{8}$
1440–1	41	$110\frac{1}{2}$	44	30	$225\frac{1}{2}$
1441–2	$47\frac{1}{2}$	$105\frac{1}{4}$	$38\frac{1}{4}$	$23\frac{1}{2}$	$214\frac{1}{2}$
1442–3	45*	?	41*	$26\frac{1}{2}$*	?
1443–4	29	84	32	26	171
1444–5	36	$105\frac{3}{4}$	$30\frac{1}{4}$	22	194
1445–6	$36\frac{1}{2}$*	?	41*	$24\frac{3}{4}$*	?
1446–7	30	$77\frac{1}{4}$	37	$16\frac{1}{2}$	$160\frac{3}{4}$
1447–8	23	$87\frac{1}{2}$	$33\frac{1}{4}$	22	$165\frac{3}{4}$
1448–9	32*	?	$37\frac{1}{4}$*	17*	?
1449–50	30	$103\frac{1}{2}$	$32\frac{1}{4}$	$12\frac{3}{4}$	$178\frac{1}{2}$
1451–2	30	$111\frac{3}{4}$	30	20	$191\frac{3}{4}$
1452–3	29	107	30	20	186
1454–5	$25\frac{1}{8}$	$131\frac{1}{4}$	$33\frac{3}{4}$	24	$214\frac{1}{8}$
1457–8	26	$142\frac{1}{4}$	$37\frac{1}{4}$	19	$224\frac{1}{2}$

NOTE: figures marked with an asterisk are estimates from the quantity of seed sown.

SOURCE PRO, SC6 939/7–13, SC6 940/2–11, SC6 941/1–2.

agriculture were used to grow barley and wheat for shipment from Great Yarmouth. This was a manor likely to be affected by the European recession since grain from this part of the world went across the North Sea as well as along the coast to English port towns. Operations here were particularly restricted in the late 1440s. Unfortunately the story cannot be carried through to the end of the continental recession because the demesne was leased after the harvest of 1458. However, the *Paston Letters* show that arable farming in this region was severely depressed in the early 1460s.[26]

The cattle trade mostly stood up better to the fluctuations of the mid-fifteenth century, chiefly because of the sustained domestic demand for beef. The prices of oxen, and by implication beef prices, were little affected by the crisis of 1437–43 and tended to rise slightly from the 1450s (Table 2, column 4). Expansion of cattle-grazing was not new. Cattle-rearing was already a principal element in the economy of the monks of Jarrow when the cell was reoccupied in 1432 after having been abandoned for nearly seven years.[27] At the other end of the kingdom, in Tottenham, the conversion from a predominantly arable to a predominantly pastoral agriculture, presumably to fatten beasts for the London market, was already achieved by 1440.[28] In some grazing country the peak of prosperity had come before the mid-fifteenth-century recession. Dairying in the East Anglian Brecklands was at its peak before 1400. On the prior of Durham's vaccary at Muggleswick the number of cows declined from 600 in 1436 to 433 in 1446 and 159 in 1464. The Vernon family of Derbyshire stocked more cattle in 1423–4 than in 1445–6.[29] However, there were parts of the country where the changing balance of profitability towards cattle-grazing may have continued to favour agrarian investment. The Forest of Arden, in Warwickshire, perhaps saw an expansion of cattle-grazing in the second quarter of the fifteenth century. As a successful grazier, John Dey built up a large estate around Drakenage between 1440 and 1472, and the village disappeared as its lands were converted to pasture. In the same region, the accounts of John Brome of Baddesley Clinton between 1443 and 1458 show another cattle-raising estate; his principal customer was Henry VI's household (when in residence at Coventry or Kenilworth), but other sales were to graziers and butchers supplying Coventry, Kenilworth, Warwick and London. Stock-raising on the estates of Richard, duke of York, seems to have made him 'a significant cattle baron' in the 1450s.[30]

Despite the good prices paid for cattle, and the relatively mild decrease in cereals prices, a gentle downward pressure on rents was not uncommon during the period 1430–70. Free rents were characteristically low in comparison with contractual ones; there was no reason for them to change, though even some of them simply stopped being paid in moments of financial hardship.[31] Some customary rents had always been low, some had been lowered before 1430, and some could only be maintained by modifying other incidents of tenure. However, from all parts of England the stagnation, reduction or non-payment of rents was more common than their increase. This was partly the result of the working out of earlier changes in price levels; particularly in the case of customary lands, there was no close relationship between market values and rents. Other declining rents were direct responses either to epidemics that reduced the number of available tenants or to the changing price structure of the period.

In the north there was an exceptionally severe and widespread drop in rents following the demographic crisis of 1438–40. The finances of Durham Priory, already in a confused state in 1438, were further impaired by seven exceptionally difficult years between 1438 and 1445. The priory's receipts from properties south of the Tyne dropped by 14 per cent between 1436 and 1446. The income from the bishop of Durham's estates suffered a severe permanent reduction of about a quarter at this time.[32] The income of Henry Percy, earl of Northumberland, from his manors in the barony of Alnwick in Northumberland fell by a quarter between 1435 and 1450. In Derbyshire, outside the High Peak region, rents were universally declining during the 1430s and 1440s, though opportunities for pasture farming were able to some extent to offset this decline in these decades. Widespread waste was recorded on the estates of Lord FitzHugh around Richmond in the North Riding of Yorkshire, where decays and allowances reduced the income from various manors by amounts varying from 11 to 20 per cent. The trough of this northern depression came in the 1440s and some partial recovery was possible during the 1450s.[33] The north was much less directly affected than the south by the effects of contracting exports in the 1450s and 1460s.

Meanwhile in other parts of the country, though a mid-century recession was general from the 1430s or 1440s it was generally milder than in the north. In East Anglia a drop in land values is apparent after about 1440. In Kent, rents, even for pasture, were falling from the 1430s and 1440s. In Worcestershire a mid-century depression can be dated from the later 1430s. On the east Cornish manors of the Duchy of Cornwall, where rents had been exceptionally favoured by the development of the local economy in the late fourteenth and early fifteenth centuries, rents stagnated or dipped from about 1434.[34] In these parts of the country the trough of the depression came with the decline of cloth exports and the unprofitability of sheep-farming in the period 1450–65. This was the pattern in the High Peak region of Derbyshire, where animal husbandry was of particular importance. Here there were few falling rents in the 1430s and 1440s, but there is more evidence of recession, especially in sheep-farming, from 1450.[35] Further south, in Wiltshire, the 1450s and early 1460s were a period when landlords found it exceptionally difficult to collect debts to which they were entitled, and falling rents were more generally characteristic of these decades than of any other period of the fifteenth century. This was especially so in textile regions where rents had earlier been static or rising. The village of Durrington, ten miles north of Salisbury, had benefited from local industrial development, and from the growth of Salisbury in particular, during the early fifteenth century. But the depression in the textile industry in the 1450s led to arrears of rent, and in 1461 the warden and fellows of Winchester College were obliged to lower the rents on their manor there from 20s. to 16s. a virgate. Even these reduced rents were not easy to collect during the 1460s.[36]

Landlords who had properties in Wales had a particular long-standing problem. At the opening of the fifteenth century the rebellion of Owen Glyn Dwr had shaken some Marcher lordships to the point that they never recovered. In part this was the result of destruction and desertion, but it was also due to the resistance of tenants to seigneurial authority. Despite some recovery from the days of the rebellion, when revenues from Welsh lordships had been wholly unrecoverable, the situation in the mid-fifteenth century was a source of frustration. Richard, duke of York, with eleven out of his nineteen receiverships in Wales and the Welsh March, was the greatest of the Marcher lords. These properties were said in 1443 to be worth £2,879 a year net of upkeep and administrative costs, but a large part of this income was in arrears. Humphrey, duke of Buckingham, with two Welsh receiverships of Brecon and Newport, found the 1440s and 1450s a period of disorder and mounting arrears.[37]

There were ways, of course, in which landlords could hope to counteract the tendency of rents to fall. Mostly they involved putting more time and effort into negotiations with tenants, collecting arrears, and the scrutiny and compilation of records. A general enquiry into the management of the estates of the bishop of Worcester was held about 1450, using local juries to identify rents that were too low and properties of which the administration had lost track, and new rentals were compiled as a result. Leases were more tightly controlled and some unsatisfactory tenants were removed. The leasehold rents of the demesne lands of the bishopric went up by varying degrees as a result. A prolonged renegotiating of rentals was conducted on the estates of Richard, duke of York, during the 1440s and early 1450s.[38] Yet good estate management was not without its costs in travel and manpower, and even if effective it was unlikely to enable landlords to offset all the effects of falling prices and rising wages.[39] Moreover, this was a period in which tenants were in a strong position to counter anything that savoured of high-handed lordship. On the bishop of Worcester's estates, for example, arrears mounted up during the 1450s notwithstanding the attempted reforms, and it may be that aggressive administration had backfired by fuelling tenant resistance. Tenants were particularly resistant to dues that implied their dependent personal status, such as head money and tallage.[40] Even the best administered estates found the middle decades of the fifteenth century difficult to weather.

The end of the mid-century recession is difficult to define exactly both because its causes and chronology were different in different parts of the country and because recovery was generally weak and discontinuous. In the north, as we have seen, some recovery was possible in the 1450s. In some places, as in northern Derbyshire, the rising profitability of stock-raising meant that the recession lifted in the 1460s.[41] Revival of output and rent levels was reinforced more generally from the later 1470s by the renewed growth of cloth exports, with an accompanying improvement in the profitability of sheep-farming.[42] Even then, however, agrarian growth was hesitant and geographically patchy, so that not all estates can be shown to have benefited from it.

The relevance of the recession of the mid-fifteenth century to the incomes of landowners varied from family to family, chiefly because landlords' total incomes were affected by so many other things. The inheritance of property, a fortunate marriage, political favour, were all things that could improve an individual's fortune enough to offset the effects of falling rents. In 1438, for example, on the eve of a severe economic crisis, the fortunes of Humphrey Stafford, duke of Buckingham, were improved by his inheritance of lands worth about £2,400 a year.[43] On the other hand, the adverse implications of falling rents might be as nothing compared with those of financial incompetence or political miscalculation. The problems of the royal demesne in this period have been more usually attributed to these causes than to economic change.[44] On grounds such as these it could be argued that because of these varieties of fortune, which meant that some men were richer than their fathers, the movement of rents was not a prime determinant of landed incomes and cannot be considered to have had any general significance for the thoughts or actions of the nobility.[45]

The argument is not a conclusive one. Even amongst the upper lay nobility, there were men like Henry Percy, earl of Northumberland, who were no richer than their fathers and whose incomes were adversely affected by economic recession.[46] The argument is of dubious relevance even in the case of more fortunate landlords. What they thought they ought to be receiving was a more immediate concern, and a more relevant yardstick of how the world was treating them, than their fathers' total income, especially when dissatisfaction was sharpened by envy of the good fortune of others. The accounting systems that fifteenth-century landlords adopted were almost guaranteed to create a sense of hard times. Estate accounts recorded what estate officers thought their lord's income ought to be, even when much of what was supposedly due had to be written off. The 'true value' of an estate was commonly some level of rent that had been paid at some time in the past, when land had been more in demand. So, for example, the estates of the dukes of Buckingham in 1447–8 were 'worth' £5,020, but the actual income they yielded was only about £3,700.[47] The shortfall here represented either rents that had been lowered, or uncollected rents from tenants who made difficulties about paying, or rents that had lapsed because properties were no longer tenanted. These uncollected rents sometimes made a long list, as in the accounts from the scattered estates of Edmund Grey, earl of Kent, in 1467–8.[48]

Nor can this argument be confined to landlords. No one doubts that rents were exceptionally low, by historical standards, in the mid-fifteenth century and that real wages and standards of living were high. Yet that did not preclude bitter resentment of economic setbacks amongst tenants. In periods of low prices tenants' incomes were bound to suffer, and there were many years in the 1450s and 1460s when arrears of rent arose simply because tenants felt too hard up to pay. The arrears of rent on the Paston estates in the 1460s were clearly in part due to the difficulties tenants had in marketing their crops and their malt. The court rolls of Alciston (Sussex) between 1440 and 1470 frequently speak of losses of seigneurial income that resulted from the poverty of tenants.[49] The fact that shortages of cash did not often amount to starvation or destitution is irrelevant to the question of how they were perceived. Expectations had risen to the point that country people were disgruntled with levels of income quite unattainable by their forefathers. Unemployment, too, was bound to be a source of discontent in regions where, until only recently, there had been scarcities of labour.

The Wars of the Roses cannot be understood simply as a consequence of economic discontent. For one thing, earlier periods of economic dislocation and falling seigneurial incomes between 1348 and 1437, had not been associated with any breakdown of political consensus. Adjustments to aristocratic life-styles imposed by falling revenues were probably more extensive in the period 1380–1420 than during the forty years following.[50] Moreover, the origins of political crisis in Henry VI's reign are explicable by referring to non-economic causes, which include England's humiliating withdrawal from France, the incompetence of Henry VI and the aggressive disaffection of Richard, duke of York. Any attempt at thorough-going economic determinism must founder on these objections. However, this conclusion does not rule out the possibility that dissatisfaction with Henry VI's regime was deepened and broadened by economic discontent. The economic problems of the day, in other words, were one of the causes of his political weakness.

It is a commonplace of fifteenth-century political literature that prosperity was one of the fruits of good government.

And as a body which that stand[eth] in health
Feeleth no grief of no froward humours,
So every commune continueth in great wealth
Which is demeaned with [*i.e. ruled by*] prudent governors.[51]

The king's subjects were similarly disposed to believe that some aspects, at least, of economic recession were the result of misgovernment. For want of better analysis, it was common amongst all ranks of society to blame economic misfortunes on excessive taxation. For example, the author of the so-called *English Chronicle* introduces Cade's Revolt by explaining that 'all the common people, what for taxes and tallages and other oppressions, might not live by their handwork and husbandry, wherefore they grouched sore against them that had the governance of the land'.[52]

In popular politics the case for a strong relationship between insurgency and economic crises is not difficult to argue. In Cade's Rebellion, which occurred during a severe dip in cloth exports during the years 1448–50, the most troubled parts of Wiltshire were the western clothmaking centres (especially Trowbridge, Westbury and Bradford) and Salisbury. In Sussex economic grievances figure prominently amongst the rebels of 1450–1, a large proportion of whom were artisans. Both the number of rebels and the exceptionally radical character of their demands can be explained by their perception that the government had exacerbated rather than solved the economic problems confronting them. Thomas Bright, a fuller of Canterbury, was accused of raising rebellion in Kent on behalf of the duke of York in August 1452. In 1453 the Percy cause in Yorkshire was supported by citizens of York and rural textile workers whose interests were damaged by commercial recession. The widespread agitation against Edward IV's government in 1463–4 again coincided with a crisis in the export economy and involved clothmaking centres in the West of England. One of the ringleaders in Gloucestershire was Robert White, fuller, who was accused of inciting men to rebellion. In the anti-Yorkist rising of 1471 the Essex rebels were said to have made their way to London determined 'that they would be revenged upon the mayor of London for setting of so easy pennyworths of their butter, cheese, eggs, pigs and all other victual', implying that economic grievances were the dominant cause of their unrest.[53]

Men from higher social ranks were not liable to sudden unemployment or destitution, and it is not to be expected that their attitudes should be closely governed by fluctuations in business activity. Economic grievances do not figure prominently amongst complaints against the rule of Henry VI and Edward IV. At most it can be argued that economic discontent sharpened criticism of royal policy and can help explain some of the unusual willingness of landowners to get embroiled in tussles for power between 1450 and 1471. Lawlessness in the country at large, and the acquisitive policies of court cliques, two of the main sources of political discontent, were regarded both as absolute evils and as causes of impoverishment, so that the dividing line between political and economic grievances cannot be finely drawn. In the parliament of 1461 economic grievances were implied, alongside much else, in the denunciation of the Lancastrian period as one of 'misery, wretchedness, desolation, shameful and sorrowful decline'. In 1469 Warwick attacked the Woodvilles, and other figures close to the king, for causing 'our said sovereign lord and his realm to fall in great poverty and misery' through their failure to administer the laws and their personal greed.[54] Such propaganda does not suggest that political opposition was primarily driven by economic grievances, or that it had any precise economic content. However, it confirms that economic adversity was one of the signs by which people identified misgovernment.

Besides blighting attitudes to the king's government, these economic considerations are likely to have increased the bitterness of disputes between his subjects.[55] They enhanced the indignation of provincial landowners who saw individuals using influence at court to obtain grants of lands, wardships and offices under the crown. They may, too, have sharpened antagonism between families in dispute over coveted properties. These two issues often came together. For example, a severe loss of estate income after 1438–40 exacerbated the animosity felt by the Percies towards the Nevilles, who were much better positioned at court. The title to Wressle (Yorkshire) and Burwell (Lincolnshire), former Percy manors which the family had been hoping to recover, was secured by Lord Cromwell for life in 1438. It was the threat of permanently losing these properties to Sir Thomas Neville and his descendants in 1453 that provoked open violence between the two families at Heworth.[56]

Another way in which economic change affected the stability of the political order was through its direct and indirect effects upon royal funds. The decline in Henry VI's income from the royal estates is attributable to his alienation of property rather than to any general economic trends, and the historian of the royal demesne in the period is one of Henry's unkindest critics. It was commonly perceived that Henry was being impoverished by the acquisitiveness of his courtiers.[57] It would therefore be unwise to put much stress on agrarian recession as a direct source of falling royal income. Meanwhile, the king's main regular source of income was from customs duties. He undoubtedly suffered a loss of revenue directly because of the recession in international trade. From the beginning of the Hundred Years War the king had received a large subsidy on the export of wool, and high rates of duty were retained through the later Middle Ages. English merchants paid 40s. a sack on all exports throughout the period 1422–85. Foreign merchants paid even more. Yet, chiefly because of declining exports of wool, income from customs duties fell from £40,677 in 1421 to £28,100 in the years 1446–8.[58] Henry's period of personal rule began badly, in that a sharp drop in wool exports between 1436 and 1439 forced him into a financial crisis and immediate dependence upon parliamentary grants. This inevitably squeezed the credit of the crown and its capacity to defend possessions in France. As Table 1 shows, wool exports increased from the disastrous level of the later 1430s, and never again sank so low in the period under observation. Yet wool exports never returned to the level known during the reigns of Henry's father and grandfather. The number of sacks sent overseas during the thirty years between 1440 and 1470 was 43 per cent below that between 1400 and 1430.[59] This means that even in the absence of any drop in revenue from the royal demesne, the king's normal income would have declined by nearly a fifth since the beginning of his reign.[60] This was not a short-term crisis or one with easy remedies. Edward IV suffered the same financial disabilities as his predecessor. Current estimates imply that the crown's annual income from customs between 1461 and 1470 was only about £25,000 a year.[61]

Henry VI's net annual revenues between 1428 and 1454 perhaps averaged only 60 per cent of those of his father between 1413 and 1422.[62] Such a reduction in ordinary royal income was bound to have political effect. Either the king had to spend less, or he was obliged to negotiate with his subjects for a higher income from taxes. Both courses were dangerous. There can be no doubt which alternative his subjects preferred. They expected the king to economise. On the other hand, the political system of the fifteenth century, in which both the conduct of war and the exercise of royal patronage depended upon the resources at the king's disposal, made it difficult for a king to make drastic reductions in his expenditure without incurring some loss of authority. It was unfortunate for Henry VI that his capacity to perform miracles became effective only after his death.

Neither Henry VI nor his successor was successful in increasing the crown's income from assessed taxes; indeed the level of taxation in this period sank to an extraordinarily low level. Direct taxes on laity and clergy averaged only about £19,000 a year between 1436 and 1445 and £25,000 a year between 1445 and 1453. Even Henry IV, despite his subjects' suspicions of his financial rectitude, had been able to get an average annual income from taxation three times as great.[63] Up until 1450 Henry VI was able to obtain a grant of half a 'fifteenth and tenth'[64] in most years, that is, about £16,500 up to 1445 and about £15,500 thereafter (Table 6). Even this modest expectation was no longer met after 1450. The niggardliness of grants to the king in the mid-fifteenth century is in turn to be attributed in part to the economic characteristics of the age. Economic discontent not only made Members of Parliament less willing to grant taxes. It also encouraged petitions for relief from taxation on account of poverty. The yield of a fifteenth and tenth was reduced by £4,000 in 1432, and a further £2,000 was remitted in 1446.[65] In 1450, when the king was granted a newfangled income tax, he was asked to 'consider the universal poverty and penury of your liege people', and economic hardship was given as a reason for not imposing heavier charges. It is difficult to know what to make of

TABLE 6: *Taxes on the lay wealth (other than taxes on aliens) levied in England, 1437–85*

date granted	date due	rate of taxation	approximate yield £
27.3.1437	11.11.1437	half fifteenth and tenth	16,500
"	11.11.1438	half fifteenth and tenth	16,500
14.1.1440–24.2.1440	24.6.1440	quarter fifteenth and tenth	8,250
"	11.11.1440	half fifteenth and tenth	16,500
"	16.4.1441	quarter fifteenth and tenth	8,250
"	11.11.1441	half fifteenth and tenth	16,500
27.3.1442	28.5.1442	eighth fifteenth and tenth	4,125
"	11.11.1442	three-eighths fifteenth and tenth	12,375
"	11.11.1443	half fifteenth and tenth	16,500
15.3.1445	11.11.1445	half fifteenth and tenth	16,500

Table 6 *continued*

date granted	date due	rate of taxation	approximate yield £
9.4.1446	11.11.1446	half fifteenth and tenth	15, 500
"	11.11.1447	half fifteenth and tenth	15, 500
"	11.11.1448	half fifteenth and tenth	15, 500
12.2.1449–1.4.1449	11.11.1449(a)	quarter fifteenth and tenth	7, 750
16.7.1449	11.11.1449(b)	quarter fifteenth and tenth	7,750
12.2.1449–1.4.1449	11.11.1450	quarter fifteenth and tenth	7, 750
16.7.1449	11.11.1451	quarter fifteenth and tenth	7, 750
6.5.1450–8.6.1450[1]	unspecified	tax on incomes	?
28.3.1453	11.11.1453	half fifteenth and tenth	15, 500
2.7.1453	2.2.1454	quarter fifteenth and tenth	7, 250
"	24.6.1454	quarter fifteenth and tenth	7, 250
28.3.1453	11.11.1454	half fifteenth and tenth	15, 500
4.11.1463	1.8.1463	half fifteenth and tenth[2]	15, 500
"	25.3.1464	half fifteenth and tenth[2]	15, 500
12.5.1468–7.6.1468	11.11.1468	half fifteenth and tenth	15, 500
"	25.3.1469	half fifteenth and tenth	15, 500
"	11.11.1469	half fifteenth and tenth	15, 500
"	25.3.1470	half fifteenth and tenth	15, 500
30.11.1472	3.2.1473	tenth of landed revenues	36, 794[3]
18.7.1474	11.11.1474	fifteenth and tenth[4]	31, 000
14.3.1475	26.3.1475	fifteenth and tenth[5]	31, 000
"	11.11.1475	three-quarters fifteenth and tenth[5]	23, 250
15.2.1483	24.6.1483	one fifteenth and tenth	31, 000

1. For the earliest admissible date, see J. H. Ramsay, *Lancaster and York*, 2 vols (Oxford, 1892), vol. II, p. 123.
2. In lieu of an aid of £37,000 granted 2.5.1463–17.6.1463 (*Rot. Parl.*, V, 497–8).
3. I. e. £31,410 14s. 1 1/2d. collected by 8.2.1474 and £5,383 15s. 0d. yet to be collected on 18.7.1474 (*Rot. Parl.*, VI, 113, 115).
4. In lieu of an earlier uncollected fifteenth and tenth granted 8.4.1474 (*Rot. Parl.*, VI, 39–41). This grant was in conjunction with a wartime subsidy that was later commuted to one and three-quarter fifteenths and tenths.
5. In lieu of the subsidy granted 17.7.1474 (see note 4).
SOURCE *Rotuli Parliamentorum*, Record Commission, 6 vols (London, 1783), vol. IV, pp. 502–3; vol. V, pp. 4–5, 37–8, 68–9, 142, 143–4, 172–4, 228, 236, 498–9, 623–4; vol. VI, pp. 6–8, 111–19, 149–53, 197.

the argument that the king's subjects could 'afford' to pay more taxes. Of course some of them could. The question for the king was whether they in fact would, given the widespread (erroneous) belief that excessive taxation was a principal cause of lower incomes.[66] This belief, incidentally, coloured all contemporary criticism of the extravagance of Henry VI and his court, and so continues to haunt histories of his reign.

While recognising that some extravagances of expenditure were Henry VI's own fault, and that his priorities were out of line with those of his subjects, it is difficult to avoid the conclusion that shortfalls of royal revenue, accompanied by insistent allegations that the kingdom was over-taxed, fed directly into the discrediting of his government. It is reasonable, in other words, to attribute some of Henry VI's difficulties as king to the problems of defending England's position in France, and establishing his own position in England, at a time of falling royal income. In the first place, the contraction of his income, in a time of foreign wars, made him more indebted to some of his leading subjects, and in ways that created lasting political tensions. By September 1443 Richard, duke of York, was owed £38,666 13s. 4d. as king's lieutenant in France, and his inability to recover all this money turned into a sore political grievance. Meanwhile Cardinal Beaufort, because it was difficult to fund the war without him, was able to engineer his nephew, the duke of Somerset, into a position of military command rivalling that of York. In 1443 Somerset led an expensive and futile expedition to Anjou and Maine that did little to further England's interests but which did permanent damage to relations between York, on the other hand, and the king and his Beaufort relatives, on the other.[67] Obviously these events cannot be attributed wholly to declining royal income, since the war itself was a major independent cause of Henry's financial difficulties. However, at this stage Henry was politically committed to the war, and it cannot be without significance that his freedom of action was so clearly constrained by the unprecedented inadequacies of his personal income between 1437 and 1443, the first six years of his personal rule.

Secondly, attempts to extricate himself from the financial quagmire in which he was sinking led Henry into difficulties of other sorts. The sale of Chirk, Chirkland and some manors in Dorset, Somerset and Wiltshire to Cardinal Beaufort for £8,667 in 1439 has been generally condemned as one of Henry's wilder acts of profligacy, and yet on closer observation it appears to have been the only way, in the financial crisis of 1439, in which he could finance the earl of Huntingdon's campaign to Guyenne, a direct result of the Council's commitment to defending England's stake in France. There can be no wonder if, already in 1440, the king's friends thought that war in France was impoverishing both the king and his kingdom.[68]

The third political problem arising from shortage of funds was the problem of handling patronage. Henry VI is open to criticism for the policy he chose to pursue, the chief argument against it being that it did not work. He built up a patronage network centred on his household, and because of his inability to reward his dependants adequately in other ways he authorised an unprecedented flood of alienations of land and offices to the detriment of his normal revenues. In the process he antagonised landowners in the shires, many of whom had a long-established interest in working with the crown, often with the Lancastrian dynasty in particular.[69] However, a severe shortage of funds was bound to make it more difficult than in the past to maintain a crown interest, especially given that the king's expenditure, and the way he managed his estates, were subject to comment and criticism to an extent none of his subjects ever had to endure.

Finally, the king's poverty encouraged the abuse of his right to purveyance. He was entitled to make compulsory purchases of food throughout the countryside to feed his household, but from the late thirties the purveyors responsible for exercising these powers became notorious for their rapaciousness. Those surrendering produce often went unpaid. Despite parliamentary attempts in 1442 and 1445 to limit the burdens this practice imposed, the problem became more acute rather than less, and reached a peak of public outcry in 1450. The problem was a direct result of the inability of the king to pay his way, and it inevitably turned into a grievance against the royal household.[70]

Historians who prefer to understand the fifteenth century solely in terms of conflicting personalities can always write the events leading to the Wars of the Roses as a self-contained political narrative, making the necessary counterfactual assumptions. An abler man than Henry VI – Richard, duke of York, perhaps – might have survived the financial squeeze of the 1440s and 1450s with better grace. Nevertheless, something is lost in ascribing all the political problems of the 1440s and 1450s to Henry's inanity.

Such an analysis greatly exaggerates the differences in quality between Henry VI's rule and that of his successor. It plays down the intractability of the financial problems that both these kings and their advisers faced. It also implies that economic change did not affect the way in which fifteenth-century people evaluated the governments under which they lived. In fact, in this respect they had certain similarities with ourselves.

4. The Origins of the Wars of the Roses

KEITH DOCKRAY

Even historians of the highest calibre put their reputations on the line when they choose to investigate the causes of wars, as A. J. P. Taylor proved so dramatically in 1961 with the launch of his controversial *Origins of the Second World War*. Lesser practitioners need entertain fewer qualms. Nevertheless, the task is always awesome, particularly when, as with the Wars of the Roses, there is no agreement even on the date the wars commenced. 1399 long enjoyed favour as their true beginning: both Lancastrian and Yorkist partisans were wont to find the seeds of conflict in the upheavals of that year; Tudor writers, too, felt powerfully drawn to 1399 as the commencement of almost a century of domestic turmoil; and, in 1888, William Denton could still confidently declare that 'the deposition and murder of Richard II and the usurpation of Henry of Lancaster led to the struggle between two branches of the royal family, which is known as the War [sic] of the Roses'.[1] In the twentieth century, however, 1399 has largely been abandoned and, instead, historians have offered a variety of dates between 1450 and 1459.

Many have settled for the First Battle of St Albans, a major brawl in an English market town fought on 22 May 1455: on one side were Edmund Beaufort, duke of Somerset, Henry Percy, earl of Northumberland, and Thomas, Lord Clifford, committed upholders of the Lancastrian regime; on the other was Richard, duke of York, in alliance with Richard Neville, earl of Salisbury, and his son Richard Neville, earl of Warwick. During the action Somerset, Northumberland and Clifford were all killed; Henry VI fell into the hands of York and his Neville allies; a precarious and short-lived Yorkist administration was set up; and the fate of leading Lancastrian magnates may have set in motion a series of blood feuds of prime importance once the wars commenced with a vengeance in 1459. Certainly, the engagement's most eminent modern historian, C. A. J. Armstrong, believed that, although its military significance was negligible, 'the battle proved to be a mile-stone marking the start of the most extended period of civil war in English history'.[2] Yet was it really so significant? The numbers involved were small and it was not the prelude to a bout of sustained fighting: the next significant battle to be fought, in fact, was Blore Heath in September 1459. Moreover, there are several alternative starting-points available.

The year 1450 is certainly in the frame, seeing, as it did, a powerful parliamentary onslaught on the recent Lancastrian record both at home and abroad, the disgrace and assassination of the king's chief minister William de la Pole, duke of Suffolk, the rebellion of Jack Cade, when men in South-eastern England took up arms in a determined if largely futile effort to remedy the shortcomings of Henry VI's government, and finally, the eruption onto the political stage of a mightily disgruntled Richard, duke of York. Professor Anthony Goodman settles for 1452, the year of Richard of York's first armed challenge to the Lancastrian regime at Dartford, since this campaign was 'the first large-scale one, with more magnates and soldiers involved than in 1455'.[3] Or, perhaps, we should follow an anonymous near-contemporary annalist in regarding the onset of private war between the great northern families of Percy and Neville (specifically, events on Heworth Moor near York in August 1453 when the earl of Northumberland's sons Thomas, Lord Egremont, and Sir Richard Percy attempted to ambush the Nevilles) as 'the beginnings of the greatest sorrows in England'.[4]

The most recent historian of the wars, A. J. Pollard, will have none of these dates. Events in Yorkshire in 1453 (or in 1454, for that matter) cannot be regarded as the beginning of the Wars of the Roses; nor, realistically, can the First Battle of St Albans in 1455 since, although 'a major civil disturbance', it was no more than 'an isolated clash, part of a long prelude to the sustained conflict which broke out four years later'.[5] 1459, in fact, is Pollard's preferred year for marking the onset of civil war proper, and he makes a compelling case for it. In the last analysis, however, it is probably misleading to put too much emphasis on any specific date or event – except, perhaps, Henry VI's mental collapse in August 1453 or, even more, his recovery at the end of 1454 – during a decade that saw mounting political turmoil, rising civil disorder and military confrontation, and eventually culminated, in 1461, in the deposition of the last Lancastrian king of England.

I

Contemporary and near-contemporary sources provide a range of indications as to why civil strife broke out in the 1450s, and although most are critical of late Lancastrian government at best (particularly chronicles written after Henry VI was deposed in 1461) or overtly propagandist in the Yorkist interest at worst, they do pioneer in microcosm virtually every avenue of causation since pursued by historians. Direct criticisms of Henry VI *personally* are relatively rare, but even his admirers (like John Capgrave and John Blacman) tended to remain largely silent on his record as king; while, on occasion, Yorkist partisans deliberately highlighted the central importance of his manifest shortcomings. In about 1460, for instance, Richard Neville, earl of Warwick, declared in a letter to a Papal legate that 'our king is stupid and out of his mind, he does not rule but is ruled'; Warwick's brother George Neville, bishop of Exeter, wrote in similar vein, on 7 April 1461, of 'that puppet of a king ... that statue of a king'; and the anonymous but firmly pro-Yorkist author of the *English Chronicle* recorded, under the year 1459, that 'the realm of England was out of all good governance, as it had been many days before, for the king was simple and led by covetous counsel, and owed more than he was worth'. The *Register* of Abbot Whetehamstede of St Albans, again notably sympathetic to the Yorkists, applauded the king as 'honest and upright' but nevertheless considered him to be 'his mother's stupid offspring', a son 'greatly degenerated from the father who did not cultivate the art of war', a 'pious king' admittedly but 'half-witted in affairs of state'. The Burgundian chronicler Jean de Waurin perhaps got to the heart of the matter when he remarked that:

> because King Henry VI has not in his time been such a man as is needful to govern such a realm [as England], each one who has had power with him has wished to strengthen himself by getting control of the king. So much so that, by reason of the envy which was occasioned between the princes, there arose the dissensions such as you have heard of above.[6]

There are frequent references in anti-government progaganda in the 1450s to the loss of English possessions in France as a cause of discontent at home: major defeats at Formigny in 1450 and Castillon in 1453 resulted in the loss of Normandy and Gascony respectively (leaving England in possession of Calais alone). Richard of York was certainly inclined to make much of this, particularly stressing Edmund Beaufort, duke of Somerset's dismal record in France compared with his own period of service there in the early 1440s. In a manifesto directed to the citizens of Shrewsbury early in February 1452, for instance, he remarked on the 'derogation, loss of merchandise, lesion of honour and villainy' resulting from the loss of Mormandy, placing the blame firmly on Somerset. York's ally John Nowbray, duke of Norfolk, in a petition to the Council in 1453, castigated Somerset in similar vein for 'the over-great dishonours and losses that be come to this full noble realm of England' as a result of 'the loss of two so noble duchies as Normandy and Guienne'. In a later manifesto, this time issued from Calais in 1460, York and his aristocratic supporters were still attacking those 'enemies of the common weal' who 'have suffered all the old possessions which the king had in France ... to be shamefully lost or sold'. And, by the time Polydore Vergil penned his *English History* in the early sixteenth century, the connection between English failure abroad and the onset of civil war at home could be confidently asserted. The battle of Castillon and the fall of Bordeaux to the French, Vergil declared, was 'the end of foreign war, and likewise the renewing of civil calamity: for when the fear of outward enemy [was] gone from the nobility, such was the contention among them for glory and sovereignty, that even the people were divided into two factions'.[7]

Another area of failure by late Lancastrian government often commented on by contemporaries in the context of the slide towards civil strife was the chronic condition of the royal finances in the 1450s. Sir John Fortescue certainly believed regal poverty was a fundamental weakness of Henry VI's government. If a king be poor, he remarked in *The Governance of England*, this can only be highly prejudicial to his prestige and power; worse still, it is 'most to his insecurity' since 'his subjects will rather go with a lord that is rich and may pay their wages and expenses, rather than their king that has nought in his purse'. The Yorkist manifesto of 1460 commented on 'the poverty and misery in which the king our sovereign lord finds himself', while, according to the *English Chronicle*, the king's debts:

increased daily [by 1459] but payment there was none. All the possessions and lordships that pertained to the Crown the king had given away ... so that he had almost nothing to live on. And the impositions that were imposed on the people, such as taxes, tallages and fifteenths, all that came from them was spent in vain, for he maintained no household and waged no wars.[8]

Clearly, the perceived personal inadequacies of Henry VI lie behind the stress in several contemporary sources on the importance during the 1440s and 1450s of growing resentment at the power, wealth and influence of those around the king. A manifesto circulating during Jack Cade's rebellion in June 1450, for instance, expressed the belief that the king has been 'betrayed by the insatiable covetousness and malicious purpose of certain false and unsuitable persons who are around his highness day and night [who] duly inform him that good is evil and evil is good'. Thomas Gascoigne, a convinced Yorkist partisan writing shortly before his death in 1458, portrayed Henry VI even more graphically as a pathetic and gullible figure liable to blatant manupulation by his advisers, who deliberately excluded from the royal presence men who might 'preach anything against those who were around the king, or against the actions of the king, or against the actions of his privy – or more truly his evil – council'. Whetehamstede's *Register* portrayed the Yorkist lords, in 1459, as stiffening their necks 'in order to chastise with rods of iron those familiars of the lord king who had the daily custom of calling those lords false and betrayers of the lord king', while the *English Chronicle* particularly highlighted James Butler, earl of Wiltshire, Treasurer of England from 1458 to 1460, as a man who, 'to enrich himself, fleeced the poor people, and disinherited rightful heirs and did many wrongs'.[9]

Private aristocratic feuds and escalating lawlessness did not escape attention. John Hardyng's *Chronicle*, for instance, contrasted the ineffectual leadership of Henry VI with that of his father Henry V; it resulting, he believed, in increasing misrule and lawlessness in the shires and a notable failure of the legal processes to cope. The Yorkist manifesto of 1460 certainly, and predictably, made much of the notion that 'all righteousness and justice are exiled from the land and no man is afraid to offend the laws', while Sir John Fortescue was much exercised by 'the perils that may come to the king by over-mighty subjects'. Richard of

York in his own propaganda, and chroniclers of a pro-Yorkist bent thereafter, frequently stressed the bitter personal feud between himself and Edmund Beaufort, duke of Somerset. York certainly blamed Somerset for the collapse of English power in France, a matter that clearly rankled deeply with him, as in 1452 when he identified his rival as the 'means, consenter, cause and mediator' of the loss of Normandy. John Mowbray, duke of Norfolk, in 1453, castigated Beaufort no less vigorously for the 'great bribes' by which he had turned men's hearts 'from the way of truth and justice'. The *English Chronicle*, reviewing the political situation on the eve of St Albans in 1455, remarked that the duke of Somerset, by whom 'the king was principally guided and governed', invariably 'kept near to the king, and dared not depart from his presence, dreading always the power' of the duke of York and his Neville allies. Even the early Tudor historian Polydore Vergil, while firmly putting the alternative view of York as the aggressor and Somerset as the 'good councillor' of the king, recognised the vital importance of the powerful personal antagonism between the two men. Nor was the York/Somerset feud the only aristocratic confrontation seen as feeding into burgeoning civil war. In the north of England, for instance, bitter dispute raged between the great families of Neville and Percy from at least 1453, resulting in the Middleham Nevilles forging an alliance with York in the winter of 1453/4, while the Percies threw in their lot with the Lancastrian regime; in the west country, similarly, the rivalry between Thomas Courtenay, earl of Devon, and William, Lord Bonville, clearly did much to influence their response to national developments; and the mutual antagonism of Henry Holland, duke of Exeter, and Ralph, Lord Cromwell, helped determine their political affiliations in the early 1450s as well.[10]

II

For much of the last five hundred years the Wars of the Roses have been portrayed as a dynastic struggle, originating in the tragic circumstances surrounding Richard II's deposition and Henry IV's seizure of the throne in 1399. Indeed, such an interpretation is already to be found in Yorkist propaganda in the later fifteenth century, with the house of Lancaster (in the person of Henry VI) pictured as being rightfully deprived of the throne by the Yorkist King Edward IV: the civil wars are dramatically portrayed by Yorkist apologists as God's punishment on England for the unnatural usurpation of Henry IV and the sinful murder of Richard II.

As early as March 1450, interestingly enough, Richard of York's chamberlain Sir William Oldhall and others were alleged to have been plotting 'to depose the king and put the duke of York on the throne'. In 1451 Thomas Young, one of York's councillors, proposed in Parliament that 'because the king as yet had no heir' it would 'promote the security of the kingdom if he openly established who was his heir apparent', and Young then 'nominated the duke of York'. York himself, in the early 1450s, certainly had the succession to the throne in mind in his manifesto to the citizens of Shrewsbury in February 1452 when he accused Somerset of labouring 'continually about the king's highness for my undoing [and] to disinherit me and my heirs'. York, indeed, seems to have feared that his own powerful claim to be heir-presumptive might be set on one side, Henry IV's act barring the Beauforts from succession to the throne reversed, and Somerset's own merits as the king's rightful heir promoted. And, it is clear, Henry VI's government was notably sensitive on the issue: Oldhall and his associates were indicted on treason charges and Oldhall himself attainted in 1453, while, in 1451, Young was sent to the Tower for his pains. Once Prince Edward of Lancaster was born in October 1453, of course, Richard of York's claim to be next heir to Henry VI disappeared: henceforth, if he were to aspire to the throne, it would have to be entirely in his own right on the basis of his descent from Edward III's son Lionel of Antwerp, duke of Clarence (the so-called Mortimer claim).

Contemporaries were certainly aware of the Mortimer claim and its significance. The *English Chronicle*, for instance, tells us that the rebel leader Jack Cade in 1450 'called himself Mortimer for to have the favour of the people', while an anonymous Chancery memorandum of July 1456 recorded that 'from the time that Jack Cade or Mortimer, called captain of Kent, raised a rebellion in Kent, all disturbances are at the will of the duke of York, descended from the Mortimers'. Sir John Fortescue, it seems, found the existence of rival claims to the throne both fascinating and challenging: indeed, he composed no fewer than four tracts on the dynastic question, as well as devoting a great deal of attention to it in his major work *De Natura Legis Naturae*. In three of the tracts, and in the *De Natura Legis Naturae*, he set out arguments in favour of the Lancastrian title, rejecting Richard of York's main line of descent from Edward III on the grounds that, containing as it did two female links, it was invalid under the Law of Nature. Only after Edward IV's restoration to the throne in 1471 did he pen a fourth tract refuting his own earlier arguments. Pro-Yorkist chronicles written after 1461 certainly tended to draw attention to both the invalidity of the Lancastrian succession and the importance of Richard of York's dynastic aspirations in the lead-up to civil war. The *English Chronicle*, for example, reported how, in the later 1450s, Queen Margaret of Anjou was 'defamed and denounced, that he who was called prince was not her son but a bastard gotten in adultery'; while the *Register* of Abbot Whetehamstede, discussing the motives of Yorkist partisans in 1459, identified a group who 'said that they had risen chiefly for this reason, that the lord duke of York might sit on the throne of the lord king, over his kingdom, and that this should be confirmed and strengthened in him and in his heirs by hereditary succession, from now on and for ever'. And, when Edward IV's title to the throne was proclaimed in Parliament in November 1461, the new king and his advisers cited recent disorders as God's judgement on the country for tolerating Lancastrian rule and denying rightful inheritance to the house of York for so long.[11]

The dynastic approach to fifteenth-century English history in general, and the origins of the Wars of the Roses in particular, admirably suited Tudor propaganda needs after 1485. Early Tudor writers soon took to portraying Henry VII as the agent of divine retribution at Bosworth, the man who rescued England from dynastic conflict after decades of bloodshed, and the king who, by his marriage to Elizabeth of York (Edward IV's eldest daughter), at last united the warring houses of Lancaster and York. Polydore Vergil, for instance, believed that the original cause of division was Richard II's deposition and Henry IV's seizure of the throne in 1399. The wars as such began when 'King Henry [VI], who derived his pedigree from the house of Lancaster, and Richard duke of York, who conveyed himself by his mother's side from Lionel, son to Edward the Third, contended mutually for the kingdom'; even as early as 1450, according to Vergil, York 'aspired to the sovereignty', conceiving an 'outrageous lust of principality' and never ceasing thereafter 'to devise with himself how and by what means he might compass it'. The very title which Edward Hall, writing in Henry VIII's time, gave to his chronicle shows his firm commitment to the notion that the wars were dynastic in origin: *The Union of the two noble and illustrious families of Lancaster and York, being long in continual dissension for the crown of this noble realm ... beginning at the time of King Henry the Fourth, the first author of this division.* Sir Thomas Smith, in 1551, declared his commitment to the dynastic interpretation in no uncertain terms:

> From the time that King Richard II was deposed ... unto the death of King Richard III ... by reason of titles this poor realm had never long rest ... Now this king prevailed, now the other. ... These two blades of Lionel and John of Gaunt never rested pursuing the one the other, till red rose was almost razed out and white made all bloody.

Similar sentiments permeate the pages of the Elizabethan chroniclers Richard Grafton and Raphael Holinshed and, of course, William Shakespeare's cycle of history plays. During the early seventeenth century, too, the Italian Giovanni Francesco Biondi, in his *History of the Civil Wars of England between the two houses of Lancaster and York,* clearly believed the wars began with Richard II and ended with Henry VII; while another commentator, in 1685, traced 'that bloody, unnatural and fatal war' between York and Lancaster which 'lasted about 106 years' from Richard II's reign to the execution of Edward, earl of Warwick, in 1499. In the nineteenth century William Stubbs could still portray the Battle of Bosworth as 'the last act of a long tragedy or series of tragedies ... the unity of which lies in the struggle of the great houses for the crown'. Even as late as 1966 A. L. Rowse remained firmly captivated by traditional notions of the 1399 revolution resulting in the deposition of a lawful king, insecure tenure of the throne by his usurping successors, dynastic wars and constant domestic upheaval.[12]

III

The modern debate on the origins of the Wars of Roses can largely be traced back to two influential studies published in the 1960s: K. B. McFarlane's lecture, 'The Wars of the Roses' (1964) and R. L. Storey's monograph, *The End of the House of Lancaster* (1966). However, its genesis can be found earlier. David Hume, in his *History of England* first published in 1762, when seeking to explain the wars, put a good deal of stress on the importance of aristocratic turbulence in the later Middle Ages. In the introduction to his 1885 edition of Sir John Fortescue's *Governance of England*, Charles Plummer put even firmer emphasis on 'the overgrown power and insubordination of the nobles', and, in the process, coined the term 'bastard feudalism' to describe what he observed in the upper echelons of later medieval English society. The reign of Edward III, he suggested:

> saw the beginning of bastard feudalism which, in place of the primitive relation of a lord to his tenants, surrounded the great man with a horde of retainers, who wore his livery and fought his battles ... while he in turn maintained their quarrels and shielded their crimes from punishment. This evil ... reached its greatest height during the Lancastrian period.

C. L. Kingsford, in 1925, believed that 'in the middle of the fifteenth century governance was the chief thing that was lacking'; however, he also linked social disorder in the 1450s to the ignominious end of Lancastrian rule in France, economic and social change, and political discontent which 'afforded the occasion for the beginning of the Wars of the Roses'. The eminent economic historian Michael Postan concluded, in 1939, that the dwindling resources of landlords in an era of agricultural depression contributed to the 'political gangsterism' of the times; while, in 1953, C. D. Ross and T. B. Pugh suggested not only that financial crisis made lords increasingly desperate to obtain royal patronage but also that the Wars of the Roses were probably fought 'not because magnates could afford to hire armies of retainers to fight their battles but rather because they could no longer afford to pay them'.[13]

Despite an obstinate perfectionism resulting in a remarkably slender corpus of work published during his lifetime (he died in 1966), K. B. McFarlane is the most respected of all modern historians of fifteenth-century England and his 1964 lecture on the Wars of the Roses contained his final considered judgement on the wars.[14] He set the scene by clearing away what he regarded as the many misconceptions and misunderstandings surrounding the wars in general and their origins in particular. For a start, he put on one side the dynastic issue: the Wars of the Roses were not, in his opinion, primarily a dynastic struggle. Nor would he accept the idea that overmighty subjects were a fundamental cause: 'only an undermighty ruler had anything to fear from overmighty subjects', he declared, 'and if he were undermighty his personal lack of fitness was the cause not the weakness of his office and its resources'. Equally misleading, McFarlane thought, is the notion of a causal connection between the end of the Hundred Years War and the outbreak of civil strife in England soon after. In particular, he firmly rejected the suggestion that magnates 'deprived of the profits of war which had compensated them for falling rents' sought to 'escape threatened ruin in the lottery of civil war'. Surely, he argued, the fact that men like York, Salisbury, Warwick, Somerset and Buckingham were richer than their fathers had been belies any suggestion that economic difficulties drove them to political gangsterism. No less unsatisfactory, he believed, is the notion that 'the very existence of armed bands of retainers caused the war', especially if this involves blaming the return of 'a demoralized, unpaid and mutinous soldiery' from France. McFarlane certainly refused to accept that the existence of retainers as such was significant since, after all, such men had been around for centuries without bringing civil war. Nor could he approve the stress by some chroniclers on the importance of local disputes between families as a cause of conflict: the wars did not grow out of quarrels like that between Percy and Neville in the north or Courtenay and Bonville in the south-west. Rather, such feuds 'grew out of the paralysis at the centre induced by the struggle of Somerset and York for control'. In fact, McFarlane concluded, the basic cause of the Wars of the Roses was simple enough: 'Henry VI's head was too small for his father's crown' and the wars were fought because 'the nobility was unable to rescue the kingdom from the consequences of Henry VI's inanity by any other means'. The king's incompetence had so divided the aristocracy that those who had profited from the Crown were completely at odds with those who had not: civil war was therefore neither more nor less than 'a conflict between ins and outs', between those who had the king's ear and those who found themselves out in the cold.

In 1964 McFarlane felt able to declare that it still had to be demonstrated that private feuds between great families did much to influence the alignment of Lancastrians and Yorkists. Two years later, in 1966, R. L. Storey set out to show that such feuds were, in fact, crucially important.[15] Drawing heavily on unpublished judicial records of Henry VI's reign (deposited in the Public Record Office), Storey concluded that the outbreak of civil war can be explained very largely in terms of an escalation of private feuds. It resulted, in fact, from the collapse of law and order in the context of the 'parasitic' and 'retrograde' urges of bastard feudalism: retaining and the lack of good governance, rather than the undermightiness of the king, eventually brought conflict to a head. Private aristocratic feuds, he declared, were very much the order of the day in the 1450s, with a strong tendency for protagonists to resort to violence, as in the clash of Thomas Courtenay, earl of Devon, and William, Lord Bonville, in the west country. The key conflict, he thought, was that between the great northern families of Neville and Percy, at any rate once the Nevilles began backing Richard of York and the Percies, Edmund of Somerset. Bastard feudalism did the rest:

> Gentry, with understandable lack of confidence in the processes of law, attached themselves to lords who could give them protection against their personal enemies and in return supported their patrons in private wars with their peers. These baronial hostilities similarly resulted in the contestants aligning themselves with the major political rivalries, and thus drawing their retainers into the conflict of Lancaster and York.

This, then, is a grass-roots hypothesis: the true causes of the wars should be sought in the shires, in the tensions of magnate and gentry society, Henry VI's personal inadequacy primarily of significance as facilitating 'a steady increase in local violence and a deterioration in men's ability to gain redress at law'.

Historians writing since 1966 have certainly admired and drawn heavily on Storey's diligent researches into private feuds and their consequences. Maurice Keen, in an excellent textbook on *England in the Later Middle Ages* published in 1973, largely endorsed his conclusions indeed, backed up as they were by 'an impressive body of evidence drawn from an intensive study of the local and family rivalries of both the gentry and the peerage in the 1450s'. Since Storey wrote, moreover, there have been a series of further studies of particular aristocratic feuds which, in part at least, have served to reinforce his thesis. In 1968, for instance, R. A. Griffiths, while concluding that it would be a mistake to suggest that feuds such as that between Percy and Neville could *cause* the Wars of the Roses, nevertheless considered their northern dispute to be 'unusually crucial in the passage of events towards the outbreak of war'. Martin Cherry, in 1981, analysed the 'process of polarisation' developing within the Devonshire ruling class over fifteen years until, in December 1455 (when forces led by Thomas Courtenay, earl of Devon, and William, Lord Bonville, fought each other at Clyst), the 'conflict and tension inherent in the group degenerated into civil war'. S. J. Payling, in 1989, while remarking that it may be going too far to suggest that an escalation of private feuds was the *primary* cause of the fall of the house of Lancaster, nevertheless opined that 'there can be no doubt that these feuds undermined traditional Lancastrian loyalties, exacerbated existing divisions within the baronage and provided many with a motive for supporting the Yorkist cause which drew its strength from its foundation in self-interest'. Certainly, he argued, Ralph, Lord Cromwell's efforts in the 1450s to retain possession of a valuable Bedfordshire estate in face of the rival claims of the tempestuous Henry Holland, duke of Exeter, tested profoundly his hitherto firm support for the Lancastrian regime.[16] And, in recent years, the conclusions of both K. B. McFarlane and R. L. Storey have been much cited and discussed in a renewed scholarly debate concerning the origins and nature of bastard feudalism.[17]

In the final analysis, however, most recent historians of the Wars of the Roses have preferred to line up behind McFarlane rather than Storey. Even Maurice Keen, in 1973, had certain reservations about Storey's thesis, particularly in view of bastard feudalism's being 'a constant of the late medieval social and political scene' and the fact that 'contemporaries, though they were aware that the civil wars were closely bound up with struggles for private influence among the great, believed that other and more serious issues were at stake as well'. Charles Ross, in a splendid illustrated history of the Wars of the Roses published in 1976, declared himself impressed by Storey's investigations of private feuds and convinced that local rivalries did help explain the eventual alignment of parties in the national struggle; nevertheless, he rejected the idea that bastard feudalism (which, after all, had been in existence since the early fourteenth century) and private feuds were a prime cause of the wars. Rather, Ross concluded, uncontrolled bastard feudalism and the escalation of aristocratic feuds were a consequence of weakness at the centre: and 'adequate explanation' for civil war can be found in 'personal and political factors, especially those stemming from the weakness of the king and the impossibility of finding a political, non-violent solution to the problems which this involved'. A. J. Pollard, in 1988, remarked in similar vein that itwas 'undoubtedly lack of royal authority, lack of government, lack of firm control from the centre which allowed private feuds and wars to grow unchecked and the kingdom to collapse into civil war'. And even R. L. Storey himself has now partially retracted his earlier conclusions.[18]

Debate has continued as vigorously as ever in recent years, resulting not least in the restoration to prominence of factors both McFarlane and Storey were inclined to play down. As early as 1973 Maurice Keen was already suggesting that the importance of the collapse of English power in France had been unduly neglected when, in fact, the loss of Normandy and Gascony was a wounding blow to national pride and did more than anything else to destroy the Lancastrian regime's credibility. Even more positively B. P. Wolffe, in his 1981 biography of Henry VI, concluded that the fall of Lancastrian France was of central importance in explaining the decline of the king's authority in England: apportioning blame for the disasters in France *circa* 1449 to 1453, he argued, was a major issue in domestic politics for the rest of the reign and must certainly figure in any explanation of the outbreak of civil war.[19]

In 1989 Michael K. Jones suggested a different emphasis again: the real key to the onset of the Wars of the Roses, he suggested, should be sought in the quarrel of Edmund Beaufort, duke of Somerset, and Richard Plantagenet, duke of York. The origins of their mutual hostility, he believed, can be found in Lancastrian France in the 1440s: York could never forgive Somerset's role in easing him out of his command there, a resentment accentuated by Beaufort's dismal record of failure as his replacement . Then, in the early 1450s, he found himself thwarted again and again at home, as Somerset not only turned the king against him personally but also helped deprive him of the fruits of royal patronage. Eventually, finding himself increasingly isolated and fired by an ever more intense personal animosity towards his rival, he resorted to armed force.[20]

Nor should economic factors be neglected, particularly the implications of the increasingly chronic condition of the royal finances in the 1450s. Under these circumstances, as J. R. Lander emphasised in 1976, those whose influence at Court was strongest would always receive priority when it came to the allocation of scarce Exchequer funds: indeed, in the early 1450s, only Somerset could confidently expect his financial needs (which were considerable, given the paucity of his landed endowment) to be met, while York's exclusion from Court probably meant financial hardship. A. J. Pollard believed, in 1988, that 'in the 1450s royal finances were in chaos, the king's credit was negligible and the Crown was virtually bankrupt': this, inevitably, had profound implications both for Henry VI's 'ability to assert his authority over his subjects and for his capacity to satisfy their intensifying demands on him', especially since the harsh economic climate meant 'royal favour was of critical material importance to all magnates'. And, in 1993, G. L. Harriss concluded that the bankruptcy of Lancastrian government by 1450 'undoubtedly contributed to its overthrow'.[21]

Perhaps the most interesting historiographical development in recent years has been a revival of interest in the dynastic dimension of the Wars of the Roses. In 1973 Mortimer Levine could confidently assert that the wars 'did not originate out of any dynastic rivalry': whatever the 'secret ambition' of Richard of York, 'no dynastic issue was involved at St Albans'. In 1979, however, R. A. Griffiths set himself to restore the dynasticism missing from most twentieth-century interpretations. Henry VI and his advisers, he argued, proved to be notably sensitive about the king's dynastic position as long as he had no direct male heir. Hence the reason why, conscious as they were of Richard of York's claim to be recognised as heir-presumptive, they turned 'cautiously, yet unmistakably, to the wider royal family of Lancastrian blood in order to secure dynastic support': the Hollands, the Staffords and , most particularly, the Beauforts. Richard of York, moreover, had a powerful sense of dynasty himself and an acute awareness of the royal blood flowing through his own veins. Even after the birth of Prince Edward of Lancaster in October 1453, Griffiths thought, the issue did not go away – not least because of Queen Margaret of Anjou's emergence onto the political stage as an indefatigable champion of her son's right to the succession – until finally, in October

1460, York came right out into the open and claimed the throne in Parliament. And A. J. Pollard, in 1988, was sufficiently impressed to caution against dismissing out of hand 'the original idea that England fell into civil strife by reason of titles'. As for his own conclusion concerning the origins of the wars, it was masterly to say the least:

> In the mid-fifteenth century many circumstances combined to undermine the authority of the Crown – growing economic and financial pressures, material loss and humiliation in France, the lurking doubt concerning Henry VI's title. They made civil war more likely. In the last resort it was Henry VI's incapacity after 1453 which tipped the balance. In the end, to use a metaphor much favoured at the time, the ship of state was without a captain and, while the crew fell at each other's throats, she drifted onto the rocks.[22]

IV

If the Wars of the Roses had deep-rooted origins, and it is by no means clear they did, they can only be found in the nature of English political society and how it developed in the later Middle Ages. Historians have always, and rightly, highlighted the role of the king himself in the state: power remained very much concentrated in the Crown and the consequences could be catastrophic if a monarch proved unfit to rule. Here, indeed, is the key to much of the political turbulence and social disruption in later medieval England when, whether by reason of tender years, personal ineptitude or mental incapacity, kings too often proved singularly ill-equipped for the job they had to do. Such rulers, inevitably, had problems when it came to controlling political society in general and the great landed aristocracy in particular. The monarchy found itself having to resist the claims and contain the ambitions of nobility and greater gentry while, at the same time, being quite unable to function effectively without their support, especially when it came to fighting the French or the Scots. In fact, success or failure at ruling in the later Middle Ages is almost indistinguishable from success or failure in handling the magnates: thus, in the fourteenth century, two kings who failed to cooperate with the baronage (Edward II and

Richard II) were deposed (in 1327 and 1399 respectively), while a third (Edward III) who, for most of his reign, managed to achieve an effective working relationship with his great men was still England's unchallenged ruler at his death in 1377; in the fifteenth century, similarly, Henry V's military achievements in France depended on his ability to work hand-in-glove with the nobility, while Henry VI's failure to contain baronial rivalries eventually brought him (in 1471) to the same fate as Edward II and Richard II.

Scarcely less significant as a determinant of monarchical success or failure was warfare. Medieval kings were expected to lead their great men in war and, if they did so triumphantly, their reputations were assured. Both Edward III and Henry V scored notable successes against the French – including victory in great pitched battles like Crecy (1346), Poitiers (1356) and Agincourt (1415) – and these ensured an enthusiastic verdict in many contemporary and near-contemporary sources. Edward II, by contrast, failed dismally against the Scots at Bannockburn (in 1314), while Richard II's predilection for peace rather than war mightily aroused the misgivings of his magnates. Henry VI, too, had no aptitude or enthusiasm for war: indeed, his pursuit of peace at any price in the 1440s eventually brought the end of the Lancastrian empire in France. War, moreover, whether successful or not, frequently brought financial problems and these, in turn, proved a major factor in the evolution of Parliament as a means of raising extra cash through the medium of taxation. And later medieval governments, by and large, had an appalling record in matters financial: even Henry V was heavily in debt by the time of his death in 1422.

All this, no doubt, provides an essential political context for the onset of civil war in the 1450s. Does it, however, do more than that? The history of Henry VI's minority (1422–37), on the whole, suggests not. Minorities were always potentially difficult times in the Middle Ages and this one was no exception. In particular, there developed a bitter feud between the young king's uncle Humphrey, duke of Gloucester, and Henry Beaufort, bishop of Winchester, which for a time, in 1425 and 1426, did seem to threaten out-and-out civil war in England. That no war ensued is largely down to the Council. In 1422, although Gloucester had been designated Regent in England by Henry V before his death, the Council had set on one side the late king's wishes: Gloucester was accorded limited authority as Protector but, in fact, it was the Council that ruled on Henry VI's behalf during the minority and, for the most part, it ruled well. Both Henry VI's recent biographers, B. P. Wolffe and R. A. Griffiths, are in agreement that the period of 'collective rule' (as Griffiths calls it) saw notably responsible – if hardly inspired – government: Council members showed a considerable determination to function in a business-like and impartial manner even when confronted by major problems such as preserving law and order, keeping the government solvent and defending Henry V's conquests in France.[23] Thus when, in 1437, the king's minority came to an end, the options open to him were virtually the same as they had been at the time of his father's death: it was the failures of Henry VI and his government *after* 1437, not those of the Council during the minority, which eventually brought England to civil war in the 1450s.

Clearly, the personality of Henry VI, his political agenda (if he had one!) and the character of the Court clique which increasingly came to envelop him are crucial to understanding both the politics of the period *circa* 1437 to 1453 and, ultimately, the outbreak of civil war. Unfortunately, it is far from easy to establish convincingly just what Henry VI was like or exactly what his role was during these years. The most intimate surviving portrait is provided by John Blacman, a Carthusian monk who served as the king's chaplain for a while and probably put pen to paper towards the end of the Yorkist period. Here we have Henry as both 'upright and just' and a man 'more given to God and to devout prayer than to handling worldly and temporal things'; he enthusiastically embraced the virtues of humility, even off-setting the pomp of crown-wearing by donning 'a rough hair shirt' next to his skin; and not only was he personally 'chaste and pure from the beginning of his days' but also 'took great precautions to secure not only his own chastity but that of his servants'.[24] Could such a king have ever been actively involved in politics? Or was he, as another contemporary cleric John Capgrave strongly implied, entirely and exclusively a royal personification of conventional religious piety? Or was he both? J. W. McKenna has certainly suggested that the reality of Henry VI's personally pious and politically perverse personality bears only passing resemblance to the later saintly image encapsulated in Polydore Vergil's reference to there not having been 'in this world a more pure, more honest and more holy creature'. Rather, according to McKenna, he was a mixture of 'charming indifference and exasperating incompetency'; even some of his contemporaries found him dour and puritanical; and, all in all, he was 'the greatest single disaster' in saintly royalty since Edward the Confessor.[25] Henry VI's modern biographers have suggested that, until 1453 at least, he did aspire to be a hands-on king, albeit a disastrously inept and unsuccessful one. From the end of his minority until the early 1450s, B. P. Wolffe has argued, the king himself was 'the essential unique feature of the reign', actively presiding over the liquidation of the Lancastrian empire in France. Rather than the pious, non-worldly paragon of virtue depicted by Tudor historians, or even the negative tool in the hands of his favourites, the real Henry VI was a positive (even sinister) political menace. From 1437 there was truly personal rule; Henry VI's own unwise exercise of royal patronage seriously weakened the Crown's financial position (as well as its political reputation); and, worst of all, from 1444 until 1453, the king took the initiative frequently and with dire consequences in foreign policy. Henry VI's own 'wilful efforts', concluded Wolffe, 'divided, demoralised and hamstrung the English war effort in France, so that it dissolved in defeat and recriminations'. Moreover, the king's conduct simultaneously led to 'creeping paralysis in home affairs and a consequent collapse of respect for law and order by the great'.[26] R. A. Griffiths, in his 1981 biography, was more cautious, arguing that, in many instances, it is not possible to be certain of Henry's *personal* intervention (rather than his passive assent to policies formulated by the Council). Nevertheless, he too concluded that Henry VI rejected his father's militarism, proved himself extravagant and wasteful, and, while lacking the wilful and vindictive streak detected by Wolffe, was certainly thoroughly incompetent.[27]

The year 1450, in particular, was a disaster for the Lancastrian regime. There is evidence of seditious bills, anti-government propaganda and rioting in London early in the year, as well as a substantial demonstration of hostility to the king's men in Kent: most dramatically, Henry VI's Keeper of the Privy Seal (Adam Moleyns, bishop of Chichester) was lynched by an enraged mob of unpaid soldiers and sailors (in January 1450). Mounting discontent with both failure in France and misgovernment at home resulted, in February 1450, in the impeachment of the king's chief minister William de la Pole, duke of Suffolk, by the

Commons in Parliament. Henry VI, in fact, only saved Suffolk from almost certain execution by hastily sentencing him to be banished: even so, while in the very act of sailing into exile (in April 1450) he was seized and beheaded. Most serious of all, Jack Cade's rebellion – a formidable popular uprising – broke out in May 1450. Centred in the south-east of England, and involving gentlemen and yeomen as well as peasants and artisans, this rebellion was clearly a major challenge to the authority of Henry VI's government: indeed, the rebels succeeded in getting into London, amidst a good deal of violence, and it was only with the utmost difficulty that the citizens were able to get them out again. Jack Cade, mysterious leader of the rising, put it about that he was cousin to Richard of York, and rebel propaganda laid particular stress on York's 'true blood' and demanded that he be given a prominent place on the Council. It is clear from a rebel manifesto of June 1450 that the grievances and objectives of the rebels were highly political: for instance, there is much criticism of oppression and corruption in the shires (especially in the administration of the law), of the 'false traitors' around the king, and of England's recent record in France. The king's 'false council', declared the manifesto, has 'lost his law, his merchandise is lost, his common people are destroyed, the sea is lost, France is lost', while the king himself is 'so placed that he may not pay for his meat and drink'. The only solution, the rebels asserted, was that the king should 'send away from him all the false progeny and affinity' of the duke of Suffolk and 'take about this noble person men of his true blood', especially 'the high and mighty prince the duke of York'.[28]

The Lancastrian regime, although now lacking its wildly unpopular former Treasurer James Fiennes, Lord Saye and Sele (who had been seized and beheaded by the rebels), managed to survive this onslaught but, with the return of Richard of York from Ireland (where he had been in virtual exile) in September 1450, there came a fresh assault on its prestige and authority. Yet, despite the deaths of Moleyns, Suffolk and Saye, despite Cade's rebellion, despite recent disasters in France (culminating in the loss of Normandy), and despite powerful criticisms by both York and the Commons in Parliament, the old Court clique continued to flourish around the king. Moreover, the failure (only too evident in 1451) of a petition to remove Edmund Beaufort, duke of Somerset (newly returned from France and widely perceived to be Suffolk's political heir) and other 'familiars' from the king's presence probably reflects the continued determination of Henry VI to protect his chosen men. In February 1452, having failed to make progress by constitutional means, York resorted to armed force. It proved a costly miscalculation. The attempted *coup d'état* of 1452 attracted virtually no support from the nobility (not even the Nevilles had broken ranks at this stage): York was forced to surrender at Dartford, suffer the humiliation of seeing Somerset triumphant, and retire to his estates with his tail firmly between his legs. By the summer of 1453, in fact, the victory of Henry VI and the Court seemed complete, while York appeared hopelessly isolated and thoroughly discredited. Despite all his personal shortcomings and the manifest failures of his government over the years, the king had apparently risen phoenix-like from what, at the beginning of the decade, appeared to be the ashes of his regime: if England had been hovering on the brink of civil war in 1450 or 1452 (even enduring preliminary skirmishings, indeed), she now appeared safe again.

V

Two dramatic, and possibly connected, events in August 1453 changed the situation beyond all recognition: first, news reached England that the veteran John Talbot, earl of Shrewsbury, had been defeated and killed at Castillon, Gascony lost, and the Lancastrian empire in France reduced to Calais alone; secondly, a few days later, Henry VI himself collapsed into a condition of complete mental torpor. Even before August 1453, rumours concerning the king's mental shortcomings had occasionally surfaced: in 1442, for instance, a Kentish yeoman had been charged for saying that 'the king is a lunatic'; in 1447 a London draper was alleged to have remarked that Henry 'is not as steadfast of wit as other kings have been before'; and, in 1450, two Sussex husbandmen were indicted for declaring that 'the king was a natural fool, and would ofttimes hold a staff in his hands with a bird on the end, playing therewith as a fool, and that another king must be ordained to rule the land, saying that the king was no person able to rule the land'. Recent historians have perhaps been too ready to dismiss such snippets out of hand as mere hearsay but, clearly, in 1453 Henry VI suffered a full nervous breakdown (even, possibly, an attack of catatonic schizophrenia).

John Blacman related later how, for a time, the king was 'not conscious of himself, or of those around him, as if he were a man in a trance' (although, for Blacman, this was not so much insanity as spiritual rapture!); even more graphically, Whetehamstede's *Register* described how 'the king lost his wits and memory for a time, and nearly all his body was so unco-ordinated and out of control that he could neither walk, nor hold his head upright, nor easily move from where he sat'.[29] Clearly, the king was utterly incapable of governing the country now, whatever the situation before, and he was destined to remain in this condition until the end of 1454.

To make matters worse, at any rate as far as Richard of York was concerned, in October 1453 Queen Margaret of Anjou gave birth to a son: this served to both negate York's claim to be heir-presumptive and bring the queen into politics as a ruthless, even fanatical, supporter of Prince Edward of Lancaster's right to succeed his father. During the next few months, in fact, she attempted, initially, to conceal her husband's condition and, when this inevitably failed, made considerable efforts to prevent the Council (or, worse still, Richard of York) taking power by securing it for herself: a newsletter of January 1454 reported that she had 'made a bill of five articles ... whereof the first is that she desires the whole rule of this land'. The same letter also described Henry VI's entire lack of response to his newly born son and highlighted the increasingly dangerous political climate.[30]

Richard of York was determined, at all costs, to prevent either Margaret of Anjou or his hated rival Edmund of Somerset obtaining the upper hand during these faction-ridden months. Initially, his wife Cecily (no doubt with his connivance) put out feelers concerning the possible rehabilitation and reconciliation of her husband with the royal household: perhaps this helps explain why Somerset not only failed to ensure York's absence from a Great Council meeting in November 1453 but also, two days later, found himself a prisoner in the Tower of London.[31] More importantly, and certainly ominously for the future, the winter of 1453/4 saw the forging of a political alliance between Richard of York and the Nevilles (Richard Neville, earl of Salisbury, and his son Richard Neville, earl of Warwick, two of the most powerful nobles in England and, hitherto, attached to the Court), an alliance which could both forward York's ambitions and be of assistance to the Nevilles in their now raging feud with the Percies in the north of England.[32] The sudden death of Cardinal John Kemp, Chancellor of England and a powerful opponent of York, on 22 March 1454, finally precipitated matters in favour of the York/Neville alliance: a few days later York became Protector of the realm (but not Regent) and Salisbury succeeded Kemp as Chancellor. And, perhaps, there is some truth in a contemporary chronicler's claim that, in the months that followed, York 'governed the whole realm of England most well and wonderfully subdued all rebels and malefactors in accordance with the laws and without great harshness'. Nevertheless, throughout, his position was far from secure, not least because, as R. A. Griffiths has emphasised, the Protectorate had been 'unenthusiastically established, partly to forestall a regency by the queen, and the supporting Council preserved a strong element of men who had served Henry VI well before he became ill'.[33]

As R. L. Storey memorably remarked in 1966, 'if Henry VI's insanity had been a tragedy, his recovery was a national disaster'.[34] Although the king never again enjoyed robust health (if he ever had) and, as the years went by, became so withdrawn into himself as to be rendered a mere political cipher, even his partial restoration to mental normality had profound implications. Somerset was released from prison early in February 1455 and now, if not before, became a fully committed ally of Margaret of Anjou in her objective of making the house of Lancaster unassailable once and for all. Before the month was out York's Protectorate was terminated and, as a result, the Nevilles found themselves excluded from the magic circle of high favour as well. Feeling seriously threatened, and with justification, all three magnates retired to their estates, proceeded to arm and, about three months later, successfully confronted their rivals at the First Battle of St Albans. Another Yorkist administration followed but, by the autumn of 1456, York and his allies were once more out of office and had been replaced by men loyal to the queen. Margaret of Anjou, in fact, now threw herself into factional politics with renewed vigour; by 1459 she was ready for a further showdown; and, whatever the claims of 1450, 1452, 1453 or 1455 to be regarded as the true beginning of the Wars of the Roses, there can be little doubt that civil strife erupted with a vengeance on the battlefields of Blore Heath and Ludford Bridge.

In conclusion, it must be said that the origins of the Wars of the Roses remain as complex, confusing and controversial as ever.[35]

Dynastic considerations cannot be ignored: there was an enormous reluctance to remove Henry VI from the throne in the 1450s (for all his manifold shortcomings as a ruler) on the grounds that he was England's rightful and anointed king; yet there is evidence, as well, that the house of Lancaster was only too conscious of its dynastic weakness when faced by Richard of York's claim to be, first, heir-presumptive and, ultimately, king in his own right. Recently, indeed, historians have begun to display a notable revival of interest in dynastic, constitutional and ideological matters. Economic factors, likewise, should not too easily be set on one side: the Lancastrian government's financial situation was chronically weak by the early 1450s, while Henry VI's exercise of royal patronage, partisan and divisive as it was, clearly helped foster jealousy and rivalry between great men. Certainly, too, aristocratic feuds, often both personal and political in derivation, have their role to play in explaining the wars, as does failure by government adequately to maintain law and order. Equally clearly, apportioning blame for the disasters in France was a major issue in domestic politics during the 1450s, and the collapse of English power on the Continent perhaps did more than anything else to discredit the Court party at home. Yet, in the end, all avenues of investigation lead back to the king and central government and it is difficult to avoid the conclusion that, if Henry VI had not been the man he was and if his government had not developed along the lines it did, the Wars of the Roses might never have happened.

5. Personalities and Politics

ROSEMARY HORROX

Medieval politics were built on personal relationships. At the king's coronation the great men of the realm did homage to him one by one, and it was as individuals that the king would have to deal with them for the rest of his reign, alert (if he was doing his job properly) to their influence, their interests, and their abilities – as they, of course, would be aware of his. But the relationships acknowledged in the coronation ritual were only the central strands of a far wider network of connections, once stigmatised as 'bastard feudalism', in which men rendered service to a social or political superior in return for support and favour. Those connections might not necessarily be close, but they were never impersonal, and they meant that for contemporaries political action was almost always an expression of personal service, in which the performance of that service consolidated the underlying relationship by creating a degree of obligation. In the crisis of 1471 Richard Neville, earl of Warwick, ended a letter to Henry Vernon of Haddon: 'Henry, I pray you fail not now as ever I may do for you.'[1] Even kings, who could call upon the loyalty and support of their subjects without invoking a personal relationship, utilised a similar nexus of personal service in matters which touched them particularly closely.

For contemporaries, therefore, personal relationships within the political arena were not simply a complicating factor to be minimised if possible. On the contrary, it was received wisdom that they should be strengthened. Social or political ties would be made stronger by their transmutation into affection. 'Obeissance done for love is more steadfast than that which is done for lordship or for dread.'[2] This did not mean that such affection was essential, only that without it something was lacking. The chronicler John Warkworth, describing the progressive breakdown of relations between Edward IV and the earl of Warwick from the mid 1460s, commented simply 'And yet they were *accorded* [brought to agreement] divers times, but they never loved together after.'[3] Where it could be achieved, the transmutation of obedience into love was one step on a ladder from self-interest to the creation of an ordered world: 'Largesse engenders *familiarite*, that is true service; true service engenders friendship; friendship engenders counsel and help; by these things is all the world made stable.'[4]

In that stable world, affection was reciprocal. Like God himself, a lord should rule his people with a loving authority which would call forth their dread – the awe and respect due to legitimate authority – but also their love. John Russe, writing to his absent master John Paston I, could thus say, 'Sir, I pray God bring you once to reign among your countrymen in love and to be dreaded.'[5] The love of his subjects was the reward which could (indeed *should*) be earned by a just lord, but dread was his due. A resort to threats to achieve the same end was a tacit admission of failure, which might well be counter-productive. Before Bosworth, Richard III threatened his servants with 'forfeiture to us of all you may forfeit and lose' if they did not bring out their forces for him, and although one recipient later claimed that 'for dread whereof he was in the same field sore against his will', others were evidently less impressed.[6]

For medieval writers, reciprocated affection was the highest model of political life, and one which carried a considerable emotional charge. Personal harmony was presented as the proper goal of all public life. Civic rulers defined their purpose as the promotion of 'unity, concord and amity', and when disputes did arise it was the responsibility of those in authority to restore friendship, and hence harmony, through arbitration. The ordinances of Our Lady's Guild at Wymondham (Norfolk) forbade guild members to go to law with each other until the rulers of the guild had attempted arbitration 'to make an end, and unity and love between [the] parties'. Only if that proved impossible could the guild members resort to the common law.[7] Confrontation, whether in the legal or political arena, was an admission of failure.

Of course, the reciprocal 'love' which was meant to characterise political relationships had a material dimension as well. Lords were expected to reward service performed on their behalf by extending favour and help in return. When a servant of the duke of Suffolk spoke warmly of his lord's 'good and trusty lordship, which I have ever before this found steadfast, stable and ready, to my weal and worship' he was thinking of something of more practical consequence than simple affection.[8] Exactly what that lordship entailed is almost invariably, as here, left unstated; but a lord's obligations to his servants were no less real for that, and his honour would be impugned by a failure to meet his side of the bargain. Love – the prerequisite, as contemporaries saw it, of political stability – manifested itself in favour. Royal and aristocratic patronage was conventionally granted 'in consideration of the good and laudable service done unto us by our trusty and welbeloved servant'.

It was at this point – at what, rather anachronistically, might be called the boundary of public authority and private obligation – that the blurring of political and personal relationships began to cause problems. How far did a lord's obligation to his servants extend? Or, to put it slightly differently, how far should the personal relationships which were so integral a part of political life be allowed to determine political action?

Contemporaries were aware of the problem. Some lords were careful to cover themselves, promising their servants 'the accomplishment of all your *reasonable* desires' [my italics]; just as Malory's King Arthur marked his wedding to Guinevere by offering to grant any man's desire 'except it were unreasonable'.[9] But in fact it was not the meeting of a specific request which was likely to cause problems, so much as the lord's general obligation to uphold the interests of his servants. This obligation could manifest itself in ways which ranged from the admirable, such as the countess of Oxford's solicitude for James Arblaster in his 'troubles, losses and adversity',[10] to the downright illegal; with a large grey area in the middle where propriety was in the eye of the beholder.

This is not to suggest that contemporaries had no sense of a limit beyond which lords should not go. In theory, the limit was clear. A lord should not allow affection or obligation to compromise his judgement. This meant that he should not have favourites among his servants, and it also meant that he should not invariably uphold his own men against others. The issues are spelt out in a letter from Margaret of Anjou to the duke of Exeter. The duke had been enfeoffed in the manor of Aspenden (Hertfordshire) by a group of unnamed men, presumably his associates, who were trying to bring a claim against the manor's owner, a kinsman of one of Margaret's own servants. The queen wanted Exeter to back down, and she adopted the familiar tactic of praising him for the virtues she wanted him to display: 'knowing verily your good and natural disposition towards the favour and tenderness of truth and justice'. Exeter's reply is unrecorded, but he seems to have yielded, perhaps in this case because the queen represented too powerful an adversary for him to do otherwise. But lords were prepared to act without that pressure on occasion, as Richard, duke of Gloucester, demonstrated when he decided against one of his own servants in a case which he was adjudicating.[11]

Gloucester was in effect putting one criterion of honourable behaviour – the obligation to give right judgement – before another – the obligation of a lord to look after his servants' interests. Not all lords were willing to observe the same priorities. To uphold a servant's interests was not only a duty, but (if it was done successfully) a valuable expression of the lord's power. Standing by while a servant was defeated entailed a corresponding loss of face. One of the most extreme examples of a lord's maintenance of his servants' interests was the earl of Suffolk's backing for Thomas Tuddenham and John Heydon. Their depredations in East Anglia were perhaps exceptional, but they were a chilling demonstration of what might happen when a lord chose to parade his own power by putting it unequivocally at the disposal of his servants. In such a case the victims had two possible courses of action: to complain to the lord himself under the tactful pretence that he must be unaware of his servants' actions; or to secure the intervention of a yet more powerful figure, to whom the lord could yield without losing face. Usually that person was the king, and it was Henry VI's total failure to perform that role which made Suffolk's men such a threat.

If lords should not allow favour to override right judgement, their servants were not meant to allow duty to override morality. The Church was adamant that obeying orders was no defence, and that it was the servant's own soul which would be in hazard if he did wrong on his master's behalf. More positively, contemporary writers were unanimous that it was the job of a good servant to tell his lord honestly if something he wanted doing was wrong, and this was not mere wishful thinking. John Paston I, deeply troubled by the earl of Oxford's treatment of Agnes Denys, took it upon himself to spell out the grounds for his uneasiness, although he manifestly found the letter hard to write. 'Right worshipful and my right especial good lord, I recommend me to your good lordship, beseeching your lordship that you take not to displeasure though I write to you as I hear say.' Agnes, who was pregnant, had been thrown into prison as part of the earl's campaign against her husband Thomas – whom, as Paston reminded the earl, she had married on their urging. Paston concluded his account of her woes, 'For God's love, my lord, remember how the gentlewoman is accumbered only for your sake and help her.' It was with evident relief that, having got the criticism down on paper, he finished his letter, in more fulsome terms than usual: 'Right worshipful and my right especial lord, I beseech Almighty God send you as much joy and worship as ever had any of my lords your ancestors, and keep you and all yours.'[12]

If registering criticism was difficult, actually saying 'no' must have been even harder. When John Paston I tried to enlist Sir John Heveningham's help in taking possession of one of the disputed Fastolf manors, Heveningham refused; mainly, one imagines, because he simply did not want to get involved in such a dangerous dispute, but perhaps also because he disbelieved Paston's claim to the land. His letter exudes embarrassment:

> Sir, you sent me a letter of attorney to receive and to occupy in your name the manor called Burnvilles in Nacton. Sir, as for that occupation I can little skill on, nor I will not take upon me none such occupations; wherefore I beseech you hold me excused, for it is no world for me to take such occupations. I have as much as I may to gather my own livelihood, and truly, cousin, I cannot gather that well. And therefore, cousin, I pray you take it to no displeasure.

Heveningham softened the refusal with a promise of future help, although one which carries an implied rebuke: 'Sir, that I may worshipfully do for you, you shall find me ready.'[13]

Heveningham was Paston's equal. For acknowledged servants a straight refusal was more difficult, even though a lord could only 'pray and desire'; he could not (except with the humblest of servants) coerce. When George, duke of Clarence ordered Henry Vernon to join him with his men in 1471, Vernon stalled. He raised men, and came as far south as Lichfield, but then turned back, telling the duke that he had understood by one of

Clarence's letters that those were his instructions. Clarence denied any such intention, and ordered Vernon to return the letter in question. Vernon's next move was evidently to argue that although he was ready to come, pressing business was keeping him at home – a tactic which allowed him to avoid the battles of Barnet and Tewkesbury. Clarence, whatever his private opinion, accepted his excuses. Asking, yet again, for his attendance after Tewkesbury, he ended his letter: 'And you shall find us your good lord, and thereof you shall not need to doubt in any wise.'[14]

Vernon's successful efforts to avoid making a military commitment are a well-known example of the limits of lordship. But the pressure towards obedience remained strong, as Vernon's resort to excuses rather than denial shows. That, indeed, was the point. Personal service might allow servants a measure of choice over which commands they obeyed, but from the lord's point of view it was still a more effective way of getting things done than by sending impersonal commands to strangers. As royal records show, men might feel no qualms about ignoring routine commands from the central bureaucracy, but a direct personal command from the king to one of his servants was another matter. Servants usually did obey, partly because it was their duty, but also because refusal would compromise their own advancement. Any servant who wanted to prove his value would be wise to carry out his lord's instructions to the letter. He might also, as contemporaries were well aware, go beyond them in his zeal to demonstrate his usefulness. Fourteenth-century preachers warned against rapacious servants who would not be considered successful unless they enriched their masters. In his mirror for princes, *The Tree of Commonwealth*, Edmund Dudley urged the king to keep a sharp watch lest the poor people of the realm were oppressed by his servants in order to win the king's gratitude – or, he immediately added, to profit themselves.[15]

As Dudley knew, the links between service and advancement were not always under the lord's own control. A servant could exploit his lord's name and power for his own ends. This might be no more than harmless namedropping, but sometimes it could be altogether more brutal. Servants of Richard, duke of Gloucester, pursuing a quarrel on behalf of one of their number, raided a disputed manor in its owner's absence and terrorised his wife and servants. They claimed that they had orders to arrest the owner and carry him to the duke's castle of Pontefract, but they also roughed up his wife and suggested that if her husband were to die she would do well to marry the claimant to the manor – a suggestion which she, 'sore moved', indignantly repudiated.[16] Such behaviour again confronted the lord (if he knew about it at all) with a choice between different obligations: whether to turn a blind eye or to disown his servants' actions.

The underpinning of political action by personal obligation created a certain indefiniteness, if not an actual ambiguity, at the heart of medieval political life. A personal relationship, even in a society as hierarchical as that of the middle ages, can never be entirely governed by a formal set of rules. Some space always has to be left for imponderables like the degree of mutual trust or liking between the people concerned. Similarly, no rigid parameters can be laid down for the proper exercise of political authority when any action relies on personal relationships for its efficacy. To modern eyes, used to a more defined line between private interest and public duty, the medieval blurring of the two can look irredeemably corrupt: an unprincipled trade-off between power and obedience, in which the only goal, and the only yardstick by which success was to be measured, was self-advancement. This is precisely how the fifteenth century was once presented. It was taken for granted that all politics were a battle for personal power or wealth, but it was assumed that this struggle intensified in the late Middle Ages when weakening tenurial bonds allowed men to go where they pleased in search of lordship. 'Loyalty' became something to be bought – or, more accurately, hired, since a single down-payment was not enough to secure continuing obedience – and there was nothing to stop lords greedy for power from buying a retinue with which to terrorise their weaker neighbours; or to stop retainers taking themselves off in search of more money elsewhere.

The last fifty years or so have seen a steady retreat from this image of late medieval political life as an ugly free for all. The shift in emphasis began with an awareness that there was not, in fact, a free market in political loyalties. Given the importance attached to local knowledge and connections it made no sense for local landowners to ally themselves with men right outside their own area, and gentry families often built up long-standing connections with a neighbouring lord because it suited both of them to do so. Even men who enjoyed greater room for manoeuvre, either because they were landless themselves or because there was no pre-eminent lord nearby, were well-advised to forge lasting relationships. The greatest rewards came to those who had built up a track record of consistent service, not to men who were endlessly changing masters in search of a better deal. But this is still assuming that political behaviour was dictated by the search for reward – what has changed is the historian's perception of the behaviour most likely to be rewarded.

Recent writers have become increasingly impatient with this emphasis, which reduces political action to (at worst) a Pavlovian response to the possibility of reward, or (at best) the calculating pursuit of self-interest. There is a growing insistence that idealism needs to be written more securely into the equation – 'idealism' here being a useful shorthand for a whole range of values spanning the private and public spheres. Fifteenth-century correspondents appealed repeatedly to concepts of truth and justice, or pleaded the dictates of conscience and reason. These were not empty words. Men and women were sensitive to what would and would not be considered honourable conduct, and to characterise a course of action as dishonourable (or unworshipful) was clearly expected to be the clinching argument in influencing the behaviour of others. When a servant of the bishop of Lincoln asked his lord for the repayment of money laid out on his behalf, he concluded, 'Sir, I am sure you will not grudge so to do, well advised, for it were too much against your worship, good conscience and all *gentilnesse* that I should thus strangely be quit for my kindness.'[17]

In a world where political action relied so largely on personal obligations, the existence of a code of private behaviour inevitably had an impact on political conduct. Private morality impinged directly on public standing, as the letter just quoted makes clear. The servant was appealing both to his master's conscience – which is essentially a private matter – and to his worship, which has a public dimension since it carries connotations not only of personal honour, but of the respect in which an individual is held by other people. That public dimension, which is only implicit in the passage quoted, was made explicit in the following sentence, where the servant added that if the bishop did not do what was right in this instance, other men would become wary of doing him service.

Men were thus expected to observe certain standards of behaviour in their public as well as their private lives. But this is not the same thing as saying that the Middle Ages had developed a distinctive public morality. Indeed, it is almost tantamount to saying that they had not – and that it was an essentially private morality which prevailed in both spheres. Or, to put it another way, the emphasis on honour and conscience could seem to reinforce the traditional perception of political activity as the interplay of the aims and ambitions of individuals – albeit of individuals whose pursuit of power and influence was responsive to contemporary opinion about what constituted proper behaviour.

There is one sense in which contemporary writings seem to endorse this interpretation of political life as the enacting, on the public stage, of private preoccupations. Because the parameters of acceptable political behaviour were so flexible, complaint was always highly specific: a *particular* action had been judged unacceptable and should be remedied. In high politics, as well as at the local level where most service relationships manifested themselves, political comment was thus usually negative: itemising what had gone wrong rather than declaring how matters ought to be conducted. It was also almost invariably *ad hominem*. What was being criticised was not 'the system' but the actions of individuals within it. When in 1469 Clarence and Warwick took it upon themselves to detail the 'great inconveniences and mischiefs that fell in this land in the days of King Edward II, King Richard II and King Henry VI'. their approach was simple. Everything was laid at the door of 'seducious persons'.[18]

But this emphasis is, in fact, misleading. Contemporaries were not only concerned with the proper means of exercising power – which is where personal relationships played so large a part – but with the proper ends of power as well. Clarence and Warwick were not only attacking the self-aggrandisement of the 'seducious persons' – although they certainly had bitter things to say about the resulting impoverishment of the lords of the blood. They were also arguing that the proper aims of government were not being met: that ordinary people were being oppressed and the law not enforced. However much their claims may smack of special pleading, they were appealing to a belief that government (using that word in its broadest sense) was not just an arena in which to pursue private interest, but was the means by which the well-being of the realm and its inhabitants was to be maintained.

The law provides a broader illustration of the same point. In the fifteenth century the English legal system involved literally thousands of men: from the king himself, who sat in judgement with his council, through the judges of the central courts of kings bench and common pleas and the professional lawyers (whether king's serjeants or humble local attorneys), to the non-professionals who served as jurors and assessors in local courts. The involvement of all of them had, of course, an element of self-interest. It displayed their standing, and it allowed them an influence which might be used more directly in their own affairs. But they also went to time and trouble because they genuinely believed that the law was important and needed to be upheld for the public good, or, as they would have put it, for the common weal.

In specific cases the tension between the private and the public good can never be entirely resolved. The historian studying Richard, duke of Gloucester's seizure of the throne in 1483 cannot know the precise proportions of ambition, fear, and the conviction that he was the best man to maintain political stability which motivated him – but then nor, probably, did the duke himself. Self-interest and idealism not only co-exist, but blur into each other in complex and sometimes scarcely admitted ways. But the overall balance between them has become a subject of debate among medievalists, mainly because the prevailing emphasis on self-interest has marginalised the constitutional history which used to hold centre stage. If politics are primarily the expression of private concerns, manifested through personal relationships, then one needs to study individuals rather than ideologies. In reality, of course, one has to study both. It would be as much a nonsense to exclude self-interest from the equation altogether as to insist that it was the only spur to political action; and the new constitutionalists are seeking to redress what they see as an imbalance rather than replace one absolute with another. To that extent, the debate is something of a storm in a teacup. But it does have a particular application to the Wars of the Roses because it focusses attention on precisely the area that seems to have bothered contemporaries: how far private obligations and concerns should (or could) be subordinated to the general good.

The Wars of the Roses have been seen as the direct product of rampant individualism in high places; a terrible warning of what could happen when weak royal authority allowed innate competitiveness to escape from control and escalate to the point of anarchy. In this scenario men ruthlessly exploited lawlessness for their own ends until government collapsed altogether and buried them in its ruins, leaving the Tudors a clear field in which to build the 'modern' state. A more moderate view, still widely held, is that the wars were indeed the result of a collapse of royal authority, and the consequent escalation of aristocratic feuds, but that by far the most common response was defensive rather than exploitative. All but the irrevocably committed kept their heads down and tried to get on with their lives as best they might. The constitutionalists, on the other hand, would argue that what happened between 1450 and 1485 was, at least in part, the product of men trying desperately to find some resolution of the problems posed by Henry VI's incompetence.

The three versions offer very different interpretations of the wars' causation. At the two extremes, events are presented as driven by naked power-seeking or by a sense of what government should entail; while the middle view carries the implication that events were not being 'driven' at all, but unfolded in response to circumstances while contemporaries watched in dismay. At the level of personal responses to the war, however, the three readings are by no means mutually exclusive. It is not necessary to believe that civil war was caused by unchecked self-interest to accept that once it was under way there were individuals who seized the chance to exploit the situation, or who, more commonly perhaps, felt impelled to respond in kind when confronted by the depredations of others. But what is clear is that war was not lightly or willingly entered into. Efforts were made to halt the slide into war in the 1450s and when the worst had happened, and civil war was a reality, the overwhelming imperative was to find some way of restoring order.

At the level of high politics, what this entailed in practice was a rallying around the *de facto* king. The Wars of the Roses, far from weakening the monarchy, actually strengthened it, since the king was the only man able to surmount faction. Henry VI was a disaster as king, demonstrating an appetite for intermittent and maladroit intervention which may well have been more politically unsettling than a total withdrawal. But in spite of the king's manifest failings, Richard, duke of York's criticism of the regime commanded little high-level support – and would have commanded even less but for the crown's alienation of the junior branch of the Nevilles, headed by York's brother-in-law the earl of Salisbury. York in fact never did attain the political viability to break the vicious circle of temporary ascendancy and political exclusion. It was his son, Edward, earl of March, who finally mustered enough support to take the throne. He was able to do so in part because the situation had been transformed by the country's descent into open war, which reduced the compulsion to uphold the king as the embodiment of stability. Once it was no longer a matter of averting war, but of stopping it, political opinion began to divide more evenly between Henry VI and his rival.

However, the crucial change may well have been York's own death at the Battle of Wakefield late in 1460. In the ensuing months Edward of York was able to present himself as the man who could mend the shattered political community. That self-identification with unity proved immensely potent, and it was not a role which could plausibly have been filled by his father. In the eyes of contemporaries, York had been the begetter of faction: a man tainted by his willingness to go to extremes. Equally important, there was no longer anyone on the Lancastrian side able to make the same claim. Henry VI, although he still commanded considerable personal loyalty, was now too obviously a lay figure, and his son, Edward of Lancaster, could hardly be said to surmount faction as long as he was in the custody of his mother Margaret of Anjou. The queen had never been very popular in England, and by 1461 she had become irrevocably identified with a vendetta against the Yorkists, which offered only the continuation of conflict rather than its resolution.

The desire for stability, and mistrust of those who threatened it, was not a new characteristic. But it was to be particularly marked in the two generations which followed: testimony to the extent to which the lawlessness of the late 1450s had burnt itself into the political memory. Both Edward IV and Henry VII benefited from the perception that obedience to the king was the best bulwark against disorder. Edward's destruction of his brother Clarence, and Henry's punitive sanctions against members of the nobility, could hardly have been carried through without that broadly based readiness to acquiesce in the king's actions. Conversely, men who were judged to have reopened factional conflicts for their own purposes found themselves isolated. When Clarence and Warwick moved into overt opposition to Edward IV and his advisors in 1469 they attracted almost no backing outside their immediate circle, in spite of their claims to be articulating a general grievance. They subsequently gained a precarious political credibility only by allying with Lancastrian diehards in support of Henry VI – although even then their success is likely to have owed more to Edward's tactical errors than to enthusiasm for their cause. The backlash against Richard III's seizure of the throne implies a belief that he had taken power for selfish ends – although had Richard defeated Tudor at Bosworth opinion would probably have shifted in his favour.

The judgements being made on these occasions might seem essentially pragmatic, with contemporary opinion favouring the man most likely to succeed; and that was surely an element in men's thinking. After the Yorkist victory of Towton Edward IV simply looked far more credible than Henry VI. But the example of Richard III suggests that that was not the whole story. If what was at issue was stability at all costs, the obvious strategy in 1483 would have been to accept Richard's usurpation. This seems to have been what Richard himself expected to happen – and the underlying justification of his actions was that he was the man who could maintain the stability of his brother's closing years. It was a claim which did command respect. There were plenty of men who were prepared to remain loyal to Richard, and others only reconsidered their allegiance after it had become apparent that the king was not, after all, able to provide the freedom from factional conflict which he had tacitly promised. But other men moved immediately into opposition – and the strength of their feeling is revealed by their willingness to back an outsider like Henry Tudor rather than abandon their opposition when it came to be believed that Edward V was dead.

It is one of the paradoxes of the Wars of the Roses that an earnest desire for stability through loyalty to the established monarch should culminate in the accession of a man who had virtually no claim to the throne, and who was an unknown quantity to most, if not quite all, of the men who pledged support for him. It is hardly surprising that many commentators have felt that the crown had become the discredited plaything of faction. But this misses the point. Henry VII was never seen as the puppet of the men who had backed him – and this is not (as is often assumed) because he was strong enough not to let it happen, but because no one wanted it to happen. Kings were expected to meet their obligations, and Henry was punctilious in rewarding his early associates, but there was intense resistance to the idea that a king should be identified with, let alone dominated by, a political clique. For a king to choose to favour a particular group was bad enough – although it was accepted that, in a personal monarchy, a degree of favouritism was probably inevitable. But for him to be controlled was totally unacceptable. Yorkist propaganda was not being disingenuous when it presented Henry VI as victim rather than tyrant. Henry was perceived as a failure less because of the misgovernment of the 1440s than because in the late 1450s he was demonstrably controlled by whoever had possession of him – an intolerable state of affairs given the importance attached to the king's role as arbiter.

That view of the king had obvious implications for contemporary assumptions about the proper role of the nobility. Francis Bacon's famous characterisation of judges as lions under the throne could well be applied to the late medieval nobility.[19] They were the king's natural counsellors, his right hand in the maintenance of law and order, and his war leaders. To fulfil those roles they needed to be powerful, and historians' characterisation of the nobility as 'overmighty subjects' would probably have struck contemporaries as rather odd. A nobleman filling his allotted role could hardly be too powerful. It was only if he departed from that role that his power might seem dangerous, but in practice this rarely happened – mainly because the nobility preferred to be the king's allies rather than his opponents, but also because a nobleman who tried to turn his power against the king would almost certainly find it eroded by the unwillingness of his peers (and even, in some cases, his subordinates) to back him. The late medieval nobility were not always gleefully ganging up on the king. On the contrary, a lord with pretensions of dominance would find his severest critics among his fellow nobles, who seem on the whole to have considered an inept king infinitely preferable to a colleague wielding excessive power. The isolation of Richard of York in the 1450s can be paralleled in the fourteenth century by Thomas of Lancaster, whose assumption of dominance in opposition to Edward II was much disliked, in spite of the king's own unpopularity.

Implicit in the image of the 'overmighty subject' is the belief that political authority was essentially rooted in brute strength. Although it is true that the turning points of the Wars of the Roses almost all took the form of military engagements (Towton and

Bosworth are the obvious examples), the political life of the period cannot be characterised simply as two sides slogging it out by force. If the earl of Warwick deserves the title of Kingmaker it is less a tribute to his military might than to his skills as a negotiator. At least one contemporary observer felt that the agreement of October 1460, which recognised York as Henry VI's heir and opened the way to an ultimate Yorkist victory, was the earl's doing: 'wherein my lord of Warwick behaved him so that his fame is like to be of great memory'.[20] On this basis, the other Kingmaker of the Wars of the Roses was Margaret Beaufort, who probably deserves the credit for persuading Richard III's opponents to adopt her son, Henry Tudor, as their claimant to the throne.

An appeal to force, far from being the accepted method of deciding political priorities, was always seen as an admission of failure, not least because, as contemporaries were well aware, it initiated a damaging cycle of violence which might prove difficult to check. Battles had losers, who were (at least in the short term) unlikely to acquiesce in their defeat. A great deal of energy at the high political level went into trying to ensure that disputes were mediated before they reached that stage, so that there were, ideally, no losers with an interest in perpetuating the conflict. It was in this spirit that the duke of Clarence tried to secure a concord between his brother and the earl or Warwick in 1471: 'for to reconcile thereby unto the king's good grace many lords and noble men of his land ... for the weal of peace and tranquility in the land, and in avoiding of cruel and mortal war'.[21] Peace was the proper condition of a Christian commonwealth, but it was also the state in which individuals could feel most secure in their status and possessions. Its maintenance was not only a moral duty but a practical imperative.

The traditional scenario, which sees the Wars of the Roses as caused by the lack of a strong king able to enforce the rules, ignores the extent to which the whole political community had a vested interest in observing those rules. If the great men of the Middle Ages were lions, they were not lions who responded only to the tamer's whip. They shared a sense not only of the desirability of harmony and order, but of their own proper role in achieving that end; and it is significant that when the conventions were broken the breach was not usually cynical or gratuitous, but was carefully justified by an appeal to accepted goals. Thus York's actions in the 1450s did flout convention, but it would be unfair to call them unprincipled. He presented himself as a man whose important contribution to the restoration of sound governance was being improperly rebuffed. Like his son in 1483, York was in effect claiming that breaking some rules was justified if it achieved the end to which the rules were directed. Not everyone agreed with that reading of the duke's situation, but it should not be assumed that York's appeal to principle was necessarily either factious or factitious.

Nor, in ideological terms, was it particularly contentious. York, a royal duke and an experienced war leader, had the right to be heard by his prince. Conflict arose over his means, not their ends. This was typical. The fifteenth century saw no fundamental disagreement about the proper aims of government, or even (in general terms) about how they could best be achieved; and there was, as a result, none of the public debate over matters such as the nature of honour which characterised the civil war under Charles I. The protagonists in the Wars of the Roses were talking the same language and, by and large, pursuing the same goals; something which does much to explain why the war, although deeply disturbing, failed to generate anything like the bitterness of its seventeenth-century successor.

Acknowledging the importance of shared principles is not, as argued earlier, to deny any role to personal considerations. Self-interest, no doubt, played some part, even if it was not always fully admitted. Supporting the man most likely to restore order was, after all, often tantamount to supporting the man most likely to safeguard one's own livelihood. But personal decisions were not necessarily made on the basis of self-interest. The conflict brought private loyalties into play. Chroniclers took it for granted that this should be the case. Edward Hall is responsible for the story that when Lord Clifford killed the earl of Rutland at the Battle of Wakefield he declared, 'By God's blood, thy father slew mine, and so will I do thee and all thy kin.'[22] The reliability of the story matters less than Hall's assumption that Clifford would see matters in that light. The same perception was shared by the architects of the abortive 'loveday' of 1458, when the Yorkist victors of the First Battle of St Albans agreed to make reparation to the heirs of the Lancastrian dead to try to prevent a personal vendetta taking root.

Alongside family loyalties were the ties of service and a more generalised sense of what behaviour would or would not be deemed honourable. These did not always point in the same direction, and individuals could find themselves confronted by a bewildering array of competing arguments. The author of the *Arrivall*, describing attempts to reconcile the earl of Warwick with Edward IV, was quite clear why Warwick should have accepted. It would have saved his life and that of his followers; it would have restored them to grace; it would have brought peace to England; and it would have satisfied family ties, since Clarence, who had initiated the attempt, was married to the earl's eldest daughter. But the writer also had no trouble in coming up with a range of possible reasons for Warwick's ultimate refusal: the earl might have doubted that the reconciliation could endure; he might have felt himself bound by the oaths he had taken to Queen Margaret; he might have hoped to save his life anyway by making his escape to Calais; or his own inclinations might have been overruled by the Lancastrians in his company.[23] The account was designed to present Edward IV's view of events, but even so at least one of the writer's suggested arguments against acceptance (the oaths to Queen Margaret, which it would have been dishonourable to break) had a moral force which most contemporaries would have acknowledged.

Shared principles thus did not mean that men escaped difficult choices – or that they would necessarily all come to the same decision. Men were not ideological clones. Even if self-interest is left out of the equation, legitimate obligations might well be pulling them in different directions, with no self-evidently 'correct' solution. When men came to different conclusions about whether or not to back Richard III in 1483, for instance, it was not a case of one course of action being right and all the others wrong, let alone one being principled and the others self-interested. Even cases where there was, in theory, a right answer, must often have seemed less clear-cut at the time. The obvious example is that of the retainer who found his lord marching against the king. On one level there was no problem. Hierarchy demanded that obedience to the king took priority, and indentures of retainer formally embodied that requirement. But when it came to the issue many men put the more immediate lordship first, and few contemporaries seem to have been surprised or shocked by that. Edward IV's policy of executing defeated commanders but sparing the rank and file tacitly admitted that it was unreasonable to expect men to desert their lords. The medieval horror of treachery, the most despicable of offences, seems in practice to have meant that continuing devotion to a lord with whom the servant had a personal relationship tended to be valued more highly than the necessarily abstract obedience owed to the remote figure of the king. Under Henry VII, when the official line was that Richard III was an infanticide and usurper, Sir Ralph Bigot (who had been in the service of Richard as duke of Gloucester and as king) was admired rather than criticised for refusing to speak ill of his former master.

Contemporaries were generally prepared to be tolerant of men who found themselves having to acknowledge one duty rather than another; testimony not to an erosion of moral standards but to an awareness of the complexity of personal obligation. Even the avoidance of a decision might sometimes be viewed with a degree of sympathy. Henry Vernon's failure to bring his men to join his lord, the duke of Clarence, in 1471 took place against a background of what must have been terrifying political uncertainty. Clarence was marching up from the south-west towards the west midlands, where his brother, Edward IV, newly returned to England, was confronting the forces of the restored Henry VI, led by Clarence's father-in-law the earl of Warwick. Vernon probably had no idea which way Clarence was going to jump. The duke's formal summons was a command 'to do the king service for the universal and common weal of this land, to the resistance of the enemies thereof which be landed as we understand certainly'. Those 'enemies' who landed were the Yorkists, and so the king referred to was Henry VI, but Clarence's other letters were less explicit about his intentions. Perhaps the duke himself was still not absolutely sure what to do. In these circumstances it is hardly surprising that Vernon wanted to keep his head down – or that Clarence let him get away with it, although their relationship seems to have cooled as a result.

In the end, politics was an accretion of personal decisions, and that means that the personality of the protagonists cannot be left out of the discussion. It determined not only how they reacted to the situations in which they found themselves, but how others reacted to them. The growing support for Edward IV in 1461 must have owed something to the realisation that he would make an effective king – whereas his father never seems to have been regarded in that light. But if discussing politics in terms of self-interest is unfashionable at the moment, discussing it in terms of personalities is even more so. This is largely because of the sheer difficulty of gaining a reliable sense of the personality of medieval men and women. Where no personal writings survive, a person's actions often constitute almost the only clues to their character; but reliance on them can lead to an unhelpfully circular argument, in which the individual's actions offer the sole evidence for personality traits which are then used to explicate the actions. A circular argument of a slightly different kind is also embodied in many contemporary evaluations; where the writer's response to his subject's behaviour determines the terms in which the person is described. Margaret of Anjou is a case in point. Most contemporary accounts are hostile, and the popular modern view of her as a tigress fighting tooth and claw to defend her cub has done little to soften her image. But it is extremely difficult to decide whether Margaret was unpopular because she was brutal and abrasive or whether (because she was wielding a direct authority which queens were constitutionally not meant to hold) she was being automatically represented as the stereotypical virago: a woman who renders herself unnatural by behaving like a man. If the latter, then the comments on her character are important as evidence of how queens were not meant to behave, but say very little about Margaret herself.

For all its problems, personality cannot be ignored. The surprising persistence of loyalty to Henry VI reveals that personality might take second place to other concerns, but the collapse of good and substantial government during his reign confirms that in certain respects personality was crucial. Things would not have gone wrong in quite that way had Henry been a different man. The chequered career of George, duke of Clarence (who betrayed his brother the king and his father-in-law the earl of Warwick) can be described in a variety of ways. Most are hostile – ringing the changes on the theme of the greedy and shallow younger son – but it would not be impossible to come up with a more sympathetic reading. What is clear is that any explanation which leaves the duke's character out of the equation altogether is not going to make sense. The same could be said of Sir Nicholas Latimer of Duntish (Dorset), who managed to clock up no fewer than three attainders in the course of twelve years (1461, 1470 and 1483) and was still displaying his inimitable ability to back losers in 1497, when involvement in the Cornish rising cost him a fine and control of his estates.[24]

Keeping personality, however imperfectly, in the picture is also a reminder that political conflict does not exist in a vacuum. The events of the Wars of the Roses not only forced people to make difficult personal decisions, they also had personal implications. People died or were bereaved; land was seized and redistributed. One of Clarence's retainers was later believed to have run mad with grief when his master died. When Francis, Viscount Lovell, disappeared from view after his rebellion against Henry VII, his wife was left frantically searching for news of him.[25] It was hardly surprising that the image of Fortune and her wheel was evoked so persistently in this period, as individuals found their lives turned upside down. Many victims were men and women on the margins of political life, like Agnes Denys, whose husband was murdered in 1461 and who found herself penniless and afraid to go home for fear of being attacked herself.[26] But even the most eminent were not exempt from sudden reversals. The Lancastrian Henry Holland, duke of Exeter, who fled to Flanders in the 1460s, was reputedly reduced to begging for alms, until the duke of Burgundy came to his rescue with a modest pension. One of the most poignant documents to survive from the period of Richard III's usurpation is the household account of Edward IV's widow, Elizabeth Woodville. Barely three inches square, it seems to have been drawn up while she was in sanctuary at Westminster in May 1483.[27]

Men and women could not fail to be aware of the risks which might flow from making the wrong decision – or even, indeed, from simply being involved in public life. The penalties of treason had become terrifyingly complete: now not only the individual, but his heirs as well, paid the price of misjudgement. Even apparent success could come with a price tag attached. The most successful aroused jealousies which at best would mean relegation in the next reign, as Richard III's northerners found under Henry VII, and at worst might cost them their lives, as Henry VI's court clique discovered in 1450 and William Catesby in 1485. The modestly successful were not necessarily safe either. At least one of the men rewarded with forfeited land by Richard III later found himself being sued for the profits which had accrued to him during his brief possession. In weighing up political obligations, most individuals would surely have had some sense of what line of action would be prudent – as well as what would be proper, or profitable, or even pleasurable.

It is, as a result, impossible for an historian to do more than speculate about an individual's motivation. It would be a futile exercise to try and identify the precise proportions of opportunism, family loyalty, shame, disappointed ambition, and hostility to the house of Lancaster which brought George, duke of Clarence, back to his brother's side in 1471. The important thing is to recognise the complexity of the forces at work. It is not a matter of characterising late medieval politics as being driven solely by idealism or by self-interest. But, that said, people did have a perception of what constituted the proper means and ends of power, and of how their own actions might contribute to those ends. Unpacking that mental luggage is as crucial in understanding those men who apparently failed to observe the proprieties as in discussing those who tried to uphold them.

6. Ideas, Principles and Politics

JOHN L. WATTS

On 1 May 1450, the little fleet carrying the duke of Suffolk to the continent was waylaid by a ship called the Nicholas of the Tower, whose men came and took the duke prisoner. When Suffolk showed them the letters of protection which Henry VI had given him, the men rejected them, allegedly declaring that 'they did not know the said king, but they well knew the crown of England' and adding that 'the aforesaid crown was the community of the said realm and that the community of the realm was the crown of that realm'. Emboldened by this declaration, they went on to raise a banner of St George and to proclaim that all those who wished to stand with them and the said community should follow it, and join with them in taking and beheading all the traitors then in England.

> And, on this subject, they then said that, as the king did not wish to punish these traitors of his own will, nor to govern the aforesaid realm better, they themselves would do it. In the meantime, they would like it to be known to all and sundry standing about, that they had knowledge of another person, then outside the realm, who would punish the said traitors and better govern the aforesaid realm, and that they would bring that person into England and make him king of the aforesaid kingdom.[1]

Satisfied that they had explained and justified their insurrection, the shipmen went on to try the duke and, finding him guilty of treason, to cut off his head.

So it was that the conflict which came to be known as the Wars of the Roses – that sequence of 'savage battles', 'ruthless executions' and 'shameless treasons' (or, in a more modern idiom, that mixture of 'dynastic struggle', 'factional conflict' and 'private vendettas') – began with a series of statements of

110

constitutional principle.[2] The shipmen were arguing that it was legitimate for subjects like themselves to take away the powers of the king if he failed to exercise them properly. The 'crown' – the moral and actual source of the king's powers – was, in their eyes, nothing more than the symbol of the 'community', the body of subjects constituted for the protection of mutual interests, such as peace, justice and prosperity. If these mutual interests were unfulfilled, if the king submitted himself to the rule of traitors and failed to uphold justice, then the task of protecting the community fell to others: to common men, marching under a banner of St George (as the peasants of 1381 had done before them); or to leading individuals in whom these men had confidence (in this case, surely Richard of York, who was then 'outside the realm' in Ireland). Decapitating Suffolk was no act of murder, therefore, nor even of war: it was an act of justice, carried out by true subjects on the unimpeachable authority of the community of the realm.

Statements of this kind were to be far from unusual in the political and military struggles which followed this episode. Not only commoners, but also kings and magnates made a point of drawing attention to the ideas and principles which underpinned their actions. The disorderly events of the 1450s, 1460s, and 1480s were accompanied by a rich debate over the rights and duties of rulers and subjects, a debate recorded in the many speeches, manifestoes, newsletters, poems and treatises which have survived to the present day. Reading the words in which the politicians of the age presented their disagreements, it seems clear that this was a conflict in which political ideas and principles played a significant role. Many, echoing the shipmen, spoke of the mutual interests of the realm: the 'common weal', as they put it. Some asserted rights of self defence, or the freedom to challenge their enemies. Others made attempts to justify the exercise of royal power, or to define its proper form and extent. At times, the ideas professed by combatants were contradictory. In almost every reign, for example, the 'opposition' emphasised the paramountcy of the common weal while the 'crown' insisted on an overriding duty of obedience. Under these circumstances, it may be tempting to present the Wars of the Roses as the major conflicts of the thirteenth and seventeenth centuries have commonly been presented: wars of ideas, a clash of principles, a 'constitutional crisis'. If so, it is not a temptation to which any have so far succumbed. The civil war of the fifteenth century has, for centuries, been seen as a pragmatic and constitutionally arid struggle between overmighty noblemen, whose power to manipulate the gentry and the commons enabled them to subvert and contest the crown. Principles played little part in this conflict, because most of the participants were interested in nothing but power and its material rewards. Nor did the constitutional structures to which these principles related have any great significance: both the origins and the resolution of the wars were matters of *realpolitik*, of political management; no-one sought to change, or even to challenge, the system, it seems, only to gain advantage within it.[3]

This approach raises many problems, to which the political historians of today have begun to respond. Surely *some* principles must have governed the operation of political society, even in these desperate times. In the last ten years or so, various candidates have been discussed: the ideal of chivalry, for example, to which most leading landowners either aspired or deferred; the ethic of 'service', which appears to have governed the social and political hierarchy of kings, lords and gentlemen. Some historians have sought to show how these codes of principles bore on specific political episodes: how a leading element in York's hatred of Somerset was the chivalric offence contained in the latter's surrender of the former's garrison at Rouen; how Richard III's usurpation was fatally undermined by its disruption of the webs of personal service within the Yorkist establishment.[4] Another has approached the issue at a more communal level, seeking to find the ground rules – the 'unspoken assumptions' or 'political morality' – of fifteenth-century landowners and exploring how these affected politics, both locally and nationally.[5] Work of this kind suggests that ideas and principles could be important, that what was thought and said did relate to what was done both by individuals and by groups. So far, however, the issues which were so widely and explicitly aired in the period of the wars have received less attention. The idea of the 'common weal' and its relation to royal authority; the limits of the obligation to obey; the issue of how the king should be advised and how his judgements should be executed: these 'principles of national government', as they might be called, have continued to be portrayed as a rather meaningless cover for other motivations and dynamics.[6] In the following pages, we shall be taking a look at some of the ways in which principles of this kind did actually affect the politics of the Wars of the Roses, but, as a starting-point, it might be interesting to examine why they were excised from political histories in the first place.

Part of the answer must lie in the long tradition of scepticism about the sincerity with which politicians appeal to principles and public interest, a tradition which stretches back to the fifteenth century itself. To Polydore Vergil, author of the first historical account of the wars, the origins of the conflict lay in the Machiavellian scheming of Richard of York. Conscious of his title to the throne and consumed by 'an outrageous lust of principality', the duke set out to subvert the rule of Henry VI by sowing discord among the commons so that he could present himself as their champion. His talk of 'revenging common injuries', and of acting 'for the utility of the common wealth', was a mere pretext for gaining popular support and using it to fight his enemies about the king. By the mid-1450s and following a campaign of reporting daily 'every where to all the nobility, that the state of the common wealth was most miserable', he succeeded in dividing the magnates, gathering the Nevilles to his side and winning the Battle of St Albans. According to Vergil, these disruptions had a lasting effect on politics: from this time onwards, 'men were so nourished by factionalism that they could not later desist from it': everybody put partisan interests first, and common interests, such as order, unity and obedience to authority, were ignored. While Edward IV succeeded in taming this menace for a time, Richard III undid his work: 'by his example, [he] suggested to others the stirring up of new factions and the embarking on other schemes whereby they might acquire for themselves power or privileges'.[7] To Vergil, this gloomy state of affairs was a sign of profound malfunction, but to Sir John Fortescue, writing in the midst of the disorder, this unprincipled behaviour had come to seem the norm. For him the realities of politics were that, on the one hand, 'man's courage is so noble, that naturally he aspireth to high things, and to be exalted, and therefore enforceth himself to be always greater and greater', while on the other, 'the people will go with him that best may sustain and reward them'.[8] As a result, the king must be sure to have a higher disposable income than his greatest subjects; without it, rebellion – and successful rebellion – was almost a certainty. In this model, ideas of royal authority or common interest were of little consequence: the capacity to satisfy individual and material needs was the essence of power.

To many, these arguments have seemed strikingly modern, and Fortescue is often commended for being among the first political theorists to break away from the moralising traditions of medieval political thinking and 'to represent things as they are in real truth, rather than as they are imagined'.[9] This point of view raises another reason for the neglect of principles by commentators on the politics of the wars. Not only have twentieth-century historians seen the period much as Vergil and Fortescue saw it, they have also noted the particular unsuitability of medieval political ideas for use in the fifteenth-century political arena. The point has been neatly made by J. R. Lander, who observed that while 'theologians and lawyers had worked out extremely subtle principles of political obligation, some of which, at times of crisis, men surprisingly low in the social scale could echo, very little in the way of constitutional principles determined the course of political events'.[10] The concerns of academic theory were far removed from the needs of men of action, it appears: even 'constitutional principles' – ideas about the proper and established ways of governing the realm – bore little resemblance to the actual operations of politics.

In certain ways this is as much a comment on the historical treatment of political ideas and 'constitutional principles' as it is a judgement about fifteenth-century politics. Until recently, historians of ideas focused on the works of a small number of great thinkers, few of them English and most of them writing in Latin for an academic audience. The sort of concepts which received treatment were such as could compete in this rarefied environment, not such as could capture the imagination of shipmen, or trip from the tongues of magnates. Although many of the ideological statements made by political figures were shot through with perceptions which originated in the schools and universities, they did not receive attention in the histories of ideas and were left to be presented as 'mere rhetoric' by historians of politics. As is so often the case, the artificial barriers of the historical profession have, in this area, had a dramatic effect on the manner in which the past is interpreted: when Richard of York, for example, said that 'king or a lord lawless is as a fish waterless, for law causeth the king inheritable to the crown', it seems that he was simply posturing; but when the thirteenth-

century author of Bracton's legal treatise made the similar
observation that 'the king should be under no man, but under
God and the law, because law makes the king', it seems that he
was using a principle of Roman Law to illustrate the workings of
the English political system.[11]

More than the treatment of ideas, however, it is the past
treatment of the constitution which has had the most striking
effect on the political history of this period. 'Constitutional
History', as practised by Victorian scholars such as William Stubbs,
was an approach to the past which did bring politics and
principles together: it recognised that people thought about how
they were being governed and sought to show how their
perceptions – often their publicly-expressed perceptions – shaped
their political behaviour. Its major weakness was that the
principles to which it gave attention were those which seemed to
resemble the political principles of its own day: the rule of law;
the restraint of government by parliament; the ideal of limited
monarchy, and so on. It was axiomatic to these 'constitutional
historians' that the main theme of English history was the growing
dominance of these phenomena. Principled behaviour, therefore,
was 'constitutional' behaviour, that is behaviour which
encouraged 'constitutional' development: kings working in
tandem with parliament, or with magnate councils appointed in
parliament; noblemen pulling together, obeying the law and
using their political power to correct or restrain the king; MPs
seeking the initiative in legislation and financial matters. To his
regret, Stubbs found little of this kind of behaviour in the later
middle ages and presented it, therefore, as a generally
unprincipled age: there was, he said, 'no unity of public interest,
no singleness of political aim, no heroism of self-sacrifice. The
baronage is divided against itself, one part maintaining the
popular liberties but retarding their progress by bitter personal
antipathies, the other maintaining royal autocracy.' In this sorry
period, no event was 'more futile, more bloody, more immoral'
than the Wars of the Roses, during which self-interested magnates
cynically flirted with 'constitutional' principles when they were
out of power, only to revert to 'despotism' (tyranny), when they
obtained control.[12]

Although (or perhaps because) the twentieth century has seen
a prolonged reaction against this 'constitutionalist' approach,
some of its features continue to be influential. Stripped of its

arcane and moralistic language – 'self-sacrifice', 'liberties', 'despotism', and the like – Stubbs's picture of the Wars of the Roses is not actually so very different from most modern versions: its claim that, in this period, principles had become a simple tool of politics seems widely held. Perhaps the most significant legacy of 'Constitutional History', however, is a lingering assumption that political principles, on the one hand, and the material or personal concerns of individuals, on the other, are necessarily separate from, and opposed to, one another: for historians like Stubbs, the building of the 'Constitution' was a public task, carried out in the public interest by high-minded individuals; self-interest could only frustrate its progress. Most twentieth-century historians have reacted against this Victorian tendency to imply that altruism was the only proper course for politicians. Like Vergil and Fortescue, they have preferred to offer explanations of politics which focus on the direct and identifiable, often material, satisfaction of individual interests. Common interests have been regarded as a Stubbsian fantasy: the stuff of rhetoric, not of reality. While some commentators have begun to identify a role for principles in the politics of the period, the codes and values which have received most examination were not truly 'political' or 'constitutional' in their nature. Whatever their importance as sources of personal motivation, the ideas and conventions attached to service and chivalry, or to loyalty and Christian piety, for that matter, did not deal explicitly with government and how it ought to operate.[13] On the whole, these principles dealt with men and women as individuals, involved (at most) in *private* relationships with one another and the Deity, not as citizens or subjects, *publicly* related to each and all as participants in a political community. They may, then, be described as 'private principles' and, as such, they did not form a significant part of public or political discourse and were not generally promoted to support or explain political activity. As we have seen, the principles which dominated the political and conceptual debates of the wars were 'public' ones, 'principles of national government', ideas both political and constitutional in their meaning and their usage. Nineteenth-century historians found one way of showing how principles of this kind affected politics, but their model no longer convinces and was, in any case, unable to rescue the Wars of the Roses from their 'unprincipled' reputation. Is there another way of approaching the question, or was the language of political principle irrelevant to politics?

In fact, the question of how ideas and principles affect politics has come to attract the interest of some leading intellectual historians, notably the so-called 'Cambridge School' of John Dunn, John Pocock and Quentin Skinner. Skinner, in particular, has produced a number of studies which, among other things, are designed to show why 'it is essential, and not optional, for any political historian to be an historian of ideas'.[14] Much of what he argues seems directly relevant to the problems posed in this chapter and it may be that by examining and then applying his methodology we can arrive at some sense of how ideas and principles were important in the politics of the wars.

We have seen that the grounds on which the political historians of this period have left ideas and principles out of their accounts boil down to two: scepticism about the real influence of publicly-stated principles on the political behaviour of individuals; and scepticism about the contemporary relevance of the sort of ideas and principles on which earlier historians focused their attentions. As far as the first is concerned, Skinner has a novel and interesting answer to put forward. This is that the question of sincerity, which seems so fundamental, is actually beside the point: politicians do not have to be personally committed to the principles they propound in order for their political behaviour to be influenced by them. The private attitudes and motives of a Richard of York or a Richard of Gloucester – attitudes and motives that we cannot truly know – do not bear on the issue of the political meaning and importance of the principles they professed. Even if these men had been wholly unscrupulous, the important thing is that they found it necessary to find a description of their actions which could justify in public what they had done. Why they found this necessary is a difficult question, but an important one: it reminds us that, whatever the reserves of private power on which kings and noblemen could call, they were also forced to negotiate its use in public. As we shall see, the later medieval polity was a complex amalgam of private and public powers and obligations: people were aware of a broader politics beyond their own immediate relationships and interests; and so, if they were to manipulate them, politicians had to recognise this awareness, to justify their actions publicly. Only in rare periods of outright war – when politics were, in a sense, suspended – were politicians released from this obligation.

It was through this necessity for public justification that ideas exerted their power, because the task of finding a suitable description involved making appeals to what Skinner calls the 'accepted principles' of political society. These would tend to be established beliefs about the distribution of rights, powers and duties among the political classes; acknowledged views of how and why things should be done; a 'constitution', in the most general sense of the word. Because these principles were restricted in scope and application, they could not be used to justify all forms of behaviour, with the result that politicians were limited in what they could get away with. The knowledge that certain actions could not but be judged unprincipled was sufficient to deter most politicians from undertaking them, which means that the politics of any society were normally influenced – at least negatively, perhaps positively – by its 'accepted principles'.

We can illustrate this proposition quite effectively from the careers of the two men named above. If we assume for a moment that, as Vergil suggested, York's main aim in launching his campaign against the government of Henry VI was the acquisition of the throne, then it is quite clear that the principles he was forced to employ to justify his campaign made his 'true' end harder to achieve. All along, as we shall see, York was driven to emphasise his loyalty to Henry VI, and when – after ten years of principled opposition – he attempted to change tack and secure his goal, he found that he could not do so without rumblings from his allies and a significant loss of credibility. The principles which he had professed guided him down certain paths: when, at the last minute, he strayed from these paths, in pursuit of his 'true' ends, he paid a heavy price.[15] Gloucester was in a similar predicament. The notion that the common weal was unsafe in the hands of a king who was vulnerable to sectarian influences opened the way for his protectorate, but it did not justify the usurpation which followed a few weeks later. As soon as he departed from principled norms, the duke lost the public support which they conferred. As Rosemary Horrox has demonstrated, he was reduced to depending on his private resources and these, in fact, were insufficient to maintain him as king: on the one hand, the principles of public government made the ducal retinue a poor means of ruling that realm; on the other, the principles of personal loyalty meant that his nephew's household mostly turned against him.[16]

The fact that both York and Gloucester came to grief when they acted against the 'accepted principles' of their society suggests that Skinner's thesis works. Nonetheless, a problem clearly remains. At first sight, it appears that neither man was, in the end, dissuaded from his policy by the knowledge that it contravened political morality: even the comparatively circumspect York went for the throne in the end. Does this mean that, even if they lost out as a consequence, politicians were not capable of, or interested in, the sort of rational calculation which Skinner's model implies? I think the answer is more complicated. Not only were York and Gloucester exceptional figures, and treated as such by both contemporaries and historians, but they were caught in the crossfire of a clash of principles and found that actions which were necessary, proper and justifiable when viewed from one ideological perspective were unnecessary, improper and unjustifiable when viewed from another. To understand this dilemma, however, we need to know something about the 'accepted principles' of mid-fifteenth-century political society. How do we discover them?

One obvious answer is to begin with the various documents in which the politicians of the period sought to justify their actions. If we look at these, we find the same ideas and themes occurring time and again. It is, for example, immediately clear that the good of the community, or the 'common weal', as it was often called, was a principle which seemed to justify all manner of public action, from the ruling of the realm by a king with a shaky title, to the risings of great magnates or Kentish yeomen. Interestingly enough, we can find the same principle being advanced in sources more removed from the maelstrom of political debate: the 'mirrors for princes', for example, which were handbooks that told kings how to rule; or the speeches made by chancellors at the openings of parliaments. One mid-fifteenth-century 'mirror' reminded the king that he, and other lords, were given their power 'to govern and do well, and duly, as well as in their own persons as by other good and true deputies, to see the just governance of God's people'. Another, written earlier in the century, drew attention to the power and authority of popular feeling: quoting the tag '*vox populi vox Dei*' (the voice of the people is the voice of God), it urged the king to 'win your people's voice' or risk the damaging consequences of their dissatisfaction with his rule.[17] Even Fortescue, for all his cynicism about the self-interest of individuals, believed that their common interests were worth preserving and quoted the view of an eminent theologian, Thomas Aquinas, that 'the king is given on account of the realm, and not the realm on account of the king'.[18] Meanwhile, Bishop Stafford, describing Solomon's throne to the parliament of 1442, told MPs that the throne itself symbolised 'good rule, by which the public good of every realm may grow and be established in prosperity'.[19] The concept that royal rule was justified by its capacity to defend the community was everywhere – in the minds of academics as much as the mouths of politicians – and we may therefore take it to be one of the most fundamental 'accepted principles' of this society. In a sense, of course, the prominence of this concept vindicates the prejudices of Victorian commentators like Stubbs and therefore answers the second objection raised by political historians to using the evidence of ideas. The governments of this period were indeed, it seems, founded on a representative ideal. Politicians and academics were speaking more or less the same language. Even so, it is important to note that we deduce the political importance of this principle from its presence in accessible contemporary materials and from the realisation that politicians must defer to established principles as a matter of course, regardless of their private character and motivation. We do not see it as part of some timeless 'Constitution' and we do not assume that adherence to this principle necessarily had positive results. In fact, we shall also find that it was not the only fundamental principle of royal government and was therefore far from being the only idea of which politicians had to take account.

It was a commonplace of political thinking throughout western Europe in the Middle Ages that kings were appointed by God to advance the common interests of the people they ruled: that is, to defend them from their enemies, to pacify and judge them rightfully, and – more generally – to enable as many as possible to lead the 'sufficient life' that a well-ordered community offered.[20] In this single and general statement lie two of the most fundamental principles of English political life. The first, and more obvious, has already been introduced: it is that the king was obliged – partly through his coronation oath, partly through the simple fact that he was king – to protect or advance the common interest, or 'common weal'. This was the whole purpose of his kingship, the essence of his role in society: if he was lord of all his people, he was also their servant – 'servant of the servants of God', as Fortescue pointed out.[21] The second, and less obvious, was that as the king was God's appointee, not man's, his obligation to protect the common weal was a matter between him and the Deity, and he had full, free and absolute authority to carry out his task as he saw fit. Subjects might reasonably expect him to be guided by virtue, or by law, or by their own advice (or 'counsel') in the fulfilment of his duties, but they had no right to force him to rule in this way, or, in fact, to punish or depose him if he seemed to be failing.

Although both of these principles had, to some extent, been modified by the growth of public authority in the thirteenth and fourteenth centuries, they remained the basic norms of royal power in our period. Predictably, the rise of public and representative institutions such as parliament and, in a sense, the common law, tended to encourage the first principle at the expense of the second and English constitutional historians have given much less emphasis to the theme of royal freedom – even absoluteness – than they have to the corresponding theme of public obligation.[22] Even so, if the sense that the king was ultimately independent of his subjects was undermined by the formal depositions of Edward II and Richard II and, more frequently and prosaically, by the imposition of statutory and conciliar checks on kings who were felt to be failing, it is clear that measures of this kind were undertaken in an atmosphere of crisis. The community could claim rights and impose controls, but it could maintain either in peace unless the king chose to accept them. Invariably, the price of restoring political relations was a concession on the part of the subjects that the king was free: in the language of 1399, for example, he would not be denied his 'royal liberty', but – in return – he would undertake to use it 'to keep the ancient laws and statutes ... and to do right to all people, in mercy and truth'.[23] If the later medieval king has often appeared to be in the thrall of the community, then, the true situation was almost the reverse.

One underlying reason for this state of affairs was undoubtedly the fact that, during periods of good rule, the two principles described above helped to encourage the kind of political harmony in which kings and subjects were prepared to trust one another and work together. The people benefited from the king's obligation to uphold the common weal, because it encouraged him to keep the laws and listen to their views. More surprisingly, perhaps, they also benefited from his absolute authority. Freedom from his subjects ensured that the king would rule them impartially, because he had no need to base his power on the support of 'factions', or groups, among them. Freedom from the letter of the law enabled him to rule flexibly, making new policy to confront new problems and tempering justice with mercy and equity. All the same, during periods of bad rule these principles could be remarkably destructive. Certainly, as the king failed to defend the common weal – the sole justification for his status and powers – the fact that it remained illegitimate to act against him created profound political diffficulties. Under these circumstances, principles diverged and 'principled' behaviour was likely to be controversial; perhaps even divisive and violent. The need both to accept and to confront the dilemma posed by bad kingship was a fundamental element in causing and prolonging the Wars of the Roses, and the rest of this chapter will be devoted to tracing its political effects.

The common weal was a hard thing to define, but the comprehensive failure of Henry VI's government to satisfy the many interests of its subjects was, by 1449–50, hard to deny.[24] As Cade's rebels succinctly put it in one of their manifestoes, the king's 'law is lost; his merchandise is lost; his commons are destroyed. The sea is lost; France is lost; himself is made so poor that he may not pay for his meat or drink; he oweth more and [is] greater in debt than ever was king in England.'[25] Neither justice, nor order nor prosperity had been maintained, and Cade and his men were in no doubt about either the cause of this failure or the action it demanded. The first was the undue influence of evil men 'brought up of nought', who had monopolised the king's attentions and turned his wealth and power to their own selfish ends. The second was to achieve the downfall of these men: by royal justice, if possible; by the 'true justice' of the community, if not. If getting true justice meant going to war against the king's ministers, it would be a war fought in the name and interests of the king himself, as well as in those of the community, since he was as much the helpless victim of these 'traitors' as his subjects were. Throughout the decade leading up to 1460, and again in 1469, all the opponents of the government took up the same cry: the king was prevented from preserving the common weal by a clique of low-born 'traitors' who diverted his powers and resources to suit themselves, in response, loyal subjects could – and should – act for the common interest by opposing these 'traitors'. Whatever these statements may or may not reveal about either the true nature of government under Henry VI and Edward IV or the inner motivation of opposition politicians, they are clearly a response to the principles discussed above. Specifically, they are an attempt by subjects to justify taking action by alleging the principle that the community must be defended; to explain, in effect, why they were apparently ignoring the principle that God had bestowed the power of government on the king alone.

Politicians sought to get round this problem in a number of ways. First of all, they did what they could to demonstrate that the whole community thought as they did: if this did not give them royal authority for their actions, it did at least underwrite their claims that the common weal was not upheld and make it harder to present them as sectaries. No less than the common weal, in fact, the community was ultimately undefined and probably meant different things to different groups. Since it expressed the idea of the whole body of the realm – head and members, king and people – the claim to represent the community was most straightforwardly made by large gatherings of commoners, such as Cade's rebels. While the normal uses of the concept were royal, aristocratic and, of course, parliamentary – where MPs (not for the last time) advanced the interests of landlords under cover of communal representation – the fact that it implied a measure of 'popular' authority made it vulnerable to appropriation from below. Predictably enough, common people were largely excluded from the apparatus of national rule, but – under certain circumstances – they could be an acceptable barometer of its effects: it is, for example, a telling feature of Fortescue's *Governance of England*, that the 'commons' who are most prominently shown to profit from the political arrangements he describes are men below the level of the gentry. Even so, if peasant agitators wished to forestall the predictable and damaging assumption that they were simply out to kill and rob their social superiors, they had to publicise national and communal (rather than local or sectional) grievances, and show respect for life and property.

Dissenting magnates, meanwhile, faced a slightly different problem. They had to combat the suspicion that, whatever they professed, their real grievances were personal and selfish ones: exactly the charge that historians, from Vergil onwards, have levied against them. One way to suggest probity was to stimulate popular rebellions with a similar agenda, as York attempted to do in 1452 and 1459, and Warwick and his various allies succeeded in doing in 1460, 1469 and 1470, but there were problems with this approach. Nothing was to be gained from exposure as a rabble-rouser, and York was on surer ground in 1450, when he tried to use the popular disturbances as a shaming demonstration of the failure of government rather than as a platform for action. For the nobility could seek to represent the community in other ways. They had not altogether lost their older, feudal, distinction as the king's leading vassals: if it was the gentry and the townsmen who spoke for the community in parliament, it was the nobility – peers of the realm and, in many cases, the managers of regional power-networks – whom people expected to represent the community to the king. As Bishop Russell planned to tell the peers in 1483, 'the people must stand afar and not pass the limits: ye speak with the prince, which is quasi deus noster in terris [like our God on Earth]'.[26] The lords were the 'consiliarii nati' (the born, or natural, counsellors) of the king, and if he appeared to ignore their advice – to exclude them, or enough of them, from his daily presence – this very act was a suggestion that he was not concerned, or not able, to conduct his government in the interests of the community. In other words, excluded magnates who had never shown any disloyalty to the king possessed, by the fact of their exclusion, legitimate grounds for criticism of his government. A single excluded magnate could be dangerous enough – particularly if, like Richard of York, he spoke the language of the commons in the realm (justice upon the traitors) or that of the commons in parliament (resumption, for example, which York seems to have espoused throughout the 1450s) – but a group of excluded magnates was potentially lethal. The papal legate, for example, was probably not alone in having difficulty deciding which was the legitimate government of Henry VI in 1459–60: was it the lords about the king, whom the Yorkists presented as self-interested rogues, bent on violence and busily preventing the king from exercising power freely? Or was it York, Warwick and Salisbury, whom the Lancastrians presented as traitors, crowning their decade of subversion with a threat to King Henry himself? The wars may have been a battle of 'ins' and 'outs', in a sense, but some 'outs' were more significant than others and this for reasons of public principle as much as of private power.

Being seen to act for the community was, of course, only half the battle. To secure legitimacy, politicians had also to take account of the other important principle, that the king was ultimately above his people. Two strategies for doing so were commonly adopted during the Wars of the Roses, often in tandem. The first was to claim that what might appear to be insurrection was really a kind of petitioning, or counselling; behaviour which recognised the authority of the king to determine policy and direct public action. So it was that in 1450 Cade, as we have seen, presented himself as a 'public petitioner' and called for royal justice, while York offered himself as the king's 'humble subject and liegeman' to execute whatever Henry should ordain concerning the 'traitors': he would do nothing of his own will, but only as the king's agent or minister. In an environment where the king was cut off from his subjects by a clique of greedy courtiers, such true and loyal counsellors might find themselves in danger, and the consequent need to protect themselves explained the large numbers of armed men who characteristically accompanied their 'humble submissions'. As York pointed out in 1452, it was the 'truth, faith and allegiance that (he bore) unto the king, and the good will and favour that (he had) to all the realm', which had made the duke of Somerset so bitterly hostile to him.[27]

This feature draws attention to the second strategy adopted by the avowedly loyal dissidents of the period: the protest that their opposition was directed not against the king, but against his wicked advisers – men who had 'blinded' him, 'stirred and moved' him to destructive policies, 'estranged' him from his true lords, and even 'restrained and kept (him) from the liberty and freedom that belongeth to his … estate'.[28] While Cade and York, Warwick and Clarence asked for 'justice' on these traitors – and typically paused to allow the king to exercise this prerogative himself – it was implicit in their critique that their petitions would not be heard, that the king would be unable or unwilling to judge the 'traitors', and that they, for king and crown, for the community and for themselves, would have to go to war against these men to see justice done. Such a move was hard to justify: private warfare had been a felony since the Treason Act of 1352 and the excuse of England's peril, put forward by the Yorkists in 1455 and 1460, was scarcely equal to a further problem which the 'traitors'' argument raised, but could not overcome. This was the fact that war against people 'having the guiding about the most noble person of our sovereign lord' was likely also to involve war against the king, an almost indefensible act. It is worth noting that there were actually only five occasions between 1450 and the end of the wars on which an army headed by magnates claiming to act for the community confronted a royal army which contained a king whose right to rule these magnates recognised.[29] Arguably, there was only one such occasion on which the self-styled leaders of the community had to acknowledge that a confrontation of this kind had taken place and to find reasons for their actions. This was the First Battle of St Albans, in May 1455, and it is difficult to feel that the Yorkists were ever truly able to justify what they had done: while a heavily-guarded parliament sat patiently through their extraordinary tale of curial deceptions and misplaced letters, Warwick had already abandoned the party line and put the blame for the affray on Lord Cromwell.[30] And even if the Yorkists had been able to persuade themselves and the rest of the political nation that their actions at St Albans had been legitimate, it is not clear that their eradication of a few 'wicked counsellors' availed either themselves or the community very much. An essential problem with the devices which sought to reconcile communitarian action with the recognition of royal authority was that they had to leave the king himself untouched. Even in the wake of victories at St Albans and Northampton, the 'loyal' Yorkists of the 1450s were stuck with Henry VI, who – as they well knew – was the real source of the realm's problems. In 1469 Warwick and Clarence, on the other hand, were stuck with Edward IV, who was free of them within a matter of months and whose freedom (rather like that of Henry VI in the early months of 1461) launched his sometime captors on a more desperate course of opposition. In each of these cases, it seems, political action in the name of principle produced the results which principle dictated: the freedom of politicians to bend the rules was evidently limited.

Clearly enough, then, none of these communitarian justifications for political action by subjects was really effective. The principles of English royal government could not, beyond a certain point, be deployed to justify moves against a king and his ministers. At the same time, however, the same principles meant that moves of this kind were likely to be made whenever the crown could plausibly be presented as failing in its obligation to uphold the common weal. This was the conundrum underlying most of the political crises of the Middle Ages, and the Wars of the Roses were no exception. The governments of Henry VI in the 1450s, Edward IV in the 1460s, Edward V and Richard III between 1483 and 1485, and Henry VII (perhaps) in the 1480s and 1490s were all undermined by their inability to provide the orderly and authoritative government which was the basis of the common weal.[31] This inability made them vulnerable to anyone who could make an effective claim to be acting in the interests of the community. The prosecution of such claims was likely to cause further disruption, providing still greater licence for action on behalf of the common weal as order, justice and authority retreated further: Richard of York, in the 1450s, and Warwick, in 1469–70, were both able to exploit disturbances which they themselves had helped to create. Yet the ineradicable authority of monarchy ensured that the successes of opposition were strictly limited and that the surest chance of corporate salvation lay (as it had always lain) in the victory of the king over the men whom he regarded as his enemies, and in his willingness to reform himself in whatever ways appeared to be necessary. Since neither royal victory, nor royal wit, nor royal good will could be counted on, there was a tendency for the disorder which bad government and communal reaction generated to be prolonged.

Contemporaries were not always prepared to tackle these structural and, in a sense, conceptual problems head on. As we have seen, they often resorted to the simpler solution of decrying the political immorality of their times. It will be clear by now that this was a significant misdiagnosis. The real source of difficulty lay in public morality itself, not the immorality of individual politicians. The same principles which made for order and prosperity in periods of political harmony produced violence and division in periods of political dysfunction: this was the hard thing to accept, to understand and to explain. Principles simply dictated the lines down which politics would flow. In themselves, they were neither good, nor bad. If they proclaimed the common interest, they were not inevitably incompatible with individual interest. They were open to exploitation from all comers: the idea that lords, for example, could sometimes speak for the community was as visible to their underlings as it was to the magnates themselves. For the ideologists of the period, therefore, the task was clear: to find the means of resolution for an apparently insatiable conflict, and to find them within the stock of principles recognised by political society. In the remaining pages of this chapter, I should like to consider three of the more important solutions contemporaries devised.

In many ways, the first attempt at an ideological solution to the problems raised by the wars was the argument contained in the tract known as *Somnium Vigilantis* ('A Dream of Vigilance').[32] Written in 1459, probably to persuade the Lords – and perhaps the Commons – at the Coventry Parliament to convict the Yorkists of treason, this was a reasoned presentation of the view that nothing but obedience to the king could ever be justifiable. It is actually one of the best sources for the ideology of monarchy in later medieval England, and deserves to be more widely known, but its particular relevance to us lies in what it has to say about the common weal. The author, who may have been Fortescue, was apparently in no doubt about the falseness of the Yorkists' professed concern for the common weal: 'pure malice and long-premeditated wickedness' were, he alleged, their real motives. However, what makes his tract so interesting – indeed exemplary – is that insincerity was not the ground on which he resolved to condemn their actions. Instead, he set out to make the rather more important, and universally applicable, case that what they had done was offensive to the very principles they were professing. The essence of his argument was that it was only through obedience to the king and his laws (and, implicitly, his formally-authorised ministers) that the common weal could be served. If anyone had 'controversies or debates' to settle, he should put them before the normal authorities and be content with what was ordained. Unauthorised public action was inherently subversive. Even unauthorised judgements about the quality of government could be unacceptable: 'you say perhaps that it belongeth to every person of the community to oppose himself to the ruin of the public good. But it is not so when authority lacketh ... Who made [the Yorkists] judges?' Authority had to be preserved because, without it, there could be no government and no order. The violence which accompanied Yorkist activism on behalf of the common weal was a simple proof of its self-defeating nature: much as 'they did pretend a reformation of wrongs and extortions used, as they said, in this realm and [by] the sovereign, [actually] the most endless misrule of all the sinners of the world did rest in them and in their servants'.

As a reiteration of the old theme that it was better to endure a tyrant than to upset the order of the universe (and of the realm) by attempting to depose him, this was the most persuasive yet. People must already have seen how little was to be gained – and how much to be lost – through dissidence, no matter how principled or well-intentioned it may have been. The *Somnium* supplied them with a simple and authoritative proof that this must always be the case and, through its emphasis on the intrinsic spuriousness of all unauthorised action on behalf of the common weal, may have had a certain long-term influence on the workings of politics. What it did not do was to offer any palatable solution to the general problem of royal misgovernment or, it may be added, to the specific problem raised by Henry VI; namely, that the well known feebleness of Henry's will meant that there was no effective and convincing means by which the all-important 'authority' could be transmitted by the king to the ministers through whom he normally acted.[33] Even so, it may be that the arguments in the *Somnium* were a significant factor in encouraging the duke of York to propose a new way of reconciling the representation of the community with the recognition of royal authority: the notorious attempt to make himself king.

The coupling of professions in defence of the community with the assertion of a better claim to the throne was the second major response to the problems raised by the wars of the Roses and, of course, it was this device that lent the Wars their particular character. From Edward IV, in 1461, to Perkin Warbeck, in 1497, every claimant of the crown, successful or unsuccessful, accompanied his claim with talk of how the triumph of dynastic right would also be the salvation of *Res publica* (and how the unrightful tenure of his opponent was the explanation of the poor government he inflicted). After Richard of Gloucester's coup of April 1483, there were fewer 'loyal' rebellions: Tudor, Simnel, Warbeck, and possibly Buckingham, abandoned the notion of wicked counsellors and simple cited wicked kings. It matters little which concern – dynasty or good government – came first, or had more motivating power. It matters little whether (for example) York had always nurtured designs on the throne – as his Lancastrian opponents promptly suggested – or whether he resorted to making his claim because there was little chance of either saving himself or obtaining political control by other means. The fact is that this was a policy which both conformed to the prevailing principles of the day and answered the problems which the Yorkists and other loyal critics had encountered in the past. A title in blood, the vehicle of divine appointment, supplied the necessary authority which stewardship of the common weal, in itself, could not. By insisting that he was king, York and his supporters could abandon the unworkable posture of 'loyal' opposition and sidestep the censures contained in *Somnium Vigilantis*: the irresistible authority which it bestowed upon the king belonged to the natural successor to the crown, and York had a plausible claim to be that successor.[34] If he could secure rapid recognition of that claim and then defeat the intruding Henry of Lancaster and his remaining supporters, he could resolve the problem of misgovernment from the top: the only position, in fact, from which it could be resolved.

York's policy was not without its virtues, then. Even so, it is clear that it was also fraught with problems. The first of these was that the succession of a new dynasty was no guarantee of better government: the fact that good kingship may have been the only means of advancing or defending the common weal did not mean that a new king was necessarily a good one. Leaving aside the matter of his personal qualities – and there is every reason to assume that Richard of York would have been a better king than Henry VI, and some grounds for thinking that the rule of Richard of Gloucester was a better bet than another royal adolescence – there was the considerable problem that the new king was rarely the only person who could claim the right to rule. This meant that his subjects were not clearly obliged to obey him and could, in fact and in principle, dispense with his services whenever they chose and whenever circumstances allowed. Edward IV, Richard III and Henry VII – and, for that matter, the 'readepted' Henry VI, Lambert Simnel and Perkin Warbeck – may have claimed the throne as a matter of absolute and transcendent right, but this did not rescue them from the obligation to rule in the common interest of their subjects and, with a choice of claimants available to the community, it was on their fulfilment of this obligation that they could expect to be judged. Without the normal guarantees of obedience, of course, the task of government was much harder and the obligation to pursue the common interest tended to take second place to the creation of unanswerable power, a policy which could never be justified and invited criticism and further instability. In the event, therefore, York's apparently ingenious *demarche* transformed a conventional conflict into a nuclear conflict.

A third answer to the problem of inadequate kingship was proposed by Sir John Fortescue in his treatise on the *Governance of England*. Like the author of the *Somnium* and the sponsors of dynastic legitimism, he recognised that effective government could only be restored from the top, and his solution was to devise a means of reinforcing the ruler – so as to restore some measure of order – and then of reforming his rule from within. The problems of disobedience and misgovernment would be tackled almost simultaneously: if he followed Fortescue's prescription, the king would not need to resort to unpopular devices in order to maintain himself in power, while the community, unable to counter the newly-invincible ruler, would find that this did not matter, that they were receiving better government anyway. What the *Governance* proposed was that the king should resume all the lands which had been granted to supporters and servants 'inconsiderately, or above the merits of them that have them'. This, Fortescue believed, would greatly increase the king's personal 'livelihood', so diminishing both his debts and his unpopular dependence on taxation. Once his financial health was restored, the king would be better able to protect himself from the ambitions of 'overmighty subjects'; and the Commons, relieved of the burden of supporting a 'poor king' from their own pockets, would be less inclined towards insurrection. From this time forward, the king would debar himself from granting any part of his resumed livelihood and a formal council would be established to police this understanding. This council would have other roles as well: it would help the king administer what remained of his patronage; and it would devote itself to exploring other ways by which his livelihood might legitimately be increased. It was to be an effective means of representing the interests of the community: on the one hand, it would have a significant influence over royal policy; on the other, three-quarters of its members were to be appointed on merit from among the ranks of ordinary men, only a quarter would be noblemen, because Fortescue thought this would reduce the tendency for government to serve the interests of the quarrelsome élite.

In many ways, it seems that Fortescue had found the perfect mixture of authoritarian and communitarian policies to suit the circumstances in which he wrote. The demands set by the principles we have discussed were fully satisfied. Even if he lacked the sanction of divine appointment, Fortescue's king would clearly be able to secure obedience and, assisted by his devoted and intimate council, would effectively be independent of his subjects.[35] Meanwhile, his commitment to the common weal was secured by the participation of the councillors in many of his deeds and by their guardianship of his expanded 'livelihood'. The community would feel the benefit in measurable ways: an end to internecine conflict; an end to inappropriate taxation. At the same time, the practical solutions which Fortescue recommended as the means for satisfying and reconciling the divergent principles of the period were, for the most part, reassuringly familiar: plans for resuming royal grants or improving the quality of royal government by formalising conciliar arrangements had been heard in many of the parliaments of the preceding century; the only real difference was that most kings had, in the past, regarded measures of this kind as a form of limitation, while Fortescue was arguing that they were actually the route to a greater liberty. In this very difference, however, lies an important problem with Fortescue's proposals: whatever their roots in the polity of his own day, they actually involved a significant re-ordering of its normal arrangements. Not for nothing has Fortescue commonly been regarded as the architect of a 'new monarchy'. Discreetly, tacitly, perhaps accidentally, he seems to have been arguing for the replacement of royal and noble lordship by a new and more 'republican' system, in which a council drawn from the community managed a society of free men who were more or less equal in their political status. Much as the kings of the later fifteenth and early sixteenth centuries flirted with ideas and policies similar to those contained in the *Governance*, none of them was about to implement such a wholesale change in the structure of political society. Perceptive as Fortescue was and influential as his thinking was to be, it remains uncertain what, if anything, it contributed to the restoration of political harmony under Edward IV and the early Tudor kings.[36]

The aim of this chapter has not been to explain why the Wars of the Roses started or how they were resolved, but to say something about the ways in which the basic principles of English royal government shaped the course of politics in a period of profound and lasting crisis. My purpose is not to suggest that these principles were more important in determining politics than other factors, such as the structure of society, or even – in a sense – the beliefs, capacities and deeds of powerful individuals. The point is rather to establish that these principles deserve our attention too: that the wars were as much about the achievement of the common interest, the restoration of strong government and the reconciliation of these two ends, as they were about the more easily identifiable interests of the leading participants. We have seen that it was possible for principles to influence the movement of politics at a communal level, as well as a personal one, and that for this to take place, a sincere devotion to the ideals these principles might seem to represent was not necessary. This explains how it was possible for the wars to be a highly 'principled' conflict even though, for centuries, they have been seen as a cynical and pragmatic affair. Now that it is clear that the pursuit of principle did not necessarily produce an orderly politics, the condemnation of fifteenth-century politicians seems more than ever misplaced. Not only were these men fighting to protect themselves and their interests, they were fighting for what their society professed to believe in.

7. The Church and the Wars of the Roses

RICHARD G. DAVIES

Christian life in mid-fifteenth-century England was comfortable.[1] Wool-merchants and other *nouveaux riches* led the way in building and re-building churches across the beam of England and leaving their signatures on them; a thirsty market for works of conventional personal piety was about to give William Caxton his chance; prelates, landowners and urban oligarchs endowed schools and (Cambridge) colleges in a steadily increasing flow; the even tenor of monastic life was punctuated here and there by some lively rioting from the local peasants and flare-ups of domestic disharmony, but nothing serious and nothing new. In an increasing number of towns craft-guilds were getting together to organise joint mystery plays. Rural parishes organised ales, Robin Hood plays and teenage Hoke-days as fund-raisers and splashed lively, sometimes ghoulish, wall-paintings along the naves of their churches. Tithes were generally paid without much fuss, and the parish clergy were usually regarded as good neighbours by their flocks. The church courts concerned themselves with the moral failings and marital problems of the layfolk only as and when obliged to by outrage amongst those immediately involved, their kin or their neighbours. The bishops in the mid-fifteenth century were as pastoral and unpolitical a collection as might ever have been mustered in medieval England, albeit as avaricious as usual. Even the Lollards were at ease in their heartlands, ducking down when Bishop Chedworth of Lincoln became restless over a few free spirits in the Thames Valley in 1462–4 and shocked by Bishop Hales's wickedly-precise cull of their Coventry kin in 1486, but otherwise co-existing agreeably with the wicked world.

Of course, fifteenth-century England had its professional miseries, just like the historical profession now, although rather fewer in number. It was and is said, naturally, that too much was sham, show, hypocrisy, complacency, fossilised tradition; with vested interests, rotten foundations, the masses opiated, wealth

134

and power misappropriated, the legitimisation of inequality, not 'real Christianity' at all. Well, yes, of course. However, to the chagrin of such moralists and however 'incorrect' the diet and eating-habits of the day, most people found something to respond to in the richly-varied fifteenth-century religious menu on offer, be it theodicy, identity, comfort or power. Thus, the perceived religious life of English people throve throughout the period of the Wars of the Roses. The civil conflicts had no significant cause in religion and left little specific mark on it. Some individual churchmen were made and broken, and at times the Church as an institution had to take a stand. In the very long term, perhaps the Wars of the Roses were indeed a symbol of some fundamental land-shift in which the secular authorities would re-define their relationships with the Church, and certain particular incidents can be earmarked. This, however, was *very* long-term. Arguably, the actual lack of a fundamental role played by the Church in such a time of dynastic and physical uncertainty is the most telling point.

It has been argued that the leaders of the English Church looked to drive a hard bargain for selling its legitimising unction to the House of York in 1461, just as it had done to the House of Lancaster in 1399.[2] Truth to tell, the latter hypothesis itself hardly bears close examination, save where it suited both Henry IV and the bishops to crack down on seditious and heretical preaching. As for 1461, the current complaints of the clergy concerned infuriating practical points of friction between lay and ecclesiastical jurisdiction, notably common law prosecutions of clergy and the misapplication of writs of *praemunire facias*, to which Edward IV eventually gave leisurely fair words but no effective remedy.[3] It might even be wondered whether Edward IV so resolved to base himself upon hereditary right and justice as to be determined not to extend the role of the Church beyond traditional ceremony, preferring instead to emphasise more secular attributes and acclamations. None the less, both he and Richard III took annointing seriously, and the latter, at least, touched for the King's Evil – with greater optimism than success. Predictably, neither Edward IV nor Richard III changed the established coronation rite, and, more to the point, no 'kingmaking' bishops attempted such a novelty either.[4] It was actually Henry VII who was the keenest of fifteenth-century usurpers to gain the pope's explicit support, for his title, his marriage to Elizabeth of York, and against rebels and seditious sanctuary-dwellers; which blessings, with the ground already well prepared by the future Cardinal Morton, he obtained with ease and activated.[5]

Sir John Fortescue bent his lawyer's mind to the dilemma of English monarchy and the nature of political society, whilst William Worcestre and Sir Thomas Malory composed quasi-military alternatives of raucously uneven but not unimpressive tone. None of these men found his inspiration from the Church, even Malory setting only the most nominal of overt religious parameters to his Arthurian epic. No churchman contributed anything of moment. John Blacman's memoir of Henry VI is undergoing serious reappraisal and might emerge as a significant defence of the holiness required in any king, not just one, but Blacman was also deeply aware of the drawbacks in practice.[6] During the Great Schism, there had been Englishmen to debate very well the dilemma of a split papal monarchy, if less enthusiastically the opportunity or need to set the whole body of the Church to rights, but none of this came through into the civil war period.[7] John Stanbury, bishop of Hereford and confessor to Henry VI, did write of kingship; but what, we do not know. He was extremely unpopular, but that went with the job.[8] Oxford University, far from contributing remedial wisdom, displayed only an alarmingly consistent ability to elect high-profile chancellors destined for disgrace: Cambridge, after an initial wobble, pursued a less ambitious and quieter path.[9]

If there were no intellectual contributions to the problem of the wars, the power of preachers was well-recognised, and they were expected to deal very directly with social issues. They were regarded as dangerous when their criticisms threatened real upset. It was charged – by a very adjacent witness – that the court circle had taken by 1458 to demanding advance texts of sermons to be preached before Henry VI in order to excise any adverse comments about the state of the realm. Mr William Ive, a preacher of rising fame (albeit perhaps with undetected connections with the Neville family) was invited to preach before Henry VI. Whether as general policy (our reporter's version) or because the court did know something about Ive's circle, he was asked to submit his script for censorship. He deceived them and even slipped this scandal into his sermon about the ills of the realm. It had no effect on the king, and he was packed off home unpaid.[10]

Sermons were used to assert title during the wars. On 1 March 1461 the silver-tongued George Neville persuaded a crowd of several thousands in St George's Fields near London of Edward of March's claim to the throne, most crucially the troops. 'Friar Goddard' declared Henry VI's sure title to the people in 1470 and hence would, if it were the same man, have made a peculiarly tactless choice as George of Clarence's advocate in defence of his condemned servants in 1477. In 1483, most famously, Richard of Gloucester produced preachers, notably Dr Ralph Shaa, brother of the Lord Mayor and the most famous preacher in London, to argue his slender claims to a highly sceptical audience. For his collaboration, if gossip be believed, the hapless doctor lost both reputation and his very hold on life.[11]

The long-established tradition of a sermon by the chancellor – provided he was a bishop, as almost invariably he was – to open parliament (identical, in effect, to the modern speech from the throne) enabled current royal policy and need to be cloaked eloquently in biblical, classical and scholastic justification, and allowed anticipated whinings from the Commons to be chastised. Over the years, chancellors dug up apt texts for every occasion, sometimes even of truly brazen effrontery. In 1470, to open the Readeption Parliament, George Neville rose shamelessly to the occasion: 'Revertimini mihi, revolentes filii' (rhyme, rhythm, pun *and* pungent accuracy), 'for I'm your man'.[12] Alas, we have no more of his sermon, as of the whole record of this parliament: Edward IV saw to that when he recovered his throne. From 1483–4, by contrast, there survive serial drafts of Bishop John Russell's intended sermon, as he struggled unhappily (as for the next two years) to keep up with Richard of Gloucester's unpredictable intentions.[13] Russell was a scholar, a polymath indeed, and an intelligent, honest man. In one preliminary draft of his sermon, prepared for the intended first parliament of young Edward V, he likened Richard of Gloucester to Marcus Lepidus: not Shakespeare's lumpish beast of burden but the tried and trusted third-sharer in the Yorkist family's congenital genius, the kingdom's dream stand-in between perfect father and perfect son. Was it composed with a sincere belief in Richard? Was it written with an unquiet mind about the Protector, more in hope than expectation? We just do not know: probably Russell himself did not.

The lack of an intellectual response by the clergy to the dynastic crisis has the ironic context that Henry VI, Margaret of Anjou and the duke of Suffolk had actually promoted theologians, confessors, scholars and college fellows further up the episcopal ladder than such men had been in numbers for two centuries or more.[14] It might be argued, and has been, that this merely reflected the fact that the 'civil service' was being laicised and therefore no longer full of lawyers and administrators in holy orders jostling for high preferment. However, Edward IV and Henry VII had no trouble re-discovering such traditional recruits for high office and episcopacy. Thus, whilst Margaret in fact tended to promote administrators of the usual sort, it does remain true that Henry VI and Suffolk enhanced those who had done them some personal service of an ecclesiastical kind. Politically, this did them no good at all: when the crisis came, there was not the usual episcopal cadre of hardened royal servants to counsel their benefactor and influence parliament and council to prudence. Of the six who could be brought even reluctantly to take turns on the council during York's first protectorate, only two had much experience of politics and both were of ill-repute.[15] Furthermore, contemporary ballads left no doubt what the public thought of such men: fawning parasites and insinuating poisoners of the royal ear.[16] Sad to the modern moralising mind, medieval people had few qualms about civil servants in mitres, whereas men raised by piety alone invited the most lurid of speculation. Sadder still, the king and duke had actually had a (generally) fine eye for merit. Their protégés were politically innocent in every sense of the term (as Edward IV fairly recognised). After 1461 they trooped back to their dioceses, and fine diocesans most made. One interesting corollary is that Edward IV could not use many of them in public life, not for their lack of loyalty but for lack of the right skills. Furthermore, they did tend to live a long time, so that his opportunities to replace them were belated and few. It must be noted, for accuracy, that several of these veterans did rally to Henry VI's side in London in 1470 with more affection and alacrity than proved wise. Edward IV detained some of them for a few weeks, but then let them return home again sadder and wiser men.[17]

One specific consequence of Henry VI's unusual choice of bishops was that throughout the 1460s, wherever and whenever Edward IV looked around for one, he always found Bishop George Neville of Exeter, Warwick's younger brother. Precociously talented at whatever he turned his hand to, George might well, to be fair and consider his early years, have turned his

hand with historic effect to education and Church reform if life
and his own surname had been different.[18] Edward simply had to
promote him to York in 1465, with or without regret about this
consolidation of Neville power in the north. Quite apart from
whose brother he was, George was simply more active, more
intelligent, more eloquent, more experienced and – in
intellectual circles not least – more famous than any other bishop
serving. Archbishop Bourgchier of Canterbury found him
irritating; Bishop Waynflete of Winchester apparently hated him.
He soon added wealth and flamboyance, and never feigned
modesty. In the end, he revealed one fatal flaw: total loyalty to his
eldest brother at the expense of prudence of either a personal or
political kind. In 1471 he proved out of his depth, gullible (like
his brother indeed?) to the brutal *realpolitik* of the House of York.
Imprisonment and the fall of his family reputedly broke him both
in spirit and body.[19]

Neville was the shooting star of the episcopate. The
involvement of other individual bishops in the violent moments of
the civil wars was discussed many years ago in a rightly celebrated
essay, and although much more could be said about their
responses, for example through recourse to their diocesan
records (still largely unpublished), such individual attention must
await another time.[20] None the less, one or two men must be
identified. The Wars of the Roses could not start until the peerless
Cardinal John Kemp of Canterbury died. Recalled to save a
regime in crisis in 1450, he supervised its recovery and, even when
it was crippled by the king's breakdown in 1453, he provided an
authority that none of the factions dared challenge until his
death, aged about 80, on 22 March 1454. Immediately thereafter,
and in direct consequence, politics collapsed into violence. From
then until 1486, Canterbury and the headship of the Church
rested with Thomas Bourgchier. Equipped by birth with kinship
to all the great of the realm and consequently rising through no
visible effort or talent to Worcester (aged 24), Ely (33) and the
primacy itself (44), Bourgchier turned lack-lustre mediocrity into
an art, rendering himself tolerable and even useful to any and
every faction. Like any congenital appeasor (or, apparently meant
as praise, 'a mediator, probably by temperament and almost by
profession'), he possessed an infinite capacity to forgive and
forget personal humiliation, and to rationalise and cohabit with
the brutal outcome; and likewise to feather his own nest quietly

before, during and after the event. Curiously, he has often had very distinguished defenders amongst historians, a Teflon archbishop now as then.[21] Granted it is hard to see what more he could have done at certain key moments, once violence had commenced, his wretched performance in 1483 cannot be defended even in such an old man: it was all too much in character. His dull oversight of his own province of the Church through thirty-two years serves only to confirm how little he even wanted to offer.

William Waynflete of Winchester, the truest personal friend of Henry VI, reappears below, as does Robert Stillington of Bath and Wells, who needs no accretion of myth to confirm himself as irredeemably unattractive. Lawrence Booth of Durham, for all his embarrassing background in the service of Margaret of Anjou, proved a redoubtable defender of his mighty bishopric against the encroachments of first the Nevilles and then Richard of Gloucester. Edward IV was persuaded to suspend him from his temporal authority in such a treacherous region in the early years, but thereafter found him a useful, if self-interested, ally. His promotion to York in 1476 actually testified to Gloucester's exasperation with his doughty resistance to either blandishment or pressure.[22] John Morton of Ely, a man marked out for the highest offices in the church and realm well before he even reached the bench, suffered a severe setback with the fall of Henry VI in 1461, but stood loyal.[23] His rehabilitation was swift once he admitted that Edward IV was secure after 1471. Then came a further disaster in 1483, when Gloucester feared his ability and loyalty to Edward V so much as to arrest him in his *coup* of 13 June. Whatever his role in suborning his gaoler, the duke of Buckingham, to treason within weeks, Morton entered exile once more, to play a key diplomatic part in preparing for Henry Tudor's usurpation and thereafter, if belatedly, his long-anticipated primacy in the counsels of the realm. A man of exceptional talent who eventually did achieve his predictable historic fame, none the less he lost some fifteen years of what should have been his pomp because of the wars and because of his own principled response to them. Grey of Ely; Russell of Lincoln; Lyhert of Norwich; Rotherham of York; Dudley and Shirwood of Durham, and half a dozen more: all were men of considerable talent, and all affected in person by some aspect of the wars.

In terms of personal hurt, the episcopate was afflicted surprisingly little by the wars.[24] Adam Moleyns of Chichester and William Aiscough of Salisbury had both been lynched in 1450, whilst William Percy of Carlisle fled the First Battle of St Albans in 1455 in his undershirt. Fortunately, such early alarms proved the low point, and thereafter even the most politically-committed of bishops avoided the translations to dioceses *in partibus infidelium*, i.e. loss of their sees, that their predecessors had suffered either side of 1400. Not that this was always certain. William Waynflete of Winchester's position was under some threat in November 1460, but the 'Yorkists' themselves defended his reputation to the pope against detractors.[25] John Stanbury of Hereford was rumoured to have been executed after the Battle of Northampton in July 1460 but, in fact, although he may have been in custody for a short while and openly declared his fear of dispossession, he was back in his diocese by October 1460.[26] Thomas Bird of St Asaph was deprived of his see by Edward IV in January 1463 for his obdurate Lancastrianism (he was with Margaret of Anjou in exile), but he was not actually removed by the pope until October 1471, when he himself accepted the failure of the Readeption and a pardon, but was replaced by Richard Redman in his see. On 23 July 1460 John de la Bere resigned St David's, but although he took a pardon in February 1461, his old age and ill-health had been signalled for some time.[27]

Edward IV, evidently bent on reconciliation, did not try to chastise, still less remove, any other bishops in 1461. Lawrence Booth of Durham, as has been noted, was suspended for two years as a precaution but not victimised. During the crisis of 1469–71, several bishops did align themselves unluckily and suffered briefly – Bourgchier, and perhaps Grey of Ely, being briefly imprisoned during the Readeption, up to ten even more briefly by Edward on his return. John Chedworth of Lincoln was amongst the latter and his resignation from his see was being seriously planned at the time, but there was no connection.[28] George Neville alone, after Edward had bided his time, was seriously punished, detained in one or other of the Calais castles from April 1472, and Edward IV did press a papal envoy, Pietro Aliprando, for his removal.[29] In fact, the latter was sympathetic to the archbishop, and it was thought that the pope was too, and would try to help him. The archbishop was released quite quickly, on 19 December 1474, and in theory restored to full authority.

As is well known, Richard of Gloucester's coup discomforted several bishops in 1483. Archbishop Rotherham of York was briefly detained from 13 June to *c.* 11 July and took no part in the coronation, but his position was never threatened.[30] John Morton of Ely, as noted already, was imprisoned more seriously and lost his temporalities at once. Lionel Woodville of Salisbury, by contrast, was encouraged out of sanctuary and only lost his temporalities on 23 September for further involvement in rebellion. Richard III certainly did move to have him translated out of his see, but the young bishop (he was 30) was still in formal possession when he died conveniently in autumn 1484. Thomas Langton of St David's, his designated supplanter from an early stage and a notoriously fervent admirer of Richard III, had his own setback when Henry VII won the throne, but within months was set free to enjoy Salisbury and a rich career thereafter. Robert Stillington of Bath and Wells, a more contentious adherent to Richard III, had too blemished a record to forgive, and made it yet worse by collusion in Lambert Simnel's revolt in 1487 and an embarrassing defiance of the king from refuge inside Oxford University. Even he, though, was simply held at Windsor for the rest of his life. If it might be thought that popes had defended their men well against bad times, the truth is more that Edward IV chose not to be vindictive, whilst neither the Readeption regime nor Richard III had time to show their colours. Most of all, few of the bishops were important enough or obdurate enough to merit a decisive fate.

Such a down-to-earth review of the fate of individual bishops during the wars will not please the fashion-conscious. Every so often, historians are accused of treating fifteenth-century people like twentieth-century people, by failing to take on board the cosmology of their minds, their sense of fate and providence, their superstitions, their resort to astrology, alchemy, soothsaying, the black arts, and even sometimes religion, especially in times of stress. (Apparently this all refers to the *fifteenth-century* people.) Alas, though chastened and crestfallen, we are still awaiting the incisive re-interpretation by the New Age cosmologists. Polydore Vergil's history of these times is, meantime, a more constructive guide, not only for his narrative but for the insight into his own outlook, that of an intelligent man. Certainly he acknowledged fate, providence, immutabilities and portents so readily as to have incurred many a curled lip since. Yet, in no contradiction, he elevated the personal influence of a series of individual men, the kings, to be the very demarcator of his analysis of England's history: he wrote by reigns. He collected evidence, examined eyewitnesses, and sought out empirical political causation at every turn. To him, the natural and the supernatural, the material and the spiritual did not jostle for place or each reduce the validity of the other.[31] Likewise, the academic commentator John Warkworth threaded portents and marvels through his account of how betrayal led to self-destruction, but he did not deny free will; rather, his work was a lament of its effects. All in all, the fifteenth century had fewer sacred cows than the twentieth.

There was, however, the occasional charge of witchcraft as a political weapon. Henry IV's second wife, Joan of Navarre, had suffered purely because her stepson, Henry V, wanted to re-arrange her financial settlement. The trial and imprisonment of Eleanor Cobham, wife of Humphrey of Gloucester, in 1441 was flagrantly a deliberate public humiliation by the government of her husband, the heir-presumptive to the Crown (although she may indeed have dabbled, in hopes of hastening their succession). In 1450 Jack Cade was denounced, amongst more earthy sins, for dalliance with the Devil, albeit not against the Crown.[32] Long after the event, Richard III accused Jacquetta of Luxembourg, duchess of Bedford, of conjuring Edward IV into marriage with her daughter, Elizabeth Woodville, in 1464, but Richard was dragging up everything to justify his title to the throne and evidently placed no great reliance on the charge.[33] He proved very ready thereafter to hurl moral as well as political accusations against his opponents, but he left out witchcraft. In 1477 George of Clarence, evidently a considerable sceptic even when emotionally over-wrought, only accused the attendants of his late wife of straightforward poisoning her, executing them forthwith. Perhaps predictably, then, he lost his self-control altogether in the face of counter-accusations that some of his own followers had engaged in necromancy against the king; his fury in the end cost him his own life.[34] All in all, witchcraft was not used much as an accusation against opponents, either with specific reference to its presumed target or as a general smear. Wayward or supernumerary Capetian princesses had in past times been vulnerable to the charge, but even disgraced Lancastrian and Yorkist queens and duchesses were left untarnished. Evidently the charge of witchcraft lacked credibility; presumably, by the same token, there was not much of it going on.

There was a tradition of political cults in later medieval England, and some most improbable martyrs attracted interest.[35] Initially, Richard II had been buried in Langley Priory (Hertfordshire), within the perimeter of a royal manor, possibly to deter pilgrimage, but Henry V transferred him to Westminster Abbey, probably because he had been more fond of him than of his own father, because Richard himself had very much wanted burial there, and because Henry had a very strong sense of the majesty of kings, even deposed ones. It was not to undermine any alarming Ricardian cult; although (or perhaps because?) a man of very decent conventional piety, the late king achieved only a survival legend.[36]

Much more significant, Richard Scrope, archbishop of York, whom Henry IV beheaded perfectly justifiably for rebellion in 1405, proved a considerable attraction. Even at the time it was a serious oversight to allow him a prime burial-site in York Minster (which, moreover, had a curiously gaping need for a resident saint), and the spontaneous cult severely embarrassed the government. There has recently been an interesting suggestion that perhaps in time the dynasty itself found some advantage in this standing reminder of an opponent overcome. Either way, Scrope remained a respectably lucrative draw right down to the accession of the House of York.[37] Significantly, at that point, orderly but unobtrusive plans within the cathedral chapter to have him officially canonised suddenly lapsed, as too did his fund-raising. Perhaps his work as an anti-cult was done once the House of Lancaster was laid low. On the other hand, the massacre of Yorkshiremen by Edward IV at the Battle of Towton was etched into northern minds, making the late dynasty harder to hate. It was doubtless noted as obvious how Henry VI's long-serving secretary, Richard Andrew, now the resident dean of York, built the great crossing-screen of the Minster, with effigies of English kings lined up in serial majesty across its front – from the earliest Northumbrians to Henry VI – with no niche left vacant for the current king.

Famously, Henry VI began his rapid ascent to popular canonisation immediately after his death in the Tower of London on 21 May 1471, his fate postponed only for as long as it had taken the house of York to hunt down his only son and heir.[38] Gratifyingly, he was reported to have bled throughout his funeral, as a martyr should: given the manner of his death, he may well have done. Even at the risk of stern disfavour with Edward IV, there was strenuous competition for his corpse. Whatever the truth about his character, Henry's public image as someone who had been just too good for this wicked world was well-established; a king whom anyone, however humble, might approach and relate to. However, even this is to jump to a conclusion. Whilst the psychology of sainthood is a well-advanced subject, and the relevant material exists, the nature and social bias of Henry's particular appeal has yet to be explored sharply. Clearly the dead king had a very strong capacity to heal the sick and, at least impressionistically, to do especially well by children, both signs at first sight of an apolitical cult with most appeal to the lower orders. To this extent, it would be unwise to rush to any conclusion that Henry's was, in its first years, a cult of opposition to the reigning dynasty. Obviously, after 1485, when Henry VII adopted the cause of his official canonisation, politics did come into it. Meanwhile, the most significant development was Richard III's decision to move Henry's body from Chertsey Abbey to St George's Chapel, Windsor, in 1483. Conceivably, the late king's cult was now much more dangerous politically than it had been to Edward IV, and Richard was hoping to neutralise it by dwarfing the tomb in the majestic surroundings of his brother's own shrine. Alternatively, he may have been currying favour and reconciliation: after all, this was Henry of Windsor by birth, and the house of Lancaster had established no specific mausoleum of its own. Richard had to be uneasy. His own efforts to touch for the King's Evil were proving a failure, a significant barometer of public opinion. Henry's booming general practice can only have been an embarrassment.

It would not be difficult to collect a good handful of prophecies and portents during the wars, some explicitly Christian, some not. Indeed, most obviously to a modern eye, victories in battle were sought and acknowledged through due and, who would deny, sincere Christian rituals, by no means all of them noisy public trumpetings of forthcoming might or recent triumph. Edward IV marked his campaign of reconquest in 1471 with appropriate ceremonies of gratitude along the way but no formal re-acclamation. Richard III copied his brother's usurpation with meticulous care as to rites in London and Westminster before adding a well-conceived and well-received progress through the provinces, culminating in a spectacular entry into York, where great ceremonies (but *not* a second crowning) were marred only by the continuing absence of Archbishop Rotherham.[39] Henry VII likewise made no change in his coronation but hastened similarly toward York, his triumph marred only by an outburst of simmering revolt in the area.

Most immediately because of the wars, both the Nevilles and the house of York promoted ostentatious translation of their fallen dead to their family mausoleums. The Nevilles adopted Bisham Priory (Berkshire) as heirs to the Montagues, and thither they brought the earl of Salisbury and Sir Thomas Neville, both killed at Wakefield, in February 1463 in a mighty procession and final ceremony of interment.[40] There too were buried Warwick and Montagu, and there lived Archbishop Neville in his last years to ponder over their fate and his fall. A fortnight earlier Edward IV had held a memorial service for his late father and brother too, also fallen at Wakefield, but only as late as July 1476 did he likewise bring their bones home from Pontefract to Fotheringhay (Northhamptonshire).[41] Rather curiously, he chose not to bring them on to St George's, Windsor, his own dynastic shrine. Justifiably or not, this project, Henry VI's lavish commitment to Eton College and King's College in Cambridge, and Richard III's extraordinarily ambitious plans for York Minster as some cross between university, mausoleum and Tibetan monastery must be excluded from this discussion, as too (thankfully) the much-debated personal piety of at least the first and last of these kings, as matters not immediately relating to the wars. Many and marvellous observations about such mysteries may be found elsewhere. Here, attention must turn to some of the institutional effects of the wars on the Church.

In a time of political stress, teetering towards civil war, it might seem natural that leading churchmen would be called, or feel a vocation, to intervene in hope of reconciling the factions. In fact, there was little precedent for this in England. In times past, notably in Richard II's reign, the spiritual peers had withdrawn from their place amongst the lords in parliament when judgements of blood were to be made, as their order required, and any chancellor-bishop would likewise remit such items of business. On the other hand, in 1450, all the available bishops 'in town' were ordered into the king's private apartment in Westminster with their secular colleagues to witness Cardinal Kemp (the chancellor) and the duke of Suffolk act out their charade whereby the duke cheated impeachment by submitting himself to the king's will; albeit they were not to be the judges and it was self-evident that the duke was to shed no blood (or so it was fondly imagined), the bishops were treading close to the line.[42] In 1459 the evidence is still more problematical with regard to the attainders passed in the Coventry Parliament. Maybe the chancellor, William Waynflete, did step down from these awesome judgements, and maybe his episcopal and abbatial colleagues did stand aside and protest their position: but, unlike the records from Richard II's time, there is no evidence of such rectitude.

Where there are signs of greater activity is in episcopal mediation in the field. Stafford of Canterbury, Kemp of York and Waynflete of Winchester rode out to Jack Cade's rebels on 6 July 1450 to persuade them to peace – a deed surely not without bravery, for all the insurgents' bloody check the night before and recent special pleading that revolting peasants in later medieval England would sooner kill themselves than smudge a social superior's lipstick.[43] In February/March 1452 Waynflete and Bourgchier of Ely were amongst those who went out to persuade the duke of York against armed confrontation with the king.[44] In neither case was their spiritual order cited as their qualification: personality and reputation seem the criteria. In the early morning hours of 22 May 1455 at St Albans, however, it became desperately obvious that the first direct fight between the king's personal entourage and its enemies was about to happen, in defiance of Henry's own person and royal standard; a descent into violence whose real significance is that it had taken so long to come.[45] As such, it was a tribute to the conventions for peace which ruled the English political system, but equally an impending catastrophe for that system. In these circumstances the idea was put forward, from the king's side, that there should be a pause, to allow bishops to be summoned up to mediate. Cynicism is easy, for the royal party were in a corner. None the less, there is no evidence that the call for a respite to summon bishops was just a spurious use of the moral highground to buy time to summon troops of their own. Some individuals may have calculated it this way – the Lancastrian side hardly displayed unity of mind – and evidently the enemies of the court wanted no truck with it, for whatever tactical reason. None the less, bloody violence was a desperate measure which no-one welcomed, the aggressors in particular. The situation at

St Albans was a demonstration that conventional remedies had
finally been exhausted. There was a thin tradition of mediation
before battle in England, although not a very reassuring one, but
the specifically spiritual element was not obligatory. Direct
negotiations were attempted, but broke down.

After the battle, Bourgchier, now archbishop of Canterbury,
continued as chancellor, with his brother as treasurer, before,
through and after York's unstable second Protectorate: an
insubstantial veneer of respectability behind which the factions
fought it out. In October 1456 the court party took the initiative
and dismissed them, installing Waynflete and the earl of Wiltshire
in their stead. Whilst Wiltshire's was as unpleasantly provocative
an appointment as might be imagined, Waynflete's was more
difficult to assess, and in the short term an astute ploy. Waynflete
would have been easier to deal with if he had been a fawning
court creep, an unworldly misfit or a political manipulator. He
was none of these.[46] He simply lacked the family connections or
political skills which customarily made the bishop of Winchester a
very major player in the realm. Not that he was a fool and by no
means was he an altruist to those below him, but he had no more
and no less than the conventional talents and glossy but
insubstantial reputation of the public-school headmaster he was;
that and an enduring empathy with Henry VI, which might be
weighed as a personal virtue but a mixed blessing politically.
Those in high places had his measure. The house of York simply
could not be bothered to punish him for his naive subsequent
trespasses across its path: he was more use as a living token of its
own good nature. The House of Lancaster appreciated his loyalty
and sought to make the most of his status: it had no mind actually
to listen to him, and it was desperate.

In April 1458 he and Bourgchier both worked hard to promote
the fatuous 'Love-Day' at St Paul's, the king's well-meaning final
attempt to reconcile the polarised factions but, in practice, more
like an official public weigh-in for the title-fight ahead.[47] In
October 1459 Richard Beauchamp of Salisbury was sent by the
king's party to offer an amnesty to the rebel's troops at Ludlow.
This was not mediation, and was not meant to be. In association
with other factors, it broke the 'Yorkists'' back. Thereafter,
politics moved fast and, still, puzzlingly. By June 1460 Archbishop
Bourgchier was ready, like many others, to show open sympathy
for the exiled magnates. It is unproven that he was actually a party

to their plan of return, although he would not have been a
Bourgchier if he had not his informants. He was engaged at the
time with a fractious convocation in London in which the lower
clergy were drawing up one list of problems and the bishops
another, whilst his own bout of ill-health (probably genuine but
suspiciously convenient) held up both. Once again, as before St
Albans (although he was chancellor then), the earls put their case
in an open letter to him as spiritual father of the realm, and this
time he made his sympathy public. With most other bishops, like
the lay peers, reluctant to commit themselves, his support for
drastic 'reform' around the king must be acknowledged as a bold
and significant grant of credibility to attainted rebels.[48]

Indeed, he did then try to avoid the civil conflict collapsing into
serious slaughter with a unique attempt at formal mediation by
the spiritual peers.[49] Unfortunately, he delegated the task,
sending Bishop Beauchamp with four colleagues to speak with
the king's constable, the duke of Buckingham, on the eve of the
Battle of Northampton. Accounts differ. One version is that the
duke rejected the group's competence as peacemakers by reason
of their collusion with the enemy and of their own armed escort:
to which the bishops retorted that they feared for their own safety
amidst those in the duke's camp. Another is that one bishop –
Beauchamp? – for reasons best known to himself, advised the
Lancastrians to fight: Beauchamp made a career out of reasons
best known to himself. Whatever the exact detail, the mediation
by the Church failed, and the ploy was never repeated. Stanbury
of Hereford, Henry VI's influential confessor, and another bishop
slipped over to the Lancastrian side. Inevitable it was Bourgchier
who took custody of the great seal after the battle. He then
formally received and humiliated the duke of York in parliament,
when the latter made what he hoped would be an irresistible
entry, but there is no reason to believe that he was the actual
engineer of the rebuff or of the compromise thereafter. The duke
should have known that spontaneous ovations need organisation.

There were moments when questions of canon law became
very important. In 1399, canon law *dicta* had been used explicitly
to justify the removal of a 'useless' or 'insufficient' king whose
basic legitimacy could not be denied.[50] During the wars there
was never any effort to annul that method of judgement: the
argument was over the line of succession from 1399, hereditary
right versus prescriptive right. Interestingly, though, it has been

pointed out that in 1460 the papal envoy, Francesco Coppini, apparently did add excommunication to the Yorkists' battery of weapons against Margaret of Anjou's supporters, arguing that it was a logical consequence of Pius II's call to England for peace at home and crusade abroad.[51] Much better known are the instances where the Church was required (or should have been) to dispense individuals in crucial political circumstances. First, there was the long semi-secret battle in the curia in 1468–9 between the proctors of Edward IV and of his brother, George of Clarence, over the duke's quest for a dispensation to marry Isabelle Neville. It seems unlikely that the timing of Warwick and Clarence's coup of 1469 was actually dictated by the securing of the grant but, as it turned out, the licence and immediate wedding (in Calais) did herald it.[52] The corollary came in the early 1470s when Richard of Gloucester in effect eloped with Ann Neville and demanded to marry her and enjoy rather more than her due inheritance. Clarence's outraged reaction is well-known, likewise too the quality of his formidable counter-arguments. Obviously, it was the property-settlement which really concerned the duke, and he said so, but he could point to the need for Richard to secure a papal dispensation; indeed the king's subsequent imposed settlement made it clear that such a grace seemed uncertain.[53] Ironically, something similar underlay the widespread belief in 1484 that Richard would cast Ann aside and marry his niece Elizabeth. According to the Crowland chronicler, whilst Richard foresaw no problem about gaining an annulment, opponents of the scheme claimed that even a pope could not authorise such an incestuous match.[54] Presumably, as with Ann, Richard would have married Elizabeth first and pursued a dispensation second. It all came to nothing in the end.

Meantime, Richard's denial of his nephews' legitimacy in 1483–4 might well, even should, have dragged the Church into a judgement.[55] In theory, he called on parliament only to record his title and the evidence, but the Crowland chronicler claimed that there was grumbling amongst the members that they were being asked to exceed their competence, probably in seeming to give a verdict on matters that fell within the ecclesiastical jurisdiction. Bastardy itself was something in which both lay and church courts had acknowledged areas of interest but when the case was founded upon the alleged sorcery of Elizabeth

Woodville's mother, upon the circumstances of the marriage ceremony itself, and upon the supposed earlier betrothal of Edward IV to another, the spiritual jurisdiction would be expected to decide. However, Richard did not ask, and the prelates were probably mightily relieved that he did not.

Inevitably during a civil war, losers fled into sanctuary. By the later fifteenth century the scope of sanctuary in England was already being narrowed, although there was no premonition of its virtual abolition under Henry VIII. As early as 1378 John of Gaunt had defended his servants who had entered Westminster Abbey and killed a sacristan and one of the two refugees they were hunting down. He thundered erastianism against the ecclesiastical sanctions levied against them: feet shuffled. In 1388 Richard II could only seethe when his loyal justice, Sir Robert Tresilian, was likewise snatched from the abbey and executed.[56] Tresilian, however, was being adjudged a traitor, and it was at this extreme end of the spectrum that even clergy were beginning to admit that sanctuary could not prevail – especially as disloyalty or unsuccessful revolt against the state became a far more dangerous game generally.

Sir William Oldhall, Richard of York's manipulative chamberlain, was the first to resort to sanctuary in the fifteenth-century conflicts, lodging in St Martin-le-Grand from 1451 to 1453 to avoid prosecution; he was pulled out, then returned within days by demand of the dean, but a picket was set up to stop him continuing his intrigues.[57] Such raw rubbing between respect for principle and outrage of practice was to prove the keynote. In 1454 Protector York was able to give his rebellious son-in-law and rival, the duke of Exeter, much shorter shrift as regards sanctuary but, if only for immediate reasons, punished him no further than secular custody.[58] In 1470, Edward IV's sudden flight into exile and the Lancastrians' return forced his queen, Elizabeth Woodville, into Westminster Abbey where she gave birth to his first son and found in the abbot, Thomas Milling, a godparent for him of enduring affection and sympathy.[59] Edward's chief officers – all churchmen – fled with others into St Michael-le-Grand's. Eventually, Bishop Grey was moved, or persuaded to move, from there to his cousin George Neville's opulent manor at Le More, but the rest stayed until Edward could release them.[60] Then, by contrast, those of their episcopal colleagues who had been actively delighted by Henry VI's restoration failed to get into sanctuary and had to endure temporary secular custody; but by the end of July 1471 all were free.

Others, however, were not so protected. With Edward IV's triumphant fight-back in February 1471, it was the turn of Lancastrians to hope for refuge. According to rumour, George Neville actually prevented Henry VI himself from slipping into sanctuary in Westminster, when the king himself retained the wit to want to. Certainly, Neville did offer up the hapless king to Edward IV in a bid to save himself. If he did keep a king from sanctuary, he deprived us and his contemporaries of a potentially landmark *cause célèbre*. Ann, countess of Warwick, landed in Southampton to news of her husband's destruction at Barnet: rather than flee westwards to join Margaret of Anjou, she slipped into Beaulieu Abbey, the nearest to hand and, by happy chance, amongst the greatest in privilege.[61] There she remained, under the surveillance of a 'protective' picket set up by the king, until Richard of Gloucester decided she was worth harbouring in the north in May 1473. Although she was to be declared legally dead, to sort out a bitter internal row amongst the royal family, it seems unlikely that she had ever faced physical execution. The Lancastrian lords defeated in open battle against the king at Tewkesbury on 4 May found no such succour. Edward IV simply entered the town abbey, thrust aside objection from a priest, pardoned some but either lured or dragged the greatest out for trial and execution.[62] This did cause some concern even to Edward's friends, but the official memoir of the campaign had no qualms. Not that anyone would care to argue anyway, but in fact Edward's sharper line was the one with a future: these were traitors in arms; Tewkesbury had no sufficient privilege.

On 1 May 1483, her wedding anniversary, Elizabeth Woodville fled into Westminster Abbey once more on news of Richard of Gloucester's arrest of her brother, Earl Rivers, taking with her, amongst others, her children and young brother, Lionel Woodville, bishop of Sailsbury. Richard would have been breaking new ground in breaching sanctuary against physical non-combatants, especially when the council had refused his claim that Rivers and his allies could be termed traitors for their (alleged) planned violence against himself. However, as is so famously known, by mid-June he desperately needed Richard of York, the younger of Edward IV's sons, in his immediate control. The arguments between Richard, the other councillors, and the queen have been debated – or, more accurately, guessed at – over and again.[63] It can be argued that each party had quite separate and conflicting reasons to see the boy free. Just two particular points need be mentioned here. First, it was said later that Richard (or the duke of Buckingham) put the argument that, because the lad stood accused of nothing, he could not be in sanctuary, which was a concept relative to the circumstances of the individual, not some freestanding physical edifice or umbrella over all those who happened to be within the holy place for whatever purpose. Hence, York could be fetched out without damage to the rights and reverence of the abbey. Whatever the canon law, it was an interesting point, albeit one denied flatly by Queen Elizabeth (according to Sir Thomas More anyway), who argued that the Ricardian definition was too narrow, sanctuary being for anyone in danger, not simply those accused of crime. More discussed the issue at considerable length, but perhaps because it was a hotter issue by his time than it had been in 1483, so, as ever, we have to suspend trust in his account. Presumably, Richard would have insisted that his nephew was in no danger anyway, and thus left the debate much where it was.

In the end, there seems no doubt that Richard called up troops to settle the matter; and, in consequence, that Cardinal Bourgchier persuaded the queen to surrender her son to save the abbey's sanctity. If that was all that moved Bourgchier, it was the first time in a long life that he had displayed such determination for the honour of the Church. It seems more probable that, what with the duke's obstinate refusal to allow Edward V's coronation without the presence of his brother, what with sheer disbelief that even or especially a Yorkist could or would steal the throne from the true heir – or fear that was exactly what he might do if things hung fire much longer – and maybe faced with Richard's declared aim to go in anyway, Bourgchier could do no more than persuade Elizabeth that she had no choice: at the least, he could offer her personal guarantees of the boy's well-being, whereas Richard would offer nothing. Somehow, Bourgchier escaped criticism at the time, and has since, about his woeful failure to defend his word. A few months later, the late king's daughters came out voluntarily, and then the queen herself. Ironically, the latter ended up in February 1487, shortly after Henry Tudor's triumph and her own daughter's crowning, as the life-guest of Bermondsey Abbey.

Her brother, Bishop Lionel, had slipped out of Westminster in the summer of 1483.[64] Possibly, like Sir John Fogge, he had found nominal reconciliation with Richard III. None the less, he supported the considerable southern revolt of autumn 1483, and had again to find sanctuary (in Beaulieu Abbey) when it failed. He attracted a price on his head in November. On 15 December 1483 Richard tried to challenge Beaulieu's rights; in early February 1484 he sent two chaplains to try to persuade Woodville to come out to answer charges in parliament. Both approaches failed: the bishop was attainted. His diocese was run by 'his' vicar-general thereafter, and the temporalities placed in the hands of his intended replacement, Thomas Langton of St David's. However, at least once, also in March 1484, Woodville exercised a right of nomination to a benefice, and the king, his rival in the matter, conceded it. Although deprivation was little used in the wars, Richard could not have let Woodville's tenure of his see go on indefinitely, and was indeed taking steps, but as a man of the cloth and still (just about) not a demonstrable rebel in arms against the king, Woodville might have been more of a legal and political embarrassment in custody than in sanctuary: and the king, besides, was soon trying to reconcile his family. As it turned out, Woodville died in the same year, aged 30, just about the only convenient demise for which Richard III has never been held responsible.

In May 1486, Henry VII's officers entered Abingdon Abbey's liberty of Culham to seize Humphrey Stafford, die-hard supporter of the late king.[65] There is a blood-chilling legal purity about the trial that followed. Humphrey pleaded sanctuary. The court summoned the abbot to display his charters. He did. These were examined and found insufficient. Humphrey entered no further defence. He was executed. The case of Robert Stillington, bishop of Bath and Wells, is much more problematic and has often been told.[66] A particularly detested 'adherent and assistant' of Richard III, he was indicted on the day after Bosworth and captured exhausted in York, yet surprisingly given a fresh start. Then, in March 1487, he slipped into Oxford, evidently aware of, and involved in, Lambert Simnel's forthcoming bid for the throne and perhaps aware too that Henry VII had learned of it. There followed a well-documented crisis.[67] The king demanded increasingly urgently, but clearly with some caution, that the university authorities 'find' the bishop and turn him in, whilst

they in return pleaded their fear of incurring the wrath of the
Church if they did (who or what this might be was never made
clear) and the obstinacy of the bishop himself, who was reluctant
to discuss the matter with them at all but, when cornered, claimed
that he had no fears about fair justice from the king himself but
expected to be murdered *en route* if he moved out of the university
and town, escort or not. It is not a conventional case of
'sanctuary'; the matter of the university's own privileged
jurisdiction over its enrolled students and staff was placed at the
centre: Henry irritably pointed out along the way that he himself
had yet to confirm these privileges and, more cogently, that
Stillington was not exactly using the university as a place of study.
It was a most curious stand-off, not without very modern echoes.
In the end, it rather petered out, and how is not known. At any
event, the bishop was carried off to Windsor Castle, possibly
allowed to visit his diocese in 1489 (something he had rarely
wanted to do in his previous twenty-five years) and otherwise left
in that same demi-life as other disgraced bishops, not quite
excluded from diocesan business but excluded from its wealth
and to all intents and purposes a non-person. Henry VII is not
known to have sought his translation out of the see, nor was he
convicted of treason.

If the Crown was becoming tougher in asserting that there was
no hiding-place for traitors anywhere in its realm, yet it still
preferred to gloss over such thorny problems as traitorous clerks
and the local privileges of an influential university. However, it is
worth completing the theme by noting that Henry VII was
following Edward IV in asserting tighter limitations on rights of
sanctuary and tighter disciplining on those within them, and in
the Stillington case determined to have his man even when he did
not propose to kill him. As with benefit of clergy and the
expanding applications of writs of *praemunire*, the Crown was
already drawing the line more closely around ecclesiastical
liberties both formally and by political persuasion. There was no
perceived intent to erode, still less eradicate, them, but that was
all to come soon and with a rush: hindsight is a dangerous thing,
but not always unattractive.[68]

To individual English people the papacy remained very
important, the 'well of grace' for individual petitioners seeking
pious favours or dispensation from the canonical norm across a
wide spectrum of personal, heartfelt and often vital needs.[69] In

such things as dispensations for marriage within the forbidden degrees of kinship, or annulments, for example, the pope's authority could take on considerable and controversial public importance. It is certainly true that it attracted constant criticism and complaint during the later middle ages, but this was almost all about the practices, personality and performance of the current curia, not about its primacy in principle and right to be. What with its 'exile' in Avignon from 1305 to 1378, when the English rather unfairly chose to depict it as both a French puppet and a den of pointless moral iniquity; a period of schism (1378–1418) with two or even three popes in competition, which the French equally unfairly accused the English of enjoying and perpetuating; then an era continuing down to the Wars of the Roses, when general councils of varying authenticity and ambition challenged the authority if not existence of the pope; and, throughout, a gradual realisation by successive popes that they simply had to descend to street politics, especially Italian street politics, to exercise much independence and influence in a new world of state-rivalries; it was not surprising that the papacy seemed grubby.[70]

None the less, in English eyes – England being a notably loyal part of Catholic Christendon – it was there because it was there. At times during the periods of schism and general councils it could be argued, and was, that this loyalty stemmed from nothing more virtuous than the fact that the English establishment had found the old *status quo* extremely to its liking, warts and all, and had no fancy for a regeneration of the centre that might lead to more effective reform initiatives from there into its own preserve. More bloody-mindedly, and with rather more supporting evidence, it often seemed that the English would block any reform proposal that had French parentage, regardless of its merit; and could be relied on to wreck any papal initiative for Christian crusade or conciliar programme of reform by its obdurate war-making in France. All that can be proposed here is that, amidst all this and not denying it, the English Crown, Church and articulate public opinion did grieve, consistently and genuinely, about the problems of Christendom, the papacy in particular: only deep cynicism can deny their genuine distress about the lack of spirituality at Avignon and the division of the holy and indivisible during the schism. As to the councils, there was understandable distrust of the huge numerical advantage the

French enjoyed over the English and a not unfamiliar belief that such peculiarly ill-assorted European assemblies of curious origin, packed with special-interest groups of people with no obligation to face the consequences of their idealism, were ill-equipped to dictate local practice to England. Above all, though, England simply believed in the pope.

However, the onset of the civil wars found England and the papacy in their equally familiar situation – bickering. The fall of Constantinople in 1453 had shaken the pope, parochial Italian mafioso or not by this time, and startled all Europe, including England. None the less, when successive popes tried to react, the English government and Church proved as exasperating as ever and in the usual way: fulsome welcomes for envoys and expressions of total, unqualified support for any papal initiative against the enemy; promises of a substantial delegation at the preparatory general council at Mantua – which somehow never set out; never quite an execution of the pope's call for a tax on the clergy to support a crusade but likewise never a refusal; and a weighty committee set up very urgently indeed to organise a response worthy of the crisis; above all, a congenital ability to make the whole project of council and crusade revolve around, and stumble over, Anglo-French antipathy.[71] The English Crown may have been driven out of all mainland Europe save Calais by now, but it regarded this low ebb as purely temporary. Likewise, with royal finances on the verge of bankruptcy and civil war an imminent certainty, the idea of the clergy having to export large sums abroad did not even border on reality: not that it had done for a long time: cash-strapped monarchs had long regarded any affordable clerical surplus as necessarily theirs. In terms of domestic taxation, the Wars of the Roses actually made no difference at all to the clergy, but neither dynasty at any time felt a need to buy papal support by letting the clergy's wealth pass overseas. Both uttered fine words: no parsnips were buttered.

None the less, in the summer of 1459 Pius II sent Francesco Coppini, bishop of Terni, in yet another attempt to bring England on board. The pope was well aware that things were even more complicated that they had ever been. England was in open civil war, two parties to deal with where even one had habitually proved too much. In France Charles VII was clearly growing frail but was as enigmatic as ever. His Dauphin, Louis, had taken himself off to Burgundy, so bad were father–son relations. Burgundy itself was moving into a like phase; its direction oscillated between the cautious but ailing Philip 'the Good' and his more forthright heir, Charles 'the Bold', but either way it was deeply committed to a three-way game of bluff with its French and English neighbours and anyone else rash enough to join in.

Until recently, under the influence of some uncontestably admirable scholarship, it was thought that Coppini, a little man too eager to seize his big chance, had made a fool of himself, succumbing to the blandishments of the 'Yorkist' earls in Calais in 1460 and lending them spiritual authority he did not legitimately possess as a tool in their factional assault on their domestic rivals: thereafter to be thrown aside by them when he had served his turn and angrily disowned by a pope whose heartfelt destiny to oppose the Turk he had ruined by his gauche, self-interested blunderings around England and France. Much of this still stands: Coppini was ambitious, and the 'Yorkists' did spot their opportunity – the Lancastrian side were appalled by his actions. However, the considerable point has now been made that our unusual insight into Coppini comes from the actual hand of Pius II himself: excited by so unique a record as a medieval pope's own memoir, and a great pope's at that, we have overlooked how such an able pontiff was well capable of, and had every reason for, a skilful cover-up of his own role. It is a complicated story; here can only be a skeleton.[72]

Pius II had actually visited the British Isles; Scotland to be exact, which he disliked intensely: he had caught influenza there, which perhaps allows a reason for what would normally seem a tautology. Intellectual and internationalist as he was, his pontificate was founded upon Italian politics: the Sforzas of Milan and King Ferrante of Naples were as constant allies as could be expected. This promoted in Pius as malicious a stance towards France, as well as its ally, Scotland, as ever the English had. Furthermore, he gave Coppini terms of reference which, whilst susceptible to bitter argument later – the bishop was actually condemned judicially – certainly gave the envoy grounds to believe that he was neither exceeding his discretionary powers to support and condemn domestic factions in England nor departing from his principal's political objectives. Nor, in fact, did the Yorkists spit him out, as Pius was to imply. What with the rapid changes of political fortune in

England, and the still more imponderable transition from the uncommitable Charles VII to the paranoid Louis XI in France, not to mention the time-hallowed refusal of either kingdom to give the papacy any real support for its wider dreams, and Pius's own embroilment in the snake-pit of Italian politics, it is no wonder that Coppini did flounder, fail to deliver what he thought he could, and finally become an easy scapegoat for a ruthless, time-hardened papacy.

From the present local viewpoint, it must be said that the papacy had no developed preference for either Lancaster (whom it did not much like) or York. It never threw its weight spectacularly behind one or other dynasty, even if Coppini gambled it on one faction under Henry VI. It appreciated that England – its monarchy, its Church – was a loyal subject as regards the papacy's own place, and reciprocated with compliant generosity to local wishes in such things as episcopal appointments and individuals' dispensations, save in instances where the English fell out amongst themselves. It even appreciated, but never accepted, that England was quite dreadful in rallying to any wider papal initiative – on occasion it even began by offering to settle for a lesser mandatory tax from England than from everywhere else; it still got nothing.

The papacy was tied up in domestic Italian intrigue. England was beset by internal faction, first between Lancaster and York, then within the inner circles of York alone. There were points of contact none the less at the political level. Controversial marriage dispensations are discussed elsewhere. Taxation rumbled on as an issue, with Edward IV even surprisingly keen to make a good impression by coercing the clergy into a 'voluntary donation' to the defence of Rhodes against the infidel in 1480, and a larger one than they cared to give, with ostentatious guarantees that he would not sneak in himself to redeploy the proceeds.

One final theme, interesting and even a significant illustration of the micro-politics that dominate the Yorkist era, is that it remained fully within the pope's freedom of gift to award the red hat, i.e. promotion to the cardinalate. Not very long after Thomas Bourgchier succeeded Kemp at Canterbury, moves were afoot to have him made up to cardinal. *Pace* his admirers, Bourgchier had no claim at all apart from his office; he had no European experience, interest or achievement, no intellectual

reputation. It is reckoned by some that the cause was delayed by
the dynastic turbulence; as likely, successive popes – not yet
attuned to the idea of red hats perched as pointless ornaments
on national metropolitans' heads – could see no reason to
promote him. Then came the complication that George Neville,
promoted to York in 1465, went after a red hat of his own at
once. His academic and intellectual background was infinitely
superior to Bourgchier's particularly its glowing European
dimension in his student days. He prided himself on his interest
in the maintenance of orthodoxy and of clerical standards and
the advancement of education and scholarship.[73] Oxford
University was devoted to him through thick and thin. Although
there seems no direct evidence, his brother Warwick could
probably solicit influential extra support from France in his cause
at the curia. To top all, he was chancellor of England and a
Neville. Bourgchier was a plodder. It was extremely unlikely that
the pope would issue two red hats to England in quick
succession. None the less, in 1467, Paul II rewarded Bourgchier.[74]
Edward IV's effortless capacity to give unintentional offence
lured him into sending on the pope's bull in favour of
Bourgchier for personal delivery to Neville. Apparently he
thought this an hilarious jest: others did not, and the incident
was remembered. In the end, Bourgchier still had to wait until
1472 before he could receive his red hat.

The role of the papacy in the wars needs further investigation.
Whilst it played no fundamental role, it left its mark in several
places – over dispensations given or not given, in the
manipulation of its envoys by domestic faction, in its brisk support
for Henry VII, and conversely in the way it went along as readily as
ever in the promotions of each dynasty's episcopal candidates but
either was not asked, or chose not, to remove politically-
blemished prelates. Tudor historians might see here some signs of
an apparently comfortable, distant but potentially combustible
relationship and still escape charges of hindsight. Comparably,
the English Church itself rode lightly through the wars,
unaffected in its grass-root heartland in diocese and parish. Some,
but significantly not many, of its leaders were seriously involved,
but even they were rarely made or broken in the process. The
house of York made no demand to change the relationship of
Church and State: Henry Tudor may have brought in his own
ideas from abroad but passed no judgement on the Church's

behaviour in the wars. Was all this a sign of the Church's well-being and strength or, rather, of its respectability but ultimate insignificance as an arbiter in the affairs of the state? The wars were not an immediate landmark for the Church, but, in terms of what was to come, any historian of whatever opinion might easily read some portent therein.

South East Essex College
of Arts & Technology
Carnarvon Road Southend-on-Sea Essex SS2 6LS
Tel: (01702) 220400 Fax: (01702) 432320 Minicom: (01702) 220642

8. The Wars of the Roses in European Context

C. S. L. DAVIES

The involvement of foreign troops in the battles of the Wars of the Roses is well known; so, too, the support that the protagonists received, in money and other ways, from foreign powers. In turn, events in England affected the political situation in western Europe. These themes are acknowledged in the standard accounts but rarely explored. English history tends to be discussed in insular terms; even 'insular' is an over-statement, since Anglo-Scottish relations are even more neglected than Anglo-French. What happened in England was part of a complex series of inter-related events which profoundly influenced the development of western Europe as a whole. At stake was the future power of the French monarchy: both the power of the monarchy within France itself, and with it therefore the nature of French political society. Equally important was the question of the future of the Netherlands, and whether a revived France would take over the provinces of Flanders and Brabant with their great cities of Bruges, Ghent, and Antwerp, the economic heartland of northern Europe. News of Towton, Barnet, and Bosworth were eagerly awaited in Bruges and Malines, in Nantes and Dijon, and in Paris; and were not without interest in Seville, Milan, Rome and Vienna.

France was by far the richest and most populous political entity in Europe; as it was to remain for another two centuries. Historians of France tend to see the evolution of a powerful monarchy, the keystone of French unity, as something inevitable, in the very nature of things. But the eventual emergence of the 'absolute' French monarchy which was to reach its zenith in the Grand Siècle of Louis XIV was not predetermined; that outcome was the result of a concatenation of events, in which sheer chance played a large part.

Quite how powerful the monarchy would be within 'France' was all to play for in the fifteenth century. Earlier in the century, after

162

all, following the victories of Henry V, one possible outcome might have been a strong French monarchy under an English dynasty. (This would not have been to the advantage of England; compare the unhappy experience of Scotland after its king became king of England in 1603.) Another might have been the long-term division of France between the Valois and the Lancastrian dynasties, as was in fact the case between 1422 and the collapse of English power in Paris in 1435–6. Even after the French had regained Paris it remained distinctly possible that the English would retain some territory in France. They were not expelled from Normandy until 1450, nor from Gascony until 1453. If they had retained a substantial foothold in France, as arguably with better luck or better policy in the 1440s they might have done, they would have been in a strong position to interfere in internal French politics. Even after 1453 easy communications across the Channel and the retention of a substantial military base at Calais gave the English the chance to intervene and to send troops to help rebels in France.

Politics in France revolved around the great princes, men like the dukes of Orléans, Alençon, or Bourbon, with their substantial landed possessions and political power under the monarchy. They were often of royal descent themselves, and torn between ambition and loyalty, the desire to run things their own way in 'their' part of the kingdom on the one hand, and to serve the king (and share in the profits of government) on the other. Their wealth, political influence (especially the power to raise armies), and, sometimes, possession of full sovereign power over some part of their territory outside the kingdom of France itself, made them figures to be courted on the international scene. The boundary between a great noble who was a subject – if, in English terms, an 'overmighty' one – and an 'independent' prince was not at all clear-cut; the very lack of clarity opened the way for opportunistic manoeuvre.

The greatest of these princes were the Valois dukes of Burgundy; for most of the century they outclassed the English kings as the greatest threat to the French monarchy. 'Burgundy' is a difficult concept: a conglomeration of territories acquired, largely by marriage and inheritance, since the late fourteenth century. The duchy of Burgundy itself, in eastern France, was granted to the first of the Valois dukes, the son of King Charles V, in 1361 as an 'apanage'. By marriage Philip also acquired the 'county' of Burgundy (Franche-Comté), adjoining the duchy but part of the Empire, not of the kingdom of France. More important, the marriage also brought him the very wealthy county of Flanders (forestalling English attempts at the same prize). Since then the dukes had acquired the rule (under various titles, such as count of Hainault, duke of Brabant, count of Holland) of almost the whole of the Netherlands (the great exception being the duchy of Guelders); that is, the territories that we think of as the kingdom of the Netherlands, Belgium, and a large part of what is now northern France. Jurisdictionally, part of this area was dependent on the kingdom of France (most notably, Artois and Flanders); part was in the Empire. In practice, the dukes had to contend with little in the way of interference from their legal superiors, although from time to time the kings of France asserted the appeal jurisdiction of the Parlement of Paris in the area technically part of the kingdom. But much more damaging to the attempts by the dukes to erect some form of centralised administration was the jealous assertion by each province of its own laws and privileges.

Students are often asked to debate the question of whether or not the Burgundian dukes were ever likely to fashion a 'real state' out of their various territories. The question is anachronistic. Few political entities in the fifteenth century possessed clearly defined frontiers, or a clear chain of political command; even less, that will-o'-the-wisp of modern ideologues, ethnic or linguistic homogeneity. It is equally pointless to debate whether the dukes saw themselves primarily as French princes or as independent sovereign rulers. The answer depends upon circumstances; the dukes were adept at playing whatever card would best suit their interest of the moment, and indeed the two roles could be used to reinforce each other. The essential point is that the duke of Burgundy in the 1460s was probably the richest and most powerful ruler in western Europe after the king of France, roughly equal to the king of England.[1]

Burgundy did not, as is sometimes implied, come to a sudden end with the death of Duke Charles 'the Bold' in battle in 1477. The French crown made important gains as a result, most notably by acquiring the duchy of Burgundy itself. But the duchy had never been, except in name, the most important part of the territories, and contributed less revenue than any one of the more important Netherlands provinces: Flanders, Holland, Hainault, or

Brabant.[2] Even without 'Burgundy' proper, the 'Burgundian' political power held together in the Netherlands. (And indeed elsewhere; Franche-Comté remained independent of France until 1678.) Charles's great-grandson, the future Emperor Charles V, styled himself duke of Burgundy, and loyalty to the house of Burgundy remained a rallying cry. The French indeed habitually referred to their northern opponents as 'Burgundians'.[3] Charles V represents in many ways the fulfilment of the dreams of his namesake. Of course the duchy itself mattered. Charles V hoped to be buried at Dijon and made the recovery of the duchy of Burgundy one of his main war aims in his early years. But in the long term the loss of the duchy was less important than the survival of the Netherlands free from French domination.

Why did all this matter to England? English kings naturally aimed to prevent the French crown becoming too powerful. The encouragement of opposition in France was important, and a powerful Burgundy was a means to that end. But it was even more important to safeguard the independence of the Netherlands; Flanders took the bulk of exports of English wool, and, with Brabant and Zeeland, most of the increasingly important manufactured woollen cloth. Antwerp in particular was the entrepôt through which English products reached the European markets. England and Burgundy were therefore yoked together. Relations did not always run smooth. Commercially they were rivals as well as partners. In politics, either ruler might be tempted by particular circumstances to do a deal with the French at the other's expense. But whatever the irritations of the moment, it was in the interests of both England and Burgundy to hold together and to keep the power of the French monarchy in check.

Second only in importance to Burgundy in English eyes was Brittany. The Breton situation was less complicated than the Burgundian one. The duchy of Brittany was a coherent geographical entity. The dukes held it of the French crown and had no territory outside the kingdom of France; in that sense they had less room for manoeuvre than the dukes of Burgundy. In practice, by playing off the English against the French, the dukes had made themselves *de facto* independent and had built up a remarkably strong state. The French king would get nowhere by trying to give orders to the duke. His only hope was by an appeal to the duke's loyalty or by building up a pro-French (or anti-English) party in the Breton court. As with Burgundy, popes consulted the duke, not the king, about nominations to bishoprics. To the English, Brittany was a useful ally against France; rather as the French cultivated the Scots against England. Brittany was strong in ships and sailors, while its coastline, given the prevailing south-west winds, made it an ideal base for attacks on England. When Brittany did fall to France, in 1491, the English were soon driven into creating, at considerable expense, a large and permanent navy.

The defence of Burgundy and Brittany, the containment of what was in effect geographical expansion by the French monarchy, was a vital English interest. More subtly, it was also an English interest to defend the position of the great French princes against the drive by the French crown towards greater internal control; the greater the powers and independence of, say, the dukes of Orléans and Anjou, the more room for manoeuvre they might have, the more power in their local area, the safer for England, or so at least it was thought. There were, then, two inter-related problems about the French monarchy: the extent of its territory, and the effectiveness of its rule within that territory.

In relations between rulers war was very much a last resort; destabilisation was of the essence, interfering in each other's internal affairs to promote opposition or rebellion. It makes sense to think not in terms of solid power blocks confronting each other, but rather of a series of somewhat rickety structures, with the various authorities within each structure busily stirring up trouble for their rivals while keeping a nervous eye on the reactions of their own inferiors. That is not to say that most noblemen were habitually disloyal. But there were enough examples of disloyalty to make rulers chary of assuming automatic obedience; while in many cases subjects were caught in a real clash of loyalties. Commands from on high often took on the appearance of pleas for help. Even the 'kingmaker' earl of Warwick could write in his own hand to his 'right trusty and well-beloved Harry Vernon, esquire', 'Henry, I pray you fail not now, as ever I might do for you' before the Battle of Barnet in 1471; in the event in vain, as Vernon skulked at home.[4]

The term 'international relations' is misleading and indeed anachronistic in implying that there were clearly defined 'states' or (an even more problematic concept) 'nations' in this period, and therefore a sharp distinction between 'internal' and 'external' affairs. Internal and external affairs flowed naturally into each other. England came nearer to being a well-defined political entity than any of its neighbours. Even so, the Wars of the Roses were part of a complex series of events; what happened in England affected events elsewhere, and was affected by them.

There was little direct foreign intervention in the first stages of the Wars of the Roses, up to the Battle of Towton in 1461. But the stage was set by the collapse of the English position in France after 1429, and in particular the disastrous loss of Normandy in 1449–50. This undermined the credibility of Henry VI's government, precipitating the fall of Suffolk, Cade's rebellion, and York's bid for power in 1450. The final collapse of the English in Gascony at the Battle of Castillon in 1453 was overshadowed by Henry's breakdown, and there is little doubt that Henry's mental state was the prime cause of the events of the next three years. The duke of Alençon took the opportunity of York's protectorate to suggest an English reconquest of Normandy; but York thought the time not yet ripe, and his abrupt fall in 1456, followed by the arrest of Alencon, put paid to the plan.[5]

More important than such dabblings in international intrigue was the earl of Warwick's retention of the captaincy of Calais after 1456, for much of the time in defiance of royal authority. Warwick used his private navy to attack French, Netherlands, and other shipping; the profits helped finance his political activity. He also built up a constituency among Londoners who resented the failure, as they saw it, of the government to stand up for their interests against foreigners. In any case, Londoners had little choice but to acquiesce in Warwick's activities, given his control of the shipping lanes. He was therefore in a good position to invade England in 1460, with his father and with Edward, earl of March, sweeping through Kent and gaining admission to London. There followed the Battle of Northampton, York's arrival from Ireland and claim to the throne, and the eventual compromise of October 1460. The Yorkist cause seemed lost with the deaths of York and Warwick's father, Salisbury, after Wakefield, in December 1460, and Queen Margaret's victory at St Albans in February 1461. However, London remained steady, opened its gates to Edward, who was proclaimed king, and went on to win the decisive Battle of Towton. The credit Warwick had gained as a pugnacious defender of English interests abroad, along with a justified fear of the looting propensities of Margaret's 'northerners', explains London's 'Yorkism'.[6]

Oddly, 1459–61 showed rather less in the way of foreign intervention than did later crises. Charles VII of France had every reason to support Margaret's government. She was, after all, his niece; her marriage to Henry VI in 1444 had been seen as a vehicle of Anglo-French reconciliation; while her Yorkist opponents harked back to the great days of English victories in France and blamed the court party generally for the subsequent débâcle. Charles was vividly aware that an English invasion of Normandy or Gascony could rekindle old loyalties among the inhabitants, already disillusioned by French rule.[7] There was undoubtedly some French diplomatic support for Margaret; and some surreptitious help for her followers.[8] Charles, however, was cautious. There seemed, after all, a very good chance that Margaret could win through without foreign support, which might in any case prove to be counter-productive. Only after Towton was there substantial French support, in terms of diplomacy, men and money. The immediate fruit was a successful attack on the Channel Islands, which Margaret had ceded to France, rather as she had ceded Berwick to Scotland. Further measures were cut short by Charles's death on 22 July 1461.[9]

Charles's old enemy Philip of Burgundy similarly gave somewhat hesitant support to the Yorkists. The Treaty of Arras in 1435 had ended the great Anglo-Burgundian alliance. In the first flush of enthusiasm after the treaty Philip had rounded on his previous allies by trying to take Calais by force. Since then he had maintained a precarious peace with the French king. But in 1456 the Dauphin Louis, in rebellion against his father, had fled to Philip's court. If Philip could spin things out until Charles VII died he might hope to sweep to power in Paris on the back of his protégé. Charles for his part was naturally determined to fell, sooner or later, the tree of Burgundian power. The behaviour of his son made war even more likely.[10] Philip therefore swallowed any distaste he felt for Warwick's privateering (which very much harmed his subjects). He gave diplomatic support to the Yorkists and tried to prevent Margaret's formation of an alliance with Scotland. The Dauphin sent a representative to the Yorkists in September 1460; and his banner was displayed by a band of soldiers, apparently paid for by Philip, in the Yorkist ranks at Towton.[11]

More directly important, as it turned out, was the involvement of the Papal Legate, Bishop Francesco Coppini. Coppini had been sent to England by Pope Pius II in 1459 to try and recruit English forces for the projected crusade against the Turks. His commission included helping to settle internal problems which stood in the way of English involvement in this pious work. However, he seems to have decided at an early stage that support for the Yorkist cause was the only way forward. He took part in the invasion by the Yorkist earls in 1460. His presence on the march through Kent gave credibility to the earls' claim that they had right on their side and the support of Holy Church; the more especially as, with his legatine cross carried before him, Coppini was probably mistaken by many for the archbishop of Canterbury. He continued to give active support to the Yorkist cause until February 1461, when, fearing that the cause was lost, he departed hurriedly for the Netherlands. He later attempted to retrieve the situation, but international events moved on too fast, and Coppini was imprisoned in Rome, ostensibly for exceeding his instructions. The clue to his activities probably lies in his being a loyal agent of the duke of Milan as well as a papal agent. He corresponded with the duke as well as with the pope. The duke's preoccupation (and indeed the pope's) was with preventing the French from taking over Genoa. The way to do this was by strengthening anti-French forces in northern Europe; primarily by supporting Burgundy, but an aggressively anti-French England would also be useful, and much more likely with a Yorkist government.[12]

Towton, therefore, gave a great boost to the anti-French cause in Europe. The next ten years were to see the slow forging of the Yorkist–Burgundian alliance. That in turn lead to Warwick's disillusion with the king he had helped to the throne; to French support for Warwick's restoration of Henry VI; to Edwards's exile and eventual triumphant return, with Burgundian support, to clear the field of his enemies in 1471.

In practice the new Yorkist government in 1461 turned out to be far less anti-French than propaganda had suggested it would be. An Anglo-Burgundian alliance against France certainly seemed natural, indeed almost inevitable; the more so as the Dauphin, once he had become king as Louis XI in July 1461, quickly showed that he had no intention of remaining a Burgundian puppet. While disposing of many of his father's servants he continued the general line of his father's policies. Various factors, however, cut across any clear Anglo-Burgundian alignment against the French. Caution bulked large; Duke Philip, even while disappointed in his former protégé, did not relish direct military confrontation. For his part, Louis much preferred to neutralise any potential English threat by diplomacy, if at all possible. Edward was hardly in a position to menace France, especially as until 1464 he faced obdurate Lancastrian resistance in Northumberland. The obvious ploy for Louis was to provide diplomatic, financial, and occasional armed support for the Lancastrian cause while holding out the possibility of an alliance with Edward.

Financial and commercial considerations further complicated matters. England's foreign trade had been in slump since 1437. One popular remedy was an aggressive policy against foreign merchants. If imports could be discouraged and the participation of foreigners in England's export trade decreased, that would, it was felt, be to the advantage of English businessmen and the English economy generally. An inflow of bullion to the realm would benefit the economy, while having the incidental advantage of increasing business at the mint, and therefore the king's profits. Edward's first years saw a number of restrictionist measures against foreign merchants, designed to ensure that they spent any proceeds they made from imports on buying English goods for export, rather than shipping out bullion or coin. Unfortunately among the principal sufferers were Flemings, who pressed for retaliatory measures in their homeland. Edward also became involved in a monetary war with the Burgundians when, in August–September 1464, he devalued the English pound (offering more English currency for any given amount of gold or silver), so making it attractive to bring precious metals to England rather than to foreign mints; and also giving English goods a competitive advantage over foreign goods. Anglo-Burgundian commercial relations reached their low-point in October 1464, when Duke Philip retaliated by prohibiting the import of English cloth to the Netherlands.[13]

The moment looked propitious for an Anglo-French rapprochement (the French were far less involved in trade with England than the Netherlanders were). Unfortunately one particular opening was abruptly slammed in October 1464, with Edward's embarrassed announcement of his marriage to Elizabeth Woodville, just at the time when Warwick was negotiating with Louis for a possible bride for the English king. Louis did not, however, give up hope of an alliance. But the years 1465–7 saw England's entry into the Burgundian camp. As Duke Philip's health failed, his heir Charles, count of Charolais, increasingly took over the running of the government, eventually succeeding his father as duke in 1467.

Charles was not particularly enamoured of the house of York. He prided himself on his ancestral connections with Lancaster and even kept open the option of one day mounting his own claim to the English throne. He had struck up a close personal relationship with Henry Beaufort, duke of Somerset, in 1459–60, and after Somerset's execution in 1464 supported his brother Edmund Beaufort and other leading Lancastrians at his court, and continued to do so until 1470.[14] But Charles was much more determinedly anti-French (or at least anti-Louis) than his father had been, throwing in his lot in 1465 with the League of the Public Weal ('Bien Public'), a group of French princes (including Brittany) which took the field against Louis and won a number of important concessions. When, in September 1465, Charles's wife died, his own hand became a factor in the international scene.

1465–7 saw a complicated set of negotiations. Neither Charles nor Edward was prepared to sell himself cheap. Edward, in particular, kept open a parallel set of negotiations with Louis, conducted largely by Warwick, who evidently saw them as a real policy option and not just as a blind to get better terms from the Burgundians. The Burgundian option slowly gained ground; especially as realisation dawned that commercial co-operation might be more profitable to both parties than the 'beggar-my-neighbour' policies they had been pursuing. In November 1467 a commercial treaty was concluded. Shortly afterwards agreement was reached for Edward's sister Margaret to marry Charles. The marriage was celebrated with sumptuous pageantry, and on payment of a heavy dowry by Edward, at Bruges in July 1468.[15]

This was a defeat for Warwick and the Nevilles in English politics; significantly Warwick's brother Archbishop George Neville had been dismissed as chancellor in June 1467. Warwick did not entirely give up hope of clinging to power. He was prepared to escort Margaret in procession on the first stage of her

wedding journey. He was also still sufficiently influential to help
embroil England in a war with the Hanseatic League of North
German cities in 1468, a war which helped deter Edward from the
invasion of France which he had promised Charles (and for which
he had received a substantial parliamentary grant).[16] Quite what
lay behind Warwick's determined advocacy of a pro-French policy
is unclear. There were real arguments, both political and
commercial, on both sides of the question. There may have been
personal antipathy between Warwick and Duke Charles, dating
back to 1460. Louis exerted himself to flatter Warwick to the
utmost, treating him as a great European prince rather than as
an English nobleman; personally welcoming him to Rouen in
1467, lavishing gifts on him, and arranging a ceremonial entry to
the city.[17] The rights and wrongs of a particular policy and the
self-esteem of those advocating it become inextricably entangled
in the process of decision-making. Other considerations, for
instance the question of the marriage of Warwick's heiresses, and
Edward's reluctance to have them marry his brothers, played their
part in the rift between the king and the earl. Nevertheless, it is
clear that differences on fundamental questions of foreign policy
dominated English politics in the 1460s.

Warwick's failure to re-establish his party by force in 1469 and
the early months of 1470 threw him into the arms of Louis. In
June 1470 Louis arranged the fateful interview between Warwick
and Margaret of Anjou at Angers; Louis provided Warwick with
money and ships which, with Warwick's own fleet, returned him to
England, where he drove out Edward IV and restored a surprised
King Henry to his throne. Edward fled to refuge in his brother-in-
law's domains, touching land somewhat ignominiously at Alkmaar
in Holland after being pursued by a Hanseatic squadron.

The crisis in England coincided with the outbreak of war
between Louis and Charles. Louis was smarting from the loss of
the 'Somme towns' (Amiens, Abbeville, and a good deal of
adjacent territory) to Burgundy in 1465. Louis had attempted to
reach a settlement in 1468 by a personal visit to Charles at his
fortress at Péronne. The meeting was not a success; Louis found
himself in effect a hostage, forced to accompany Charles to
suppress a rebellion in Liège, which Louis had himself initially
encouraged, and to concede all Charles's claims. Louis was bound
to try to reverse this humiliation. The collapse of the Yorkist
regime opened the way for Louis to declare war on Burgundy in

December 1470, safe from English retaliation. The war situation made Charles wary of committing himself to Edward's cause. He offered to recognise the restored Lancastrian regime, hoping to retain English neutrality. But Warwick had been won over by the vision Louis dangled before him of the dismemberment of the Netherlands between England and France, with Holland and Zeeland temptingly held out as his personal prize.[18] Charles therefore decided to back Edward in January 1471. While forbidding his subjects to give aid, (presumably so that he could disavow Edward if things went badly) he provided him with the equivalent of £20,000, and helped Edward hire some Dutch ships and assorted troops.[19]

More surprisingly, Edward also reached agreement with the Hanseatic League for a substantial fleet to escort his expedition. The League had evidently decided that the belligerent Warwick was a major threat to them. Edward set sail in March. Hopes of immediate reward for the Hanse were to be disappointed. The Anglo-Hanseatic war continued until a truce in 1473, leading to the Treaty of Utrecht in 1474, probably owing more to Edward's need to free himself from distractions before his invasion of France than to gratitude for 1471. The Hanse gained generous trading privileges which they were to defend for some eighty years, to the annoyance of the English trading community.[20]

Warwick's downfall in 1471 was due in part to his misjudgement of the attitudes of the London merchants. They had approved his aggressive policy in the 1450s, and that policy had carried forward to the protectionist commercial policy of Edward's first years. When that policy was reversed in 1467 there was grumbling in London that the terms of the new agreement could have been better for England. Such grumbles were a far cry, however, from Warwick's belief that all-out war against England's natural market in the Netherlands would be popular. Edward's return to London in April 1471, albeit at the head of a motley army including a contingent of Flemish gunners, was greeted with considerable relief, if not positive approval.[21] Similarly Edward's smashing of the Nevilles at Barnet and of Margaret and the Lancastrian Prince of Wales at Tewkesbury proved some consolation to Charles for his loss of Amiens and St Quentin to Louis; the Frenchman Thomas Basin indeed saw the battles as an example of 'divine clemency and favour towards the house of Burgundy', just when everybody was prophesying its ruin.[22]

Although the situation in England was a good deal less volatile during Edward's 'second reign' (1471–83), English reactions to the Franco-Burgundian struggle remained paramount; both sides paid pensions at various times to English councillors.[23] Louis's worst fears came to fruition in 1475, when Edward at last mounted his long-threatened invasion of France. The outcome – Edward's deal with Louis XI at Picquigny by which he withdrew his army in return for an annual French pension – is well known. The reasons are not so clear; whether Edward intended a deal of this sort from the beginning; or whether he was disappointed at the level of co-operation forthcoming from his allies, Francis II of Brittany, the Count of St Pol, and above all Charles of Burgundy. Charles's military contribution was rather paltry, probably because his army had been more badly battered at the long drawn-out siege of Neuss in the Rhineland than he cared to admit. In general, Charles's preoccupations had shifted away from the Franco-Netherlands border towards the east; adding Alsace and Lorraine to his possession of Burgundy proper, and becoming a great figure in the Empire, and preferably a king, took priority over interfering in France (though the two aims were not necessarily incompatible).[24] Significantly it was at Nancy, in Lorraine, that Charles was to be killed in battle in January 1477, plunging the Burgundian domains into crisis.

Charles was succeeded by his unmarried daughter Mary. Louis moved in quickly to take over the Duchy of Burgundy, though he was not successful in acquiring the adjoining Franche-Comté. He also managed to push back the Franco-Netherlands border, adding the Boulogne region and the County of Artois to the gains he had made in 1471. Flanders, Hainault, Brabant and the rest of the Burgundian Netherlands remained firm, however, and accepted Mary (on harsh conditions, which included the execution of some of Charles's leading ministers and the grant of a wide-ranging charter of liberties). In August Mary married Maximilian of Habsburg, son and heir to Frederick III, Holy Roman Emperor, and ruler of Austria. Frederick could spare little, if anything, in the way of resources; the successful resistance to the French was in fact due to the Netherlanders themselves. In all this, Edward's sister and Mary's stepmother, the Duchess Margaret, played a large part both in bringing about the marriage and in helping to arrange a settlement in Flanders. Margaret may have tried initially to press the claims of her brother George, duke of Clarence, for Mary's hand; a scheme which did not appeal to Edward IV, and which contributed to Clarence's arrest and execution in 1478.[25] Another possible suitor was Louis's son, the future King Charles VIII. Such a marriage would have united the whole of the Burgundian inheritance to the French crown; fortunately (at least from an English point of view), Charles was only six, to Mary's twenty.[26]

For the rest of Edward's reign the remaining Burgundian domains managed to hold together, with the advantage for Edward that he enjoyed the luxury of being courted on all sides and continued to receive his French pension, worth some £10,000 a year, while doing little in return. Things took a turn for the worse in 1482, when Mary was killed in a riding accident. The Estates of Flanders were ready to accept her infant son Philip as their nominal ruler but objected strongly to Maximilian's exercising any sort of regency. Maximilian hurriedly concluded peace with Louis XI. Edward (and England) were isolated.

Before the situation could resolve itself, Edward died (in April 1483), and England entered into crisis when Richard of Gloucester set aside his nephew Edward V; this was followed rapidly by the 'Buckingham' rebellion and eventually Richard's death on the battlefield of Bosworth. This period provides a particularly vivid illustration of the intricate connections between English and European politics.

The immediate result of the imprisonment, deposition, and eventual disappearance of the young Edward V was to draw attention to Brittany. The duke of Brittany, Francis II, had since 1471 sheltered or, perhaps more accurately, kept as a hostage the young Henry Tudor, since 1471 the most credible Lancastrian claimant to the English throne. Tudor was useful to Francis as a means of bringing pressure to bear on Edward IV if Edward should ever be tempted to leave Brittany to its fate when menaced by the French.[27]

Duke Francis's initial reaction to Richard III's seizure of the crown was to redouble his efforts to get substantial military assistance from England, pointing to his good service in resisting Louis's demands for the handing over of Henry Tudor. When English troops were not forthcoming the duke abruptly changed tactics. He had, after all, little reason to approve of the thrusting aside of Edward V, who had been betrothed to his daughter and heiress Anne in 1480. The bastardisation and deposition of Edward V hurt not only the duke's pride, but also his plans for the future of the duchy.[28] When in October 1483 the 'Buckingham' rebellion broke out he provided ships and money for Henry Tudor to join the rebellion. The defeated rebels fled to Brittany. On Christmas Day 1483 the partisans of Edward IV's children agreed to accept Tudor as king provided he marry Edward's eldest daughter; they evidently believed that Edward V and his brother were dead.

Meanwhile the situation in France had changed dramatically with the death in August 1483 of the fearsome Louis XI. His heir was the boy Charles VIII; and although Charles's sister Anne of Beaujeu, almost as formidable a figure as her father, took over the government on his behalf, the great princes were bound to try to regain some of the privileges they had lost during Louis's reign, and to claim their share in the running of the minority government. French politics, then, were to be distinctly unsettled; though the French observed smugly that, far from murdering boy-kings, the French paid them all respect.[29] At the States-General held in the New Year of 1484 a group of princes set themselves in opposition to the Regency. Duke Francis's minister, Pierre Landais, decided that Brittany should join them. This implied an alliance with England, rather on the lines of those mooted in 1468 and 1475, and once again approaches were made to King Richard; one condition which emerged, whether explicitly or otherwise, was that Henry Tudor should be handed over to Richard. This was too much for the duke's sense of honour. In October 1483 Tudor, with some 400 fellow-exiles, was allowed to make his escape across the border into France.

The French crown faced its worst nightmare; the possibility of civil war in France, accompanied by attacks by England, Brittany, and Maximilian, as ruler of the Burgundian Netherlands. A repetition of the dreadful year 1415 seemed to threaten. The reality was less bad. The French political scene was extremely volatile, Maximilian had his own civil war on his hands in Flanders, while Richard spun out negotiations with Brittany and was in no position to supply a large invading army. The French government responded by encouraging internal opposition to its opponents. Help was sent to the rebellious Flemish cities. The

Flemings reacted in their usual way to French intervention by making terms with Maximilian. In June 1485 the French army returned ignominiously from Ghent. Already, in May, the French government had promised Henry Tudor financial support. When, on 1 August, Tudor set sail it was in a fleet of seven Norman ships under a French vice-admiral paid for by the French crown. After landing Tudor and his army in Milford Haven, the fleet set off for a spell of privateering off Portugal, to the subsequent embarrassment both of the French crown and of Henry VII. The French also supplied perhaps half of the army which embarked with Henry, many of them veterans recently discharged from service, and including a contingent of Scots. These troops fought at Bosworth, and both French and Scots subsequently boasted of having won Henry's crown for him.[30]

It was a close-run thing. While Henry was preparing his expedition the French were also fomenting a move by Breton nobles against Pierre Landais. On 19 July Landais was hanged from the walls of Nantes castle; on 9 August the new Breton government signed a treaty with France. Had the French been able to hold out a little longer in Flanders, or had the Breton revolt taken place a little sooner, support for Tudor's dubious enterprise would not have been necessary. French support is not the complete explanation of Henry Tudor's success; careful planning, the sounding out of key individuals in England, was also important, as was an apparent lack of enthusiasm for Richard in England and his own fatal impetuosity in the battle. But Bosworth could not have happened without substantial French aid, and to that extent the French claim that Henry was 'king by the grace of Charles VIII' was justified.

While Bosworth is normally taken to be the end of the Wars of the Roses, dynastic armed conflict continued in England until 1497, and the threat of it lasted at least until the end of Henry VII's reign. Meanwhile there was a dramatic change on the European scene with the French annexation of Brittany in 1491; while until 1489, at least, there remained a distinct possibility that the French would successfully subvert Maximilian's position in Flanders.

The events of 1485 indeed came close to repetition in 1487, when the Yorkist 'pretender' Lambert Simnel, claiming to be

Clarence's son the earl of Warwick (the real Warwick was safely ensconsed in the Tower), was first proclaimed king in Dublin and then invaded England, to be defeated at a hard-fought battle at Stoke (near Newark). Margaret, the dowager duchess of Burgundy, was responsible for this venture, providing money and the services of (allegedly 1500) professional German troops under Martin Schwartz, fresh from the resumed civil war in Flanders. Her aim was presumably the installation of a genuine Yorkist prince on the English throne, either the real Warwick, or John de la Pole, earl of Lincoln, both of them her nephews.[31] In 1491 the French government financed the appearance of another Yorkist pretender in Ireland, Perkin Warbeck who claimed to be Richard, the vanished younger son of Edward IV. The French abandoned Warbeck at the Treaty of Étaples in October 1492, but he continued to receive substantial financial and diplomatic support from Margaret (who may, indeed, have been involved in the 1491 venture) until 1497, when Henry took him prisoner.[32] Maximilian was also intermittently involved with Warbeck, while James IV of Scotland received him at court in 1495–6, marrying him to a daughter of the earl of Huntly, and invading England on his behalf in 1496. James probably financed Warbeck's return to Cork and the successful raising of a rebellion in Cornwall in 1497.[33] Another Yorkist claimant, Edmund de la Pole, earl of Suffolk, was sheltered, part guest, part hostage, by Maxmilian and by his son Philip, now ruler of the Netherlands, from 1501 until Philip was forced by Henry to hand him over in 1506.[34] The similarity between the circumstances of the 'pretenders' and that of Henry himself in 1484–5 is striking, and underlines just how real was the possibility of another Bosworth.

However much Henry's own experiences might make him grateful to France, French policy towards Brittany and the Netherlands involved him in military co-operation with Maximilian, no doubt to his distaste. The problem of Brittany concerned the future of the duchy after the death of Duke Francis II. His heiress, his daughter Anne, was still unmarried. Ambitious suitors existed in profusion, among them the king of France, Charles VIII; in spite of the fact that under the terms of the 1482 Treaty of Arras he was already promised to Maximilian's daughter Margaret who had taken up residence in France in anticipation of becoming its queen. Parties in Brittany, broadly pro- and anti-French, contended around the feeble duke; the

French themselves intervened with an army in 1487 while Henry was busy with the Simnel invasion. An English military expedition to help the anti-French party in 1488 ended in disaster; and was diplomatically disowned by Henry. Duke Francis died shortly after. Henry concluded an alliance with Maximilian and with Spain in 1489 and sent substantial forces; but none of this prevented a French victory, leading to Anne's marriage to Charles in 1491 and, effectively, the end of Breton independence.

The Flemish civil war had continued in spite of the expulsion of the French in 1485; by 1488 Maximilian was a prisoner in Bruges, forced to witness the public execution of his ministers. The French decided to intervene once more. Henry retaliated with a small force which fought heroically at Dixmude and Nieuport, and helped bring about a settlement between France and Maximilian in 1489 (the Treaty of Frankfurt) by which the French withdrew from the Netherlands and gave a free hand to Maximilian to crush his remaining opponents.[35]

Henry's invasion of France in 1492 was a response to the humiliation he had experienced over Brittany. As part of this expedition English ships and men reduced the port of Sluys, which was still holding out in rebel hands against Maximilian, to surrender. Henry himself began a siege of Boulogne, but quickly made peace in return for generous financial compensation. Whether this result was Henry's aim from the beginning, or whether it was forced on him by circumstances, is not clear. The net result, however, was the beginning of a general settlement. Charles was anxious to involve himself in military adventures in Italy. In 1493 Artois and Franche-Comté were restored to Maximilian. In 1494 Charles launched his astonishing expedition to Naples, taking the heat off the Netherlands and allowing time for the consolidation of Habsburg power there. For the rest of Henry's reign, England was to be courted by the European powers; but, not faced with an immediate threat, could play the market to its own advantage.

Henry was punctilious in defending English interests, regardless of any personal obligations. But a sense of gratitude, allied to innate caution, may have distanced him from the aggressively anti-French attitudes which were traditional in England; and to that extent helped to bring about an outcome which would not have been possible for a less skilled or more militant king.

Overall then we see a distinct pattern. England, whatever the particular circumstances of the moment, was naturally concerned to defend the independence of the Netherlands and of Brittany; the first vital for English commerce, the second important for its security. This is not to say that any English government would necessarily respond in the same way, whatever the circumstances. But Warwick in 1470–1 was very much the exception among English rulers in aggressively supporting France against Burgundy. In general, English governments tried to achieve their aims in foreign policy by promises rather than by expensive action. Much the same applies to foreign support of the various parties in England. In a world of promises, of attempts to make policy on the cheap, suspicion between allies was rife; at any time one's partner might stitch up a deal with the enemy behind one's back.

What, from an English viewpoint, had been the net effect of these forty years of manoeuvre and counter-manoeuvre? The end of Breton independence was an obvious blow. As far as the Netherlands were concerned, the result was much more satisfactory. There is, as we have seen, a tendency to see the 'end' of Burgundy with the death of Duke Charles in 1477. In one sense this is true; 'Burgundy' largely ceased to be the force within France which, as in 1465 and 1468, could support the resistance of the French princes against the monarchy, and perhaps turn France into a federation of principalities.[36] If that had happened English kings, like Henry V before them, would have been tempted into a much more serious and continuous involvement in French affairs, pushing their own claims to the French throne, or trying to regain territory in France. Of course French resources were far greater than they had been in 1415; while England had failed to keep pace either in raising funds for war or in military technology (most notably in artillery, but also in tactical organisation).[37] Nevertheless, French power rested on internal cohesion which could not be taken for granted, even with the outsider Maximilian as 'duke of Burgundy'; especially if, as at one time seemed likely, he succeeded in marrying Anne of Brittany. At the other extreme, if, say, Louis XI had been able in 1477 to force the marriage of the Dauphin to Mary of Burgundy, or if in 1485 French pretensions had not alienated the good-will of the Flemish cities, the French might have succeeded in taking over Flanders and Brabant, with incalculable economic and political consequences. The eventual result was something of a draw.

France had emerged as a powerful monarchy (although further consolidation could not be taken for granted) and had acquired Brittany. On the other hand the Netherlands had been defended. Even though the French had managed to push the frontier back by taking Picardy and Boulogne, their further gains of Artois and Franche-Comté were to be undone in 1493. Over the next two centuries the frontier was to be pushed yet further back, most notably in the reign of Louis XIV. But the bulk of what we know of as Belgium was to be kept out of French hands, and it was a vital English interest that this should be so.

In another perspective, England's experience at this time seems less individual than we sometimes imagine. Rebellion was endemic throughout western Europe (to go no further afield). As we have seen, almost all rulers faced potential or actual rebellion; their opponents were more likely to encourage each other's rebels than to engage in frontal attacks. The 'kingmaker' earl of Warwick was a familiar type in Europe; comparable perhaps to Edward IV's uncle-by-marriage, Louis of Luxembourg, count of St Pol, whose double- and triple-crossing of Louis XI and Duke Charles drove them into unusual concerted action to destroy him in 1475.

Oddly, too, the transition from endemic disorder to a modicum at least of internal peace in the late 1490s was not peculiar to England. Again, quite why this should have happened is not at all clear. On one level it appears to be explicable in terms of chance, of just the way things happened to work out in each particular instance. On another, as we have seen, there was a good deal of interaction between the internal workings of each political unit; in general the settlements which were achieved between 1489 and 1494; the stabilisation, if temporary, of boundaries; and the shift in the focus of power politics to Italy; all contributed to a greater degree of internal peace in England, France, and the Netherlands. 'New Monarchies', in so far as they existed, were the result rather than the cause of this internal pacification and consolidation.

In one respect, England was unusual. It is striking how political struggles in England were about the control of central political power. However 'overmighty' English nobles might be, they were not fundamentally concerned with building up local concentrations of power at the expense of royal power; although naturally they might resent the diminution of such power and privileges as they already enjoyed. This was not true of France, nor of the Burgundian domains, where the authorities struggled endlessly against particularisms, against local powers and privileges. Oddly, perhaps, the closest parallel to England as a unified state was Brittany, where again rebellions were primarily about control of the central government. For its size, England was extraordinary; although it is important to realise that it is 'England' we are talking about here; conditions in the English dependency of Ireland were very different. Even here it is worth noting that English politicians and their foreign backers in the fifteenth century seem to have been much more interested in Ireland as a jumping-off point for intervention in England than as a power-base in its own right; that was to be left to the great Anglo-Irish nobles such as the Fitzgerald earls of Kildare and Desmond and the Butler earls of Ormond.

Of course the Channel was not England's only international boundary. Anglo-Scottish relations deserve much fuller treatment in their own right than they receive here.

Oddly, Scotland intervened less directly than might have been expected in English affairs; largely because the areas of England accessible to the Scots were too far away from London to have much immediate impact. The Scots were largely concerned with the recovery of the two important border fortresses of Roxburgh and Berwick, in English hands, with brief interludes, since the fourteenth century. The English routinely gave money, sanctuary, and sometimes military help to rebel Scots noblemen. Scottish kings, too, played the marriage card to keep up a high profile on the European scene. Sisters of James II were married to the Dauphin Louis, to Francis I of Brittany, and to Sigismund of Austria, while James himself was married, by the good offices of Philip of Burgundy, to Philip's niece, Mary of Guelders.[38]

James came of age in 1449 after a long minority (his father had been murdered in 1437). His first priority was to wage a ruthless, indeed brutal, war against the 'Black Douglases', the most powerful of the magnate families. News of the First Battle of

St Albans led to a proposal to Charles VII for a concerted attack on Berwick and Calais, and an attempt on Roxburgh by James alone in 1456.[39] From 1456 to 1460 James tried to keep lines open to both parties in England. News of Northampton led to a successful siege of Roxburgh, in the course of which James was killed when one of his own cannon blew up. His widow's regency government negotiated the cession of Berwick from Margaret of Anjou; and Scottish support was indispensable for the maintenance of the Lancastrian cause in Northumberland in 1461–4. Edward IV naturally retaliated by supporting rebels in Scotland.[40]

The Scots seem not to have involved themselves in the English crises of 1469–71. With Berwick in their possession, there was little to gain by interfering; while James III, who had just come of age, was too busy establishing his own authority and taking possession of Orkney and Shetland, effectively ceded to Scotland in 1469. From 1471 James attempted to run a high-profile diplomacy; negotiations with the English and plans for military adventures in Europe (prevented by the horrified reaction of his parliament in 1473). From 1474 James's policy was peace 'in the noble isle called Great Britain', cemented by numerous marriages between the royal families. This break with tradition brought down on him a mass of criticism.[41]

It was Edward IV, apparently, who upset the peace. By 1479 he felt secure enough to think of regaining Berwick, by force if necessary, encouraged by the enmity between James and his brother Alexander, duke of Albany. An invasion of Scotland in 1482 resulted in the capture of Berwick, and the arrival of English troops in Edinburgh in the hope of making Albany king, or at least governor of the realm; in return the English looked to acquire a large swathe of south-west Scotland. Albany's prospects were fading by the end of the year, and a second attempt was cut short by Edward's death in April 1483. Albany fled to England, leaving an English garrison in his castle at Dunbar. Yet another English-supported invasion by Albany, in 1484, was ignominiously defeated. James III concluded a truce with Richard III, swallowing for the moment the loss of Berwick and Dunbar.[42]

James may have had hopes that the presence of a Scottish contingent among the troops supplied from France at Bosworth might give him some leverage over Henry VII. Although the Scots did recover Dunbar shortly afterwards Henry acted quickly and decisively to defend Berwick, and showed himself determined, in subsequent negotiations, to keep it.[43]

Scottish rebels overthrew and murdered James III in 1488, in part, at least, because of his less than heroic record against the English, and installed his son as James IV. James was much more assertive in his relations with England than his father had been. In 1495–7 he was giving active support to Warbeck. Full-scale war broke out between the two kingdoms, culminating in Henry's projected invasion of Scotland in 1497 (foiled by the armed protest of Cornish taxpayers), and an unsuccessful attempt by James on the English castle at Norham.[44] Negotiations for an alliance began, resulting in James's marriage in 1502 to Henry's daughter Margaret. This did not prevent James mounting an invasion of England in 1513 while his brother-in-law Henry VIII was similarly occupied in France; and dying in the process on the battlefield of Flodden.

The sixteenth century, however, was to see large-scale English interference in Scottish internal affairs. It is worth making the point here that when Scotland, like Brittany in 1488, passed to a female ruler (in 1542), the English behaved just as the French had done in Brittany, and tried to force a marriage to the heir to the English throne, the future Edward VI. In spite of several years of hard-fought war, they were not successful, and in 1548 Mary Queen of Scots was carried off to marry the Dauphin of France. It was only the Dauphin's early death, as King Francis II of France, without children, and the return of Mary to Scotland, which prevented a dynastic union of France and Scotland and opened the way to the union of the British crowns in 1603, in itself the long-term and unlooked for result of the 1502 marriage. The union of Brittany and France could no more be taken for granted than that of England and Scotland, though in retrospect both look utterly natural.

The years of the Wars of the Roses and their immediate aftermath mark, then, a crucial period in the history of state formation. On the one hand, there was a distinct possibility that France would dissolve into a number of principalities, acknowledging the ultimate suzerainty of the French crown, but, like the principalities of the Holy Roman Empire, conducting their own independent foreign policies. On the other hand a triumphant French monarchy might not merely have reduced the pretensions of the princes and absorbed Brittany, but have spread its power to take over the Netherlands. Either eventuality, if it had come about, would have produced a European history very different from what actually ensued. Over and beyond that, the power of France profoundly affected events in Spain and Italy. Louis XI was extremely interested in both; and indeed his involvement did have significant consequences in both cases; none the less it was moderated by more pressing concerns in north-west Europe. Reactions against French involvement in Spain helped bring about an Anglo-Castilian treaty in 1466–7; eventually to be followed up in the alliance between Henry VII and the 'Catholic Kings', Ferdinand and Isabella, the rulers of Aragon and Castile now united through marriage. By the mid-nineties that union was too firmly established, for the moment at least, to be easily shaken by French interference.[45] When a long-distance adventure became possible, Italy was the obvious venue. What Archbishop Coppini had feared in 1460 had now come about.[46]

It would be absurd to pretend that all this was somehow 'the' result of the Wars of the Roses. So many chance factors were involved, so complicated the moves and counter-moves, so dependent were events on royal deaths, the accident of female succession, the lottery of dynastic marriage, and the ambitions of younger brothers, that no single explanation of the eventual outcome can be given. But it is clear that English events were an integral part of the general scene, shaping and being shaped by what was happening in western Europe; as is the importance of these years in helping to form the European state system as we know it. At a time when that state system is in the melting pot, when the familiar states are under pressure to concede power both upwards to 'European' institutions and downwards to their component parts, the 'naturalness' of those states is less self-evident now than it was in the nineteenth century. Both Burgundian straddling of linguistic and cultural frontiers and Breton or Scottish claims to independence seem more realistic than they once did. The element of pure chance, the play of the contingent, is at its greatest in a political system dependent on princely rule. The Wars of the Roses were part of the Great Game of fifteenth-century Europe.

9. The Visual Culture of Fifteenth-Century England

COLIN RICHMOND

> *Neritia:* What say you then to Faulconbridge, the young baron of England?
>
> *Portia:* You know I say nothing to him. ... How oddly he is suited! I think he bought his doublet in Italy, his round hose in France, his bonnet in Germany, and his behaviour everywhere.
>
> *The Merchant of Venice*, II.ii

Liverpool Cathedral MS 6 is a tiny and unusual book: it is of the hours of the guardian angel and no bigger than three inches by two. It was made in England in the second half of the fifteenth century. It has one illustration: of a kneeling woman, presumably the donor, presenting a book, presumably this book, to a queen, presumably Elizabeth Woodville. If one is to believe that the initial letters of a sixteen-line poem addressed to 'a Lady souereyne princess', which opens the book, spell her name, the donor is Elizabeth [a] Timraw. Elizabeth is presumed to have written the book as well as the poem, the presumption must also be that she has painted the picture, as she writes in the poems: the book 'shulde have bene moche more illumynid withe pleasure Ande if I had tyme'. Not money, we should note. The book is not striking because it was written and illuminated by a woman, but because Elizabeth was an English woman and her book is an English book. To see it, as I recently saw it at the exhibition of 'Medieval Manuscripts on Merseyside' in Liverpool, surrounded by books made in the Low Countries, France, Italy, even Germany, is to be made immediately aware of how bad a book it is. I mean: how poor in quality of production. This is particularly true of the single illustration. I am reminded of Doctor Johnson's comment on women preachers; I will not repeat his comment here. Liverpool Cathedral MS 6 is bad because it is English, not because it was made by an English woman.[1]

The badness of English art, as well as the Englishness of English art, in the fifteenth century is a theme, a text rather than a subtext, of my contribution. Edward IV, for instance, may not have read the books he owned; he did, however, know what he liked to look at: 'None of Edward's library books was produced in England.' Of the dozen or so books made for John, duke of Bedford, earlier in the century only one was made in England; it 'is associated with the London workshop of Herman Scheere'. Whatever the quality of the book illustrations Herman Scheere was producing in the first years of the century, 'English illuminators of the 1430s and 1440s had little new to offer', even if outside London there were, to paraphrase Nicholas Rogers, talented and inventive provincial schools of illumination, for example at Bury St Edmunds. From the 1440s Flemish illumination, like Flemish panel painting, caught every discerning Englishman's eye. It is not clear whose eye was caught by the work of the Master of Mary of Burgundy (or one of his colleagues), but the so-called Hastings Book of Hours is testimony to the demand at the highest level of society for the very best foreign work.[2]

That is equally true of the Register of the Luton Guild of the Holy Trinity and Blessed Virgin Mary. The Register's frontispiece is also by the Master of Mary of Burgundy (or one of his colleagues). It was painted about 1475 and deserves to be better known; it is very similar to, and as remarkable as , the frontispiece for the Register of the Guild of St Anne at Ghent, painted about 1476.[3] In the Luton picture Edward IV and Elizabeth Woodville are depicted kneeling opposite each other at prie-dieux; between them at another prie-dieu kneels the bishop of Lincoln, Thomas Rotherham, adoring the Trinity (certainly modelled on Robert Campin's St Petersburg Trinity of two generations earlier, and possibly influenced by the exactly contemporary Trinity panel of Hugo van der Goes, painted, as we will see, for a Scotsman between 1473 and 1478); the scroll issuing from Thomas's mouth reads 'Blessod lord in Trenete Save all thes Fretarnete'. Behind Edward IV kneels Master Richard Barnard, vicar of Luton 1477–92, whose chantry chapel survives in the parish church. The portraits of the master and two wardens of the guild which adorn most yearly entries of new members between 1474 and 1546 are hardly less remarkable. They are of variable quality; often the quality is high (by any standard). The similarly, though less skillfully, illuminated pages of the Register of the Dunstable Fraternity of St John the Baptist, which begins in 1506, may be modelled on those of the Luton Register. Were these quasi-portraits of Bedfordshire worthies by English hands?[4] What an English artist of these later years of the century was capable of is shewn by the Caxton Master's drawings in the Beauchamp Pageant of 1483–7. These often animated scenes have a vitality derived (though at some distance) from the mid-century work of Barthelmy de Eyck for king René of Anjou, particularly René's *Manual for the Perfect Organization of Tourneys*. It was, therefore, foreign craftsmanship which was admired by Englishmen and women. Imported articles then, as now, were regarded as far superior to home products.[5]

Englishmen, Welshmen, and Scotsmen, who could afford to, went abroad for their pictures. Cardinal Henry Beaufort, for example, was in Flanders in 1432 or 1438 to sit for his portrait by Jan Van Eyck,[6] while Edward Grimston esquire went to Bruges in 1446 to sit for his by Petrus Christus. If it were not for the coats of arms on the wall behind his head and the SS collar Edward is toying with, this Suffolk gentleman would look like a Burgundian, whereas the English cardinal, having nothing to identify him, has long been seen as an Italian. The Scotsman Edward Bonkil looks no less Burgundian kneeling before an organ played and worked by two stern angels in an austere church. The organ is likely to be that which Edward gave to Trinity College, Edinburgh, of which he was provost; the church may be, or at any rate may be intended to represent, Trinity College. If the panel in which Edward, the angels, and the organ are depicted is strange, that which shows the Trinity, to which Edward is on his knees in adoration, is weird. One wonders what James III of Scotland and his wife Margaret of Denmark, who are painted on the obverse of these two enormous panels, thought of the amazing images on the other side. Hugo van der Goes was busy on the Trinity panels at the same time as he was working on an equally amazing (and even more demanding) commission, the Portinari altarpiece of 1473–9. We might care to note that an Italian banker and a Scottish churchman shared a taste for the best in contemporary art; not simply the best, also the most avant-garde. At the same time in Flanders, but at Bruges rather than Ghent, a Welshman, or perhaps more correctly an

Anglo-Welshman, was having himself painted. The altarpiece Sir John Donne ordered from Hans Memling in the second half of the 1470s is also the best of taste. It, however, is small and private. If Hugo van der Goes went in for big, public (and possibly disconcerting) gestures, Hans Memling was a master of the small, the private, and the harmonious. As Bruce McFarlane taught us, Memling was *the* Northern painter of the second half of the century; his hopeful images were the ones men and women identified with, and not only an anglicised member of the Welsh squirearchy: Italians, Germans and Poles, as well as Dutchmen and Flemings, admired Memling's sentiments and style.[7]

A few years later another Englishman, a more obvious Englishman if there is such, went (or more likely sent) to Bruges for an altarpiece. Sir Robert Tate, alderman and merchant of London, had a triptych, probably of the Adoration of the Magi, painted for himself and his wife at Bruges just before 1500. Some of the panels survive at All Hallows, Barking by the Tower; the altarpiece originally stood in the Royal Chantry Chapel immediately to the north of All Hallows; this had a miraculous image of the Virgin which was particularly resorted to by Londoners in the later fifteenth century; Sir Robert Tate wished to be buried before the image. Sir John Weston, Prior of the Order of St John 1476–89, appears to have gone to Brussels when he wanted an altarpiece: to the workshop of Vrancke van der Stockt. Only the wings of his altarpiece survive: at St John's Priory, Clerkenwell, presumably the place for which it was intended. The Raising of Lazarus triptych at the almshouse of St John at Sherborne, Dorset, however, is complete. It also is to be associated with Vrancke van der Stockt. Was it commissioned for the hospital? The theme of the centre panel is almost too fitting for that to be the case, although (as has become clear from the preceding) there would be nothing at all untoward in a Netherlandish altarpiece being ordered by a provincial English hospital (even so modest an establishment as the Sherborne almshouse) in the 1480s. The same may be true of the remaining panels of an altarpiece at Queens' College, Cambridge, painted by the Master of Sainte-Gudule, another 'follower' of Rogier van der Weyden, who was working at Brussels in the last quarter of the century. Yet, in both instances, one is bound to ask, and leave the question hanging: who was the donor? Fifteenth-century Englishmen did not, it seems, go to Italy for art; one early sixteenth-century Londoner did: Paul Withypoll, a merchant who traded to Italy, was painted by Antonio da Solario in 1514 adoring the Virgin and Child.[8]

Is there anything to be said of English panel painters? The intriguing pictures here are, on the one hand, the distinctly Eyckian portrait of Marco Barbarigo of 1449 in the National Gallery, London, and on the other, the Santillana altarpiece, painted in Granada in 1455 by George the Englishman. Marco Barbarigo was Venetian consul in London in 1449; the inscription on the letter he holds 'would naturally mean', as the late Martin Davies wrote, 'that the picture was painted in London, where no follower of Jan van Eyck is otherwise known to have worked'. Could the painter Christian Colborne, whom Anne Sutton has brought to our notice, be that follower? Regardless of that, Christian Colborne, a German of some kind, found work in (and out of) London for over thirty years: he died in 1486. 'Christian', writes Anne Sutton, 'is another example of the direct influence of continental painters on English art and of the cosmopolitan nature of painting in London ... in the fifteenth century.'[9] If Christian is an example of an English receptivity to and demand for contemporary styles in painting, sufficient to attract and to give life-long employment to non-English practitioners of it, Jorge Inglés exemplifies its corollary: the capacity of English painters to accommodate to one of those styles, in Jorge's case also Eyckian, and to gain a livelihood abroad from producing it for discerning patrons. Christian worked for the executors of Richard Beauchamp, earl of Warwick; Jorge painted his great altarpiece for the Marquis of Santillana and his wife Doña Catalina Suarez de Figueroa. Nor should we forget that Marco Barbarigo was Venetian: fifteenth-century Venetians were among the most discerning of all artistic patrons. Outside London there was also employment to be had for good panel-painters. At Norwich, for instance, the Ocle family produced two painters between the 1380s and 1440s, the first of them, Thomas, may have painted the Despencer retable, the second, Robert, executed various works for the cathedral. At Canterbury in the 1470s, a painter working in the style of Memling produced at least two works for local patrons, in one case a local monastic patron.[10]

Both in London and outside there was plenty of wall-painting to be done. We might begin (in the 1440s) with Richard Beauchamp's showpiece chantry chapel in St Mary's, Warwick.

The manner in which the decoration of the chapel was divided between native and foreign craftsmen is instructive. John Prudde of London, for example, was to glaze the windows, but he was to do it 'with the best, cleanest, and strongest glasse of beyond the Sea that may be had in England', whereas the London carpenters who were to make all the woodwork were to take as their model the fittings of the choir of St Mary's itself. And, whereas Christian Colborne was to paint four stone images 'with the finest oyle colours', at a cost of £12, the last Judgement on the west wall was to be done by John Brentwood, citizen and 'steyner' of London, 'with finest colours and fine gold', at a cost of £13.[11] At about the time John Brentwood started work on the Doom at Warwick a very good Trinity was being painted over the tomb of James Langton in Lichfield Cathedral. James was a typical gentleman of Lancashire (rough and always ready to be unneighbourly); he was also rector of Wigan and a prebendary of Lichfield; he died in 1447. The painting must date from after 1442 when James was appointed to his prebend. Did an Englishman paint it? The same question might be asked of the somewhat later Assumption of Mary painted above the doorway into the chapter house at Lichfield. Unlike the Langton Trinity, this has neither been restored nor dated. The clerics who kneel to right and left must be the prebendaries; they seem to be headed by their long-serving and paternalistic dean, Thomas Heywood, 1457–92. We are on equally unfirm ground at Eton. The impressive wall paintings in the chapel of the college are securely dated to the 1480s by documentary evidence, but who painted them: Englishmen, Flemings, or an Italian, Ludovico Palmer [da Palma]? As at Winchester, where there is a similar, though later and now ruined, cycle of Miracles of the Virgin in the Lady Chapel of the cathedral, the inspirational patron is likely to have been the bishop of Winchester and sometime provost of Eton, William Waynflete.[12] The recently revealed (and restored) Marian paintings in the Deanery at Durham, 'as fine as those of Eton College Chapel' according to Pamela Tudor-Craig, also (and inevitably) raise as yet unanswered questions.[13] Their date, for instance, is insecure: perhaps the 1470s. As to who painted them and which prior ordered them we remain in the dark. In the end, too much wall-painting has been lost for us to do other than admire the little which has survived.[14] There must have been other secular, lineage themes on church walls, like that at the

'Camoys Mausoleum' of Trotton Church, Sussex. Indeed, there will have been other ceilings, though few if any so magnificent as Prior Senhouse's in the Deanery at Carlisle, and other painted choir stalls like those in Carlisle Cathedral, let alone painted screens (of all kind), as at Hexham and Romsey. What remains is not enough to reach any conclusions.

Painted screens do, however, bring us down to earth, even with a bump. Most painted screens, usually between chancel and nave, are what Pevsner was wont to call rustic in execution as well as character, if he did not call them something worse. Local patriotism, especially in Norfolk, less so in Suffolk, might say otherwise; none the less, with a handful of exceptions, chiefly in East Anglia and the west country, English church screens display good carpentry and bad painting.[15] What they lead us into is a more popular culture than that examined so far. One aspect of that culture which is thoroughly pictorial ought to detain us a while. Single-leaf woodcuts were the up-to-date medium of most fifteenth-century people on the continent. Were they of English people? The answer is probably no. If the answer is yes, the woodcuts they were looking at were overwhelmingly imports. English enterprise was as lacking in the production (and sale) of single-leaf woodcuts as it was in the printing of books: there were, for example, no block-books in England before 1500, and William Caxton was probably the only Englishman of the handful of printers at work in England before 1509. What the English read in that century might not nowadays be regarded as 'stuffy' and 'drab', although a considerable authority once said so; what they looked at in their own homes, to judge by the quality of surviving English single-leaf woodcuts, undoubtedly was. As another great authority wrote: 'English woodcut illustration in the xv century lags far behind contemporary work on the continent of Europe both in extent and quality, and its interest is for the most part literary and antiquarian rather than artistic.'[16] English imagery is terribly old-hat, mainly *pietàs* in surviving single-leaf cuts, when seen beside Dutch woodcuts with their Christocentric and *Devotio Moderna* imagery. It is, none the less, of considerable historical and sociological interest that the English dragged their feet where the new medium was concerned, for 'the image on paper was a new form of private object, available to a population with a growing ability to purchase. It must have formed a very different visual experience for those who had known only public works of art.'[17] Here was something revolutionary: a cheap and repeatable visual aid. Continentals had been sticking these penny-pictures up in their houses, shops, schoolrooms, and churches since at least the 1420s; there is hardly a trace of English men and women doing so; what few single-leaf woodcuts were available to them they stuck in their prayer books. Not until the early sixteenth century do we stumble on William Baret of Bishops Lynn having in his parlour 'a paper of the passion of cryst', or Lady Margaret Beaufort commissioning eighteen small images on parchment, probably for distribution among her household, and these parchment images may not be woodcuts at all.[18]

Something needs to be said concerning this particular English failure of the imagination. The piety of the late Middle Ages was a visual piety; the Lollards did not like images. Should not heretical opposition have spurred on English bishops to welcome and promote the single-leaf woodcut as a new means of teaching the faith? The ten commandments, the seven deadly sins, the sacraments, the creed were all available as single-leaf woodcuts, which could be pinned up in the vestry, church porch, or at home. English churchmen should have responded to the challenge (of heresy and novelty). They did not. It has to be concluded that they were not up to it. English businessmen were also out of touch: why were they not importing consignments of woodcuts, even if they were not financing their manufacture? There was clearly a market; this they almost entirely neglected. What were the reasons for these failures? Are we encountering those class divisions which bedevil English society (and English culture)? Was it English upper-class contempt for ordinary people which prevented churchmen and businessmen bothering with the single-leaf woodcut? It would not be the last time that the English lower classes were left to eat stale cake. What an opportunity was missed, especially by the church: the Reformation might have been averted or deflected, might any rate have been different. Sex apart, there is nothing more powerful than class: the English bishops, John Fisher excepted, show the truth of this old adage.

If what woodcuts there were in England were overwhelmingly imports, what cultural artefacts did England export? English choirboys were widely in demand on the continent. English embroidery no longer was. English alabasters, however, continued to be so. Nor was there any decline in the quality of English alabaster.[19] The English choral tradition has its admirers: a colleague, fleeing an English Christmas, discovered in a remote Portuguese village church that he had been overtaken by taped carols from King's College, Cambridge. English alabaster is more of an acquired taste: many continentals had acquired it. Still, my impression, possibly wrong where English polyphony is concerned, is that these were well-worn routes for well-worn products. I would be more convinced that English culture in the fifteenth century had been in good shape if English woodcuts had been more like German or Netherlandish, French or Italian woodcuts.

The woodcut is only one item of popular culture. What other aspects of that culture ought to be examined if we are to arrive at further conclusions about culture in general in fifteenth-century England? The dying-room in the Commandery at Worcester is a good place to begin. To this room, it may be concluded both from its position in the hospital and from the paintings on its walls and ceilings, the chronically sick were brought to die. Saints Roch, Erasmus, and Thomas Becket are on one wall: for the plague, abdominal pains, and head cases respectively. On another there is the weighing of souls: the Virgin's rosary on the scales tilts them towards salvation. On the ceiling there are the Trinity, the Five Wounds, and the words 'Jesus Mercy' and 'Lady Help'. Elsewhere in the room St Peter stands ready to welcome the saved soul. At the weighing of souls a perky demon has no chance of success: like that most popular (and much misinterpreted) block-book 'The Art of Dying Well', the message in the Commandery's dying-room is of hope. The idea that the late Middle Ages was pessimistic, morbid, and at the end of its emotional tether is wrong. Huizinga, writing his great book during the First World War, was bound to take an unhappy view of European culture. Great historians are necessarily moralists: they have a tendency, therefore, to be apocalyptic. This is not to say that wrong ideas are not fertile. Huizinga's *Waning of the Middle Ages* has been as properly influential as Spengler's *Decline of the West*.

Death and dying, of course, had a high visibility in fifteenth-century England, at any rate in their proper place. Domestic decoration, say in the hall at Bramhall Hall, or in the Catherine Room in the Canons Cloister at St George's, Windsor, or in the cottages of Silver Street, Ely, is cheerful enough. The religious painting in the hall at Piccotts End, Hertfordshire, if not cheerful, is certainly hopeful, which befits its position: the hall was in a hostel for pilgrims.[20] Elsewhere, what has survived is often misleading. William Worsley, dean of St Paul's 1479–99, kneels with a severe expression on his face in a fragment of wall-painting from the chapel of his house at Hackney (now in the Museum of London). Yet, at his Hackney house there are likely to have been merrier pictures on the walls of other rooms.[21] I am thinking of the Elizabethan painted parlour at Little Moreton Hall, or of the wall-paintings in the houses of yeomanly gentlemen at Debenham and Hacheston in Suffolk.[22] In church, on the other hand, death was everywhere; it was, after all, the moment at which eternity began. How one died was critical. How one was depicted in death was important. The proud needed to be shewn as humble, hence the cadaver tombs of the successful: the successful businessman, John Barton at Holme by Newark, the successful churchman, Thomas Heywood at Lichfield, or the successful king, Edward IV at Windsor. These tombs were visual displays (a phrase of Michael Hicks to describe the Hungerford chantry chapel in Salisbury Cathedral[23]), in the case of cadaver tombs, visual displays of pride above and humility below. Ordinary folk, like those, for example, in 'The Tale of Beryn', the fifteenth-century continuation of 'The Canterbury Tales', must have had great fun at such tombs, guffawing at the fiction of the proud being humble, chortling at the wealthy being worm-eaten. They were probably no more serious – and the snooty point of 'The Tale of Beryn' is that the lower classes were not serious – when confronted by the dance of death, which, after all, is a theme of the far more po-faced Early Modern Age than of the late Middle Ages (as James Clark pointed out more than forty years ago[24]): the dance of death panels in the Markham chantry chapel at Newark are from the 1520s; it was Thomas Cranmer, it seems, who wrote the Tudor homily, 'The Fear of Death'; and it is Robert Cecil who has a cadaver tomb at Hatfield.

Besides, in the fifteenth century life-giving saints were more in evidence in churches than death was. Jacques Toussaert may have considered late medieval popular christianity sentimental and infantile; there are, however, other words for it: robust, funny, sceptical, self-renewing, realistic. All these aspects are to be discerned in, for instance, Caxton's englished 'Golden Legend'. When it comes to culture, historians are prone to be like art historians: too respectful of the past. Henry James once wrote: 'things very ancient never, for some mysterious reason, appear vulgar'. The cult of the saints was wonderfully vulgar. Twentieth-century art historians, who genuflect before the material remnants of that cult, would have turned away disdainfully if they had been urged to buy a pilgrim badge at fifteenth-century Bromholm or Hailes, or had been required to kiss the feet of a crucifix, or had encountered Margery Kempe during one of her weeping bouts. The cult of the saints was (in art-historical terms) in the worst possible taste: it was Brighton Pier, Blackpool Pleasure Beach, and the Costa Brava rolled into one. Think of that typical fifteenth-century English 'saint' John Shorne, who cured gout, toothache, and male adolescent angst (and no doubt adolescent pimples too): there is no mysticism or mystification here, simply what the people want. Or, for that matter, think of those two other fifteenth-century 'characters', Walstan of Bawburgh and Urith of Chittlehampton: fairy-story saints for the rural labouring classes. Or think of Sacré Coeur in Montmartre. It is full of the best (or worst) religious 'art' of the last hundred years: people love it. Art-lovers, art historians, loathe it. Many English cathedrals and most English churches in 1500 were like Sacré Coeur. If we read a contemporary description of a shrine, for example the one written in 1445 of the shrines of St Chad at Lichfield, we get a glimpse of how gaudy late medieval religion was. St Chad's head shrine was of 'gilt and well adorned with collars and divers precious stones and other gold ornaments; and this reliquary can be opened into two parts', while 'the right arm of St Chad [was] adorned and enclosed with silver gilt with a hand at the upper end as if in the act of giving a blessing'. This is the world of the fairground.[25]

Popular religion was also the realm of the soap opera: take almost any saint's life from the 'Golden Legend'. Or read the plays that were so popular in fifteenth-century England: they run the gamut from obscene violence to knock-about farce. Here is the plot of a pious tale, *The Unnatural Daughter*:[26] a father debauches his daughter, who kills three children by him. Her mother discovers the intrigue, and the daughter kills her. The father repents and confesses to a priest. He rejects the daughter and plans a pilgrimage. The daughter murders him in his sleep, goes into the country, and lives in lechery. A bishop comes to preach. She enters the church. The bishop sees four fiends leading her by chains. A word he speaks touches her and she weeps. The chains are broken, the fiends flee. She confesses. The bishop bids her wait until his sermon is done, but her heart bursts. The bishop bids the congregation pray to know where her soul is. A voice declares that it is in heaven. The narrator warns sinners not to fall into wanhope (hopelessness), for they may yet be saved.

There was little chance of morbidity in a society which narrated such stories to itself. Not that we can recapture, any more than we can re-invent, the responses of fifteenth-century men, women and children to the culture available to them. We can read the Sleaford Trinity Guild Accounts and discover an entry like the following for 1480: 'Item payd for the Ryginall [original] of the play for the ascencion and the wrytyng of spechys and payntyng of a garment for god, 3s 8d.' But what it was like to perform in that play or to watch it is impossible to recover. In the same Guild Accounts, under 1483, another entry reads: 'Item, for beryng of the Baner and the mynstrell 6d.' The Fetternear Banner may give us an 'idea' of what fifteenth-century banners were like, fifteenth-century music give us a 'sense' of what popular entertainment of that century was like: but no more. We scratch, and only scratch, the surface, and only the surface, of the past. After much enquiry we might be able to learn what the Low Sunday to Lammas Day 'sportes and recreacions' of the Journeymen Weavers of Shrewbury were – the Master Weavers agreed in 1475 to find them a hall to hold them in – yet we have no hope of entering the least bit into the spirit of them. How did the owner (or owners) of a well-thumbed Norwich almanac, with its pretty pictures and prognostications, actually use it? Did the churchwarden of Acle, Robert Reynes, carry about the length of the nails that crucified Christ? Did he attempt to make an angel visible on a child's finger-nail? Visibility: all cultures are visual; some are more visual than others. Despite what art historians may say, the most visual are always the most vulgar. Fifteenth-century English culture was both.[27]

It was nowhere more so than in the higher levels of society. Indeed, one is emboldened to say that the greatest vulgarity was displayed by the highest in the land, were that not a truism applicable across time and space: from the Pyramids of Cairo to the Palace of Culture in Warsaw, from the Hanging Gardens of Babylon to the Gerald Ford Museum at Grand Rapids, from Yeavering to Windsor. If were are to examine royal culture (the taste of kings), and we must, then it is immediately across the river from Windsor that we should begin. Eton College Chapel looks modest as one crosses the Thames by train at Windsor: it is

St George's Chapel which dominates. That was not what was intended by Henry of Windsor. In a notable chapter Bertram Wolffe captured Henry VI's megalomaniac intentions for Eton. The 'grandiose scale' of the chapel (318 ft long) Wolffe catches perfectly: 'Had the whole ever been completed, across the Eton High Street, it would have been comparable to any of the medieval cathedrals, with a nave as long as Lincoln's, and would have been exceeded in width only York Minster, the whole being thirty feet longer than the comparable design for King's College Chapel as it now stands.' Wolffe is kinder to Henry VI where King's College Chapel is concerned than he is in the case of Eton College Chapel, perhaps because the result of Henry's plans is there for all to see and because King's College Chapel is so much part of the English scene. The college is not as Henry finally intended it to be, but the chapel is: 289 (or 290) ft long, 94 ft high, 40 ft wide. It was only finished in 1515. Wolffe called it 'splendid'. As, however, the chapel has become synonymous with England, it is impossible to look at it with a clear head, heart, or eye. Undoubtedly as imposing as it was intended to be, Pevsner's judgement that the chapel has 'qualities of imagination and fantasy, of richness and joy' seems cock-eyed to me; to me it looks like a fifteenth-century work-house, the equivalent of a nineteenth-century textile mill, or a twentieth-century bank, or (dare one say) a nazi *Kunstpalast*.[28]

Edward IV's architectural monument is smaller. St George's Chapel is a relatively modest 230 (or 237) ft long. Begun in 1474 (or 1475), the chapel was completed in 1511, a few years before King's College Chapel. Unlike Eton, where building was over by 1482, at St George's and at King's we are confronted by Tudor as well as Lancastrian and Yorkist taste. Those soaring vaults (fan or otherwise) are sixteenth- rather than fifteenth-century. St George's Chapel is less box-like than King's College Chapel: transepts and west and east chapels break up the un-compromising horizontal lines. It is very grand. It is, none the less, not such an imposition as King's, harmonising as it does with ground and setting. If Edward IV was more down-to-earth than Henry VI, Richard III was up in the clouds. Richard planned to establish in York Minster a college of 100 priests. Charles Ross called such a scheme 'exceptionally grandiose' and no one is likely to quarrel with his judgement. What architectural shape a college of that dimension would have taken who can say; one is simply relieved it did not take shape at all. Henry VII's chapel at Westminster Abbey, begun in 1503, is a mere 130 ft long. Pevsner called it 'both sturdy and sumptuous'. He drew attention to Henry VII's tower at Windsor as the model for the chapel's 'fanciful plan of bay-windows'. That tower no longer exists, though there are pictures of it; it too seems to have had a predecessor in Edward IV's state apartments at Nottingham Castle, also long since gone. What remains (with which to compare Henry VII's chapel) is the New Building at Edward, duke of Buckingham's Thornbury in Gloucestershire; it, however, is later, 1511–21. Henry VII's architectural (or better monumental) ambitions do, therefore, seem to fit Pevsner's description; they were not as far-fetched as those of his immediate predecessors.[29]

The royal mausolea are in the perpendicular style. 'There is little that is in every respect so completely and so profoundly English as are the big [perpendicular] English parish churches of the late Middle Ages', wrote Pevsner. I see no reason to omit the small parish churches. There is little point in making a list, but a handful have to be mentioned to remind the reader: St Mary Redcliffe; St Mary the Virgin, Nottingham; St Peter Mancroft; St Nicholas, King's Lynn; St Margaret's, Westminster, on the one hand; Blythburgh and Denston in Suffolk; Fairford, Gloucestershire; Shelton, Norfolk, on the other. Some of these churches are worrying. St Mary's, Nottingham, or Fairford, for example, seem built to measure, as if the architect had been to a Perpendicular Do-It-All Homebase. Others are far more satisfying, their harmoniousness not quite absolute, Denston and St Peter Mancroft, for instance. Shelton is (as Pevsner notes) 'one ideal of a new church of about 1480 or 1490'; nave and chancel are one, at any rate architecturally: wooden screens would have divided them internally. At Shelton the sacristy is squeezed in at the east end. The church feels as well as looks a layman's church. Sir Ralph Shelton paid for it. One might think the almost anti-clerical design gentlemanly, save for the fact that Ewelme, built by a nobleman, William de la Pole, duke of Suffolk, and St Peter Mancroft, built by the oligarchs of Norwich, are (in this regard) the same. That anti-clerical, or (better) a-clerical , shape is what might be said to make these perpendicular churches peculiarly English, at any rate from a cultural standpoint. What makes them attractive is something else, which at first seems contradictory: 'parts are left as parts, separated from each other', says Pevsner.[30]

For, if architectural flamboyance is wanting in perpendicular churches (and it most certainly is), then perhaps it is to be found in the cluttered eclecticism of their fittings. It is a pity Pevsner did not publish comment on Rosslyn: what, one wonders, did that old Bauhaus warhorse make of so flippant and un- (if not anti-) English and architectural comment? When the English do make an attempt at something more decorative in the later Middle Ages the effect is grotesque, for example Prince Arthur's chantry of 1504 in Worcester Cathedral (a box with knobbly, flowery bits stuck on), or Bishop John Alcock's chantry in Ely Cathedral, which Pevsner said reminded him 'of Spain more than of the reasonable English Perpendicular', but which in my view has mistaken quantity for quality. I suppose 'restraint' is the word tirelessly deployed to characterise English perpendicular architecture, and thus, by extension, English fifteenth-century culture. I would not quarrel with that: it is precisely 'restraint' which makes English gentlemanly culture, fifteenth-century or otherwise, so dull. If perpendicular is the *first* 'profoundly English' style it has a great deal to answer for: among the English ruling class it set (as hard as alabaster) an approach to art and life in which restraint became decorum and decorum philistinism.[31]

Such a judgement ultimately applies (I believe) to the ersatz flamboyance of English church fittings. There are exceptions: the fragments of the shrine of St William of York (designed by Robert Spillesby, master mason of the Minster 1466–73) are exciting; so are the iron gates of Edward IV's chantry at St George's, Windsor (made by John Tresilian, a Cornish blacksmith); the painted glass from Roger Wigston's house in Leicester (from continental woodcut designs) is admirable, though it is domestic and not institutional; the same is true of those few alabaster panels which survive in their wooden housings in Leicester Museum, the Burrell Collection, and at Worcester Cathedral, and which have exactly the kind of attraction of things old and different that Henry James so much appreciated and so well understood. Yet, none of these has the boldness, the effrontery indeed, of those *vierges ouvrantes* which turn up in Europe. It is, from this point of view, a pity that all the roods have gone in England: some, if not most, must have been new-made in the fifteenth century. One wonders how Christ was shewn on the rood: in extreme or restrained agony? If we are looking for flamboyance in fifteenth-century England, it is to be found in English woodwork, above all English choir stalls, those, for example, at Chester and Nantwich (both late fourteenth century), those at Manchester (early sixteenth century), and at St George's, Windsor. There are also West Country bench ends (and fronts): at, for instance, Brent Knoll, Somerset; Mullion, Cornwall; Abbotsham, Devon. Here, at last, we finally encounter exuberance (some of it sixteenth- rather than fifteenth-century it has to be said). It is, however, that true European, Nikolaus Pevsner, who sounds the warning where English wood-carving is concerned. He is discussing the stalls of 1478–85 at Windsor: 'one thought of contemporary stalls in Germany such as those at Ulm fixes the level of aesthetic value at Windsor firmly'. The carvings are not only naive, as Pevsner suggests, they want intelligence, that large intelligence which informs all South German and Netherlandish carving of this period – in stone as well as in wood. There was no Claus Sluter in England to supply inspiration. The Manchester stalls are better; they are even good; they are, however, very far from great. English timber roofs, particularly church roofs, are another matter: Pevsner calls Astbury's 'thrilling'; I would call Blythburgh's great.[32]

English brasses are fairly 'profoundly English'. They come in all shapes and sizes. They are seldom (if ever) exotic, like those fourteenth-century ones from Tournai workshops. English tomb effigies, on the other hand, especially alabaster ones, are sometimes more than humdrum shop-pieces: that of Alice Chaucer at Ewelme, or that of William Cannings in priest's robes in St Mary Redcliffe, or those of members of the Green family at Lowick, Northants. Even here, however, it was an Italian, Torrigiano, who brought to tomb effigies a vision large enough to make them moving: Margaret Beaufort, Henry VII, and Elizabeth of York at Westminster, Dean John Yonge in the Public Record Office.[33]

The tomb of Sir Robert Poyntz of Iron Acton near Bristol collapsed in the eighteenth century; we cannot see how he wished himself to be shewn upon it. His tomb was in the Jesus Chapel of the church of Gaunts' Hospital, now St Mark's (or the Lord Mayor's) Chapel, beside College Green in Bristol. Sir Robert built the Jesus Chapel. Sir Robert, knighted on the field at Redmore, died in 1520. Before describing the chapel we should listen to him speaking of it in his will:[34]

... my body to be buried within the church of the 'gauntes' beside Bristol in the chapel of Jesus which lately I have caused to be new edified and made of my costs and charges 'on the sowthsyde of the chauncel of the sayde churche in the one parte thereof behynde the presbitory there that is to witte in a vawte in the same therunto redy prepared and ordeyned ... and I will that myn executors within a convenient tyme after my disceas provide a fyne small marble stone and cause it to be leyde over the myddys of the vawte in the said chapell with a scripture makyng mention of all the bodies that lye buried in the same vawte and of the dayes and yeres of their discesses ... and for as much as the said new chapel which I late edified is not in all things provided and furnished yet according to my intent that is to witte in glasyng of the wyndowes therof and makyng of two pewes within the said chapell in the lower end of the same that is to witte on the sowthsyde of the dore and the other in the north syde of the same I will therfore that myn executors of my goodes shall fynysshe and performe all the same thinges being yett undone and also shall garnyshe the same chapell with certayn Images and the aulter of the same with aulter clothes vestmentes boke and chalys and with other thynges therunto necessary and requisite in suche maner as my said executors shall thynke best to be done by their good discresions as I have in parte declared unto them of my mynde and more shal declare unto them in that behalf with the grace of almyghte god.

'The chapel', as Elizabeth Ralph and Henley Evans write in the Guide Book,[35] 'is a beautiful example of the late perpendicular style. The fan-traceried roof is in two groups and in the centre of each is a boss in the form of a carved shield of arms. ... Eight exquisitely finished canopied niches are arranged round the walls. On the north side are two stone recesses ... in each spandrel is carved a rebus of the founder, a clenched fist (Poing), being a pun on his name.'

The niches and recesses no longer contain the images Sir Robert wished to be placed there; otherwise, one can detect in this small room the taste, the good taste, of a pious, generous, and cultured gentleman of 1500. Or was it the taste of his wife? Had she cultivated a taste in him? She was a Woodville: Margaret, illegitimate daughter of Anthony Woodville, Earl Rivers. It is an intriguing thought that in Sir Robert's Jesus Chapel we may be observing not only a woman's taste, but a Woodville woman's taste. How far women were responsible for fifteenth-century taste is impossible to say. Is St George's, Windsor, Elizabeth Woodville's creation? Is Fairford Mrs John Tame's? The glass of arcane saints at Wiggenhall St Mary Magdalene, Norfolk, was almost certainly the choice of Isobel Ingoldsthorp, wife of John Neville, Marquis Montagu, niece of John Tiptoft, earl of Worcester,[36] just as Tiptoft's tomb in Ely Cathedral was probably the choice of the earl's sister Joan Ingoldsthorp.

The absorbing question of gender and culture can only be touched on here. It would be a brave man, for instance, who maintained that John Paston was more cultured than Margaret Paston. Was it her idea to rebuild the nave and transepts of their parish church in Norwich, St Peter Hungate? When we look at their good roofs and the very good central boss in the nave of the Last Judgement we are, I believe, looking at a woman's work. We may also be looking at a work done for a woman when admiring that rarity, a fifteenth-century English pen drawing. It is of St Christopher.[37] The parchment sheet may be a design for a wall-painting, although to me it looks (in reproduction) more like the cover of a book, perhaps of a commonplace book. On the sheet beside St Christopher a number of Woodhouse names are written, John and Alice among them. John Woodhouse died in 1431; his wife, Alice Furneaux, remarried Edmund Winter and died in 1448. Who determined what, as between husband and wife, has to remain an unresolved matter (in almost every case), just as which poems in the Findern Manuscript are written for women, or by women, or by women for women is a matter of interpretation.

Gender may continue to occupy our minds when we slip down the social scale, from gentlemen to yeomen, from gentlewomen to yeowomen, and arrive at church towers. Church towers are a pre-eminent aspect of English culture in the fifteenth century (as they are of English landscape in the twentieth); they were going up everywhere from Suffolk to Somerset, from Devon to Lancashire. Gentlefolk and the nobility, of course, contributed to the costs of tower building: the Stathams at Morley, Derbyshire; Alice Chaucer at Eye, Suffolk; the earl of Oxford at Lavenham. Yet, and overwhelmingly, the work was paid for by farmers and townsfolk, and overseen by churchwardens who were either urban businessmen or country yeomen. Louth's towering spire, which cost more than £300 between 1501 and 1515, was a community undertaking orchestrated by socially unpretentious churchwardens. The contracts for the construction of church towers show that it was middle-class men who took the initiative, in Suffolk at least: at Walberswick in 1426, at Helmingham in 1488, and unsuccessfully at an unknown fifteenth-century date at Thornham Parva, where the partly built tower fell down and the unrepentant masons refused to recompense Roger Baldry, Henry Vale, and Thomas Green.[38] Towers rather than spires (despite Louth's) were all the rage in the fifteenth century because there was a mania for bell-ringing, and a peal of bells requires a strong structure to hang in. All this makes one pause. With church towers and bell-ringing we seem to be at the heart of fifteenth-century middle England. Male middle England at any rate. Should we go further: to mention phallocentrism as well as androcentrism. I doubt it, and yet the male mania for being up towers ringing bells smacks of something, something *not* European, something very English. Once again, it all gets going in the fifteenth century. If phallocentrism is not the answer, what is?

I have (possibly) gone off at a tangent, or (probably) off on a hobby-horse. I have, none the less, a point to pursue, if not to make: what was the culture of these bell-ringers, these Thomas Greens, Henry Vales, and Roger Baldrys? Were they like that credulous churchwarden Robert Reynes? Not all, for some were those Lollard churchwardens and wardens of fraternities in the Chilterns whom Richard Davies has uncovered for us.[39] Such men (and their womenfolk) demonstrate mine is not an idle pursuit. These were fifteenth-century people (Thomas Betson, Thomas Paycocke) with greater freedom than any others. They were well enough off to think about culture; they were not mentally strait-jacketed (and strait-laced) like the nobility and gentry; they were not materially at risk like rural labourers and urban workers. They were, as Ian Arthurson has said in a political, and Robert-Henri Bautier in an economic context, the people with choices. We can see them vividly portrayed in Julia Carnwath's study of the Thame Churchwardens' Accounts. Ms Carnwath shows us their dark side: tradesmen on the make and on the fiddle, running the church as they were running the town – to their own advantage. Yet, church and town *are* run and they are run successfully.[40] In the sixteenth century these are the men (and women) who made a religious (and therefore cultural) choice; the Reformation could not have been made where it mattered (in towns and villages) without them. Thus, their culture, a yeomanly culture, a small-town, small-businessman, small-craftsman culture, needs a far more thorough investigation than it has had hitherto.

Let one man close this section: John Bishop of Southwold. I came across him in the fifteenth-century church of St Edmund; the church 'was the entire (stupendous) creation of the decades 1430–1460';[41] images apart, it has virtually everything a fifteenth-century church ought to have, including a chest carved with St George and the Dragon, a Jack of the Clock, inscribed bells, and painted roof, pulpit and screens, the latter with the remains of a donor inscription with the name John, perhaps John Bishop. He was probably bailiff of the town in mid-century, as other Bishops were later (when records survive). Kneeling to receive the eucharist in the chapel at the east end of the south aisle – a mid-week communion on a brilliantly sunny day in March – my eye was caught by a brass plate on the floor: 'Pray for the Souls of John Bishop and Ellen his Wife', it said (in Latin). The effigies were gone. On such a day, at such a moment, I was bound (as an historian) to ask myself, who were these obviously fifteenth-century people. I looked to see if they had made wills. They had. Ellen's of 1473 is indecipherable. John's of 1456 is, as I had hoped, unexceptional. He owned fishing boats and fishing gear. He wished to be buried before the altar of St Anne. He was solicitous of Ellen, leaving her for life the house where they had lived together in Southwold (and everything in it), as well as other property in and around the town. Robert, his son and heir, was enjoined to behave well to his mother – as well he might be, considering how much she got. What she also got was a half-share in the Bishop fishing business with Robert; Ellen may well have run things while Robert did the fishing: he was left *all* the fishing tackle. John remembered his god-children, who each got a shilling. He left money for the repair of local bridges. A married daughter, euphoniously called Gode Joye, and her four sons were given cash. The Southwold poor were to have £1 a year between them for seven years. Two properties were to be sold immediately and £20 from their sale was to be given towards the building of the tower of St Edmund's church. Other local churches were to get small sums. John was unspecific about the prayers that were to be said for his soul: Ellen was to see to them. His executors, who accepted the administration of the will, were his son and son-in-law, Robert Bishop and Richard Joye.[42]

Despite his will, despite his being uxorious, despite his £20 for the bell-tower and £7 for the poor (the first, one suspects, from the heart, the second from the head), we know too little about John Bishop. Actually: we know next to nothing. What was the culture of this provincial businessman (and the influential thousands like him)? Was he a proto-Thatcherite, philistine and complacent? Or a proto-Majorite, even more philistine, and more nostalgic than complacent? And if he was nostalgic, what sort of England did John Bishop hanker after? Did he have any idea, let alone a vision, of England as he lay dying and dictating the last clauses of his will at Southwold on 22 October 1456? Was it a vision of a 'better' England: before First St Albans, before Jack Cade, before Joan of Arc, before Henry VI? Did he have any sense of history at all? If he were literate, we must suppose he had. Even if one wishes to disparage the John Bishops of fifteenth-century England – as I do, turning them, by post-modernist methodology, into John Bulls – their importance needs to be admitted, and admitted, in my view, as central to the English culture of that, possibly the previous and certainly the succeeding, century.

John Blacman seems a long way from John Bishop: the hard-headed businessman and the soft-hearted Carthusian. Nor could it be maintained that their devotional attitudes were similar, let alone the same. As Roger Lovatt has made plain, John Blacman's piety was characteristic of English polite devotion in the fifteenth century, and that piety was thoroughly academic in tone. It was also emotional, sentimental, and sensual, more intense than intellectual, more Rolle than Hilton.[43] What Robert Reynes (if not John Bishop) and John Blacman share is what I would call a credulous complacency. One only needs to read, I think, the travel diary to the Norfolk clergyman, Richard Torkington, of a journey of Jerusalem in 1517 to appreciate the phrase.[44] I may be close here to what Peter Heath has called 'the shallowness ... of some piety', yet, like Peter Heath, I can see the strengths (as well as the weaknesses) of so child-like and unquestioning a faith.[45] My point is that among all these academically trained monks, friars, bishops and clergy there is not one considerable thinker, let alone one great mind. That is a judgement on Oxford and Cambridge in the fifteenth century: what those two universities contributed to English culture in that century was as negligible as it has ever been between the twelfth and the twentieth. Enterprising Englishmen went abroad: Peter Payne to Prague, Leonard Coxe to Cracow, John Tiptoft and Thomas Cromwell to Italy. Where, oh where, were the English equivalents of Nicholas von Flüe, Catherine of Genoa, Nicolette Boylet (St Colette), Nicholas of Cusa, Gregory of Sanok (archbishop of Lvov), Nicholas Copernicus, Niccolo Machiavelli? The list is not exhaustive.[46]

I was tempted to include Gilles de Rais. Peter Lewis has written that 'the faith of this canon of St-Hilaire-de-Poitiers, this founder of the great chapel of the Holy Innocents at Marchecoul, this companion as marshal of France of Jeanne d'Arc, reveals in its most lurid light the later medieval psychomachy, the conflict of the soul.' With this sexual abuser and murderer of children we do indeed reach the extremities, the polarities of the late medieval mentality, for his faith was that with patience and hope in God he would achieve Paradise.[47] There is, incidentally, no calculating doctrine of good (and bad) works here, only (only?) a touching faith. We seem a continent away from the English world, where although a far bigger shipowner than John Bishop, William Cannings of Bristol, might give up all (as a widower) and become a priest, his two lives are nothing like the double-life of Gilles de Rais. There is no hint of Hell (or vision of Paradise) in the quiet transition from quayside to vestry of William Cannings. English life, religious, intellectual, cultural, knows no extremes. It is the quiet life. Think of the typical English country house of the fifteenth century; it is usually of (warm) brick, surrounded by green water (fish, ducks, swans, frogs) and green meadows (sheep and cattle grazing), deep in the English countryside, often with a tower or towers from which to view the deer browsing in the park: Rye House, Herstmonceaux, Caister, Tattershall, Baconsthorpe, Kirby Muxloe. English pastoral. But there was also English politics. There was no quiet life in English fifteenth-century politics: these houses were for escape, escape from Westminster.

I would like to think of one of the only three political Englishmen who resemble (in the slightest) Gilles de Rais, Richard, duke of Gloucester, standing at the bay-window (*his* bay-window?) in the Great Chamber at Barnard Castle and looking up the Tees to admire one of the grandest views in northern England. It is, no doubt, wishful thinking. Yet Richard of Gloucester, child murderer and book-lover, vicious politician and devoted ruler, may have been (for all we are likely ever to know) as wholly Richard of Gloucester when contemplating Nature at Barnard Castle as he was, contemplating unnatural acts in the Tower of London. The second of the two Englishmen is Anthony Woodville, Earl Rivers, wearer of a hair shirt, patron of learning and of William Caxton, tournament fighter, no murderer but murdered (by Richard of Gloucester). Are continental extremes encountered in him?[48]

The third of these men, and the most interesting, is John Tiptoft, earl of Worcester, Italianophile humanist and 'Butcher of England'. Tiptoft is at once the most cultured of fifteenth-century Englishmen, the most politically-minded, the most detested, and the most un-English. He was not at all like other English noblemen, whom the Italian Poggio experienced at first hand around 1420 and whom he said did nothing but talk about trade, agriculture, and the management of their estates at table, and waste their time in the open air, hawking and hunting. Tiptoft executed political opponents with unusual violence; when his turn came he died with a sardonic dignity, requesting the executioner to use three strokes in honour of the Trinity. Not even another a-typical Englishman, a-typical because he *was* a political thinker (and activist) of genius, could match that on the scaffold: Thomas More's joke was a joke, a good joke, but no more than a joke. The poet Geoffrey Hill, in his Wars of the Roses sequence 'Funeral Music', best captures the 'doubleness' of Tiptoft, Woodville, and Gloucester:

… blindly we lie down, blindly
Among carnage the most delicate souls
Tup in their marriage-blood, gasping 'Jesus'.

Not many other fifteenth-century Englishmen would recognise themselves here, not, I think, unless they were fifteenth-century historians.

Tiptoft wrote an English history. It has been missing since 1956. Antonia Gransden, who saw it in that year, thought it unoriginal.[49] Besides, it stopped at 1429 – curiously, perhaps, as that is the year English imperialism in France was thwarted by a woman, or, rather, a sixteen-year-old girl. Tiptoft's English history, none the less, enables me to make the connection I need for a conclusion. Poverty-stricken as English fifteenth-century culture has turned out to be, it was not poor where the writing of history was concerned. Great political thinkers there were none (until Thomas More), political historians there were. Bruce McFarlane made us fully alert to this dimension: William Worcestre was the founder of an historical tradition which McFarlane himself perfectly exemplified five hundred years later. There were others beside William Worcestre, who collected documents, checked references, sought out visual as well as other evidence, composed papers, and wrote what we would call contemporary history: John Rous, the Crowland Chronicler, John Warkworth, the writers of the 'English Chronicle', 'Gregory's Chronicle', John Hardyng, and the Pseudo-William Worcestre. English history did not need Polydore Vergil's humanist devices: Thomas More soon discovered how impossible they were for the writing of recent history. We ought to ask, if only because the answer is simple, why were there so many good historians in the second half of the fifteenth century? Was it not because English political history after 1429 had been calamitous? Calamities demand enquiry and description. Explanation is another matter. And yet, and yet, is any of these English historians as good as their great Polish contemporary, Jan Długosz?[50] It is sensible to end with a question and a comparison: cultural history is nothing other than questions, comparisons, contrasts.

List of Abbreviations

Add MS	British Library, Additional Manuscripts
Arrivall	J. Bruce (ed.), *Historie of the Arrivall of Edward IV in England* (Camden Society, old series, I, 1838)
BIHR	*Bulletin of the Institute of Historical Research*
BJRL	*Bulletin of the John Rylands Library*
BL	British Library
Crowland	J. Cox and N. Pronay (eds), *Crowland Chronicle Continuations, 1459–86* (Richard III and Yorkist History Society Trust, 1986)
EcHR	*Economic History Review*
EETS	Early English Text Society
English Chronicle	J. S. Davies (ed.), *An English Chronicle of the Reigns of Richard II, Henry IV, Henry V and Henry VI* (Camden Society, old series, LXIV, 1856)
EHD	A. R. Myers (ed.), *English Historical Documents*, vol. IV: *1327–1485* (London: Eyre and Spottiswoode, 1969)
EHR	*English Historical Review*
Great Chronicle	A. H. Thomas and I. D. Thornley (eds), *The Great Chronicle of London* (London, 1938)
Gregory	'William Gregory's Chronicle', in J. Gairdner (ed.), *The Historical Collections of a Citizen of London* (Camden Society, second series, V, 1876)
HMC	Historic Manuscripts Commission
HR	*Historical Research*
JEccH	*Journal of Ecclesiastical History*

Mancini	Dominic Mancini, *The Usurpation of Richard III*, ed. C. A. J. Armstrong (Oxford, 2nd edn, 1969)
PL	N. Davis (ed.), *Paston Letters and Papers in the Fifteenth Century*, 2 vols (Oxford: Oxford University Press, 1971–6)
PP	*Past and Present*
Polydore Vergil	H. Ellis (ed.), *Three Books of Polydore Vergil's English History* (Camden Society, old series, XXIX, 1844)
PRO, SC	Public Record Office, Special Collections
PRO, KB	Public Record Office, King's Bench
RS	Rolls Series
Rot Parl	J. Strachey et al. (eds), *Rotuli Parliamentorum*, 6 vols (London, 1767–77)
TRHS	*Transactions of the Royal Historical Society*
VCH	Victoria Histories of the Counties of England
Warkworth	J. O. Halliwell (ed.), *A Chronicle of the First Thirteen Years of the Reign of King Edward the Fourth by John Warkworth* (Camden Society, old series, X, 1839)

Bibliography

1. INTRODUCTION

For modern, academic, introductory accounts of the wars, all available in paperback, see J. Gillingham, *The Wars of the Roses: Peace and Conflict in Fifteenth-Century England* (London: Weidenfeld and Nicolson, 1981); A. Goodman, *The Wars of the Roses: Military Activity and English Society, 1452–97* (London: Routledge, 1981); A. J. Pollard, *The Wars of the Roses* (London: Macmillan, 1988); C. D. Ross, *The Wars of the Roses: a Concise History* (London: Thames and Hudson, 1976). A new account by C. Carpenter is to be published shortly in the Cambridge Medieval Textbooks series.

The principal studies of individual reigns are, in chronological order: R. A. Griffiths, *The Reign of King Henry VI: The Exercise of Royal Authority, 1422–1461* (London: Benn, 1981); C. D. Ross, *Edward IV* (London: Eyre Methuen, 1974); C. D. Ross, *Richard III* (London: Eyre Methuen, 1981); R. A. Horrox, *Richard III: A Study of Service* (Cambridge: Cambridge University Press, 1989); and S. B. Chrimes, *Henry VII* (London: Methuen, 1972). A. J. Pollard, *Richard III and the Princes in the Tower* (Stroud: Alan Sutton, 1991) deals with what is still the most controversial aspect of the subject. M. K. Jones and M. G. Underwood, *The King's Mother: Lady Margaret Beaufort, Countess of Richmond and Derby* (Cambridge: Cambridge University Press, 1992) is an important study of an influential figure. I. Arthurson, *The Perkin Warbeck Conspiracy, 1491–99* (Stroud: Alan Sutton, 1994) offers a major re-assessment of this important conspiracy.

A useful introduction to late-medieval society is to be found in M. H. Keen, *English Society in the Later Middle Ages, 1348–1500* (London: Penguin, 1990). R. Virgoe, *Private Life in the Fifteenth Century* (London: Weidenfeld and Nicolson, 1989) provides a splendidly illustrated introduction to the Paston family, whose story can be followed in greater depth in Colin Richmond, *The Paston Family in the Fifteenth Century: The First Phase* (Cambridge: Cambridge University Press, 1990), the first of a three-volume history.

For recent discussion of Bastard Feudalism see: J. M. W. Bean, *From Lord to Patron: Lordship in Late Medieval England* (Manchester: Manchester University Press, 1989); J. G. Bellamy, *Bastard Feudalism and the Law* (London: Routledge, 1989); P. Coss, 'Bastard Feudalism Revised', *Past and Present*, 125 (November 1989); and M. A. Hicks, 'Bastard Feudalism: Society and Politics in Fifteenth-Century England', in *Richard III and His*

Rivals: Magnates and their Motives in the Wars of the Roses (London: Hambleton Press, 1991); and S. Walker, *The Lancastrian Affinity, 1361–1399* (Oxford: Clarendon Press, 1990).

Among recent regional and local studies are: E. Acheson, *A Gentry Community: Leicestershire in the Fifteenth Century* (Cambridge: Cambridge University Press, 1992); C. Carpenter, *Locality and Polity: A Study of Warwickshire Landed Society, 1401–1499* (Cambridge, 1992); P. C. Maddern, *Violence and Social Order: East Anglia, 1422–1442* (Oxford: Clarendon Press, 1992); C. E. Moreton, *The Townshends and their World: Gentry, Law and Land in Norfolk, c. 1450–1551* (Oxford: Clarendon Press, 1992); S. J. Payling, *Political Society in Lancastrian England: The Greater Gentry of Nottinghamshire* (Oxford: Clarendon Press, 1991); and A. J. Pollard, *North-Eastern England during the Wars of the Roses: Lay Society, War and Politics, 1450–1500* (Oxford: Clarendon Press, 1990).

For the recent debate on politics and principle, see Chapter 6 of this book, by Dr Watts.

The history of the British Isles in the fifteenth century is yet to be written. The earlier centuries are surveyed in R. Frame, *The Political Development of the British Isles, 1100–1400* (Oxford: Oxford University Press, 1990). Medieval British history is also the theme of Professor R. R. Davies in his presidential addresses to the Royal Historical Society, which will be published in its *Transactions*, 1994–7.

2. THE SOURCES

For general background, the best collection of primary source material for the Wars of the Roses is still A. R. Myers (ed.), *English Historical Documents, IV, 1327–1485* (London: Eyre & Spottiswoode, 1969). There are longer extracts in J. R. Lander, *The Wars of the Roses* (2nd edn, Stroud: Alan Sutton, 1992). For source material on Richard III, see also P. W. Hammond and A. F. Sutton (eds), *Richard III: The Road to Bosworth Field* (London: Constable, 1985), which is comprehensive; A. Hanham, *Richard III and his Early Historians* (Oxford: Oxford University Press, 1975), which is authoritative; and K. Dockray, *Richard III: A Reader* (Stroud: Alan Sutton, 1988), which is particularly well-organised.

There are many useful essays discussing particular sources in J. R. Lander, *Crown and Nobility, 1450–1509* (London: Arnold, 1976); R. A. Griffiths, *King and Country* (London and Rio Grande: Hambledon, 1991); M. A. Hicks, *Richard III and His Rivals* (London and Rio Grande: Hambledon, 1991); and A. R. Myers, *Crown, Household and Parliament in the Fifteenth Century* (London and Rio Grande: Hambledon, 1985).

The following concentrate on battles. For First St Albans, see C. A. J. Armstrong, *England, France, and Burgundy in the Fifteenth Century* (London and Rio Grande: Hambledon, 1983), ch. 1, which prints the (French) Fastolf and Dijon Relations. For Barnet and Tewkesbury, see *Arrivall*, and P. W. Hammond, *The Battles of Barnet and Tewkesbury* (Gloucester: Alan Sutton, 1990). For Bosworth, see especially M. Bennett, *The Battle of*

Bosworth (Gloucester: Alan Sutton, 1985); C. Richmond, 'Bosworth Field and All That', *Richard III: Loyalty, Lordship and Law* (Gloucester: Alan Sutton, 1986); P. J. Foss, *The Field of Redemore* (Leeds: Rosalba Press, 1990).

For narratives, the fullest discussions of the chronicles are in Antonia Gransden, *Historical Writing in England from 1307, ii c. 1307 – the Early Sixteenth Century* (London: Routledge, 1986); A. Hanham, *Richard III and his early historians* (Oxford: Oxford University Press, 1975), and C. L. Kingsford, *English Historical Literature in the Fifteenth Century* (Oxford: Oxford University Press, 1913).

Most chronicles are readily available only as extracts in source collections listed above or in occasional reprints of ancient editions. The Arrivall, Warkworth's Chronicle and the Chronicle of the Lincolnshire Rebellion, for instance, are reprinted in K. Dockray (ed.), *Three Chronicles of the Reign of Edward IV* (Gloucester: Alan Sutton, 1988). The following are in print and recommended: N. Pronay and J. C. Cox (eds), *The Crowland Chronicle Continuations: 1459–86* (Gloucester: Richard III and Yorkist History Trust, 1986); G. L. and M. A. Harriss (eds), 'John Benet's Chronicle for the Years 1400 to 1462', in *Camden Miscellany* XXIV (London: Camden, 1972); D. Mancini, *The Usurpation of Richard III*, ed. C. A. J. Armstrong (2nd edn, Gloucester: Alan Sutton, 1984); T. More, *History of King Richard III*, ed. R. Sylvester (Newhaven: Yale University Press, 1963); D. Hay (ed.), *The Anglica Historica of Polydore Vergil* (London: Camden, 3rd ser. LXXIV, 1950); P. W. Hammond and A. F. Sutton (eds), *The Coronation of Richard III* (Gloucester: Richard III and Yorkist History Trust, 1983); P. de Commynes, *Memoirs*, ed. M. Jones (London: Penguin, 1972). For a recent discovery, see R. F. Green, 'Historical Notes of a London Citizen, 1483–88', *EHR* XCVI (1981). Some manifestoes are reprinted in I. M. W. Harvey, *Jack Cade's Rebellion of 1450* (Oxford: Oxford University Press, 1991).

On national records, the best modern discussion of central government and its records is A. L. Brown, *The Governance of England in the Later Middle Ages, 1272–1485* (London: Edward Arnold, 1989). The parliament rolls were published in the eighteenth century and the patent, close, and fine rolls before the Second World War. They are available in academic libraries but not on the open market. Other records are generally unpublished. Richard III's signet books are printed in R. E. Horrox and P. W. Hammond (eds), *British Library Harleian Manuscript 433*, 4 vols (Gloucester: Alan Sutton, 1979–83).

For local records, the best urban records are L. Attreed (ed.), *York House Books*, 2 vols (Gloucester: Richard III and Yorkist History Trust, 1991). Useful extracts are collected in Hammond and Sutton, *Richard III: The Road to Bosworth Field*. The most relevant letters are reprinted in the collections cited above: the best full editions are N. Davis (ed.), *Paston Letters and Papers of the 15th Century*, 2 vols (Oxford: Oxford University Press, 1971–6); C. L. Kingsford (ed.), *Stonor Letters and Papers of the 15th Century. 1290–1483*, 2 vols (Camden 3rd ser., XXIX, XXX, 1919); A. Hanham (ed.), *The Cely Letters, 1472–88* (London: Early English Text Society, CCLXXIII, 1975). The most celebrated household accounts are reprinted in A. Crawford (ed.), *The Household Books of John Howard, Duke of Norfolk* (Stroud: Richard III and Yorkist History Trust, 1992).

For local government, see H. M. Jewell, *English Local Administration in the Middle Ages* (Newton Abbot: David and Charles, 1972).

3. THE ECONOMIC CONTEXT

The following four titles contain discussions relating to the whole of England in the mid-fifteenth century: J. L. Bolton, *The Medieval English Economy, 1150–1500* (London: J. M. Dent and Sons, 1980); C. Dyer, *Standards of Living in the Later Middle Ages* (Cambridge: Cambridge University Press, 1989); J. Hatcher, *Plague, Population and the English Economy, 1348–1530* (London: Macmillan, 1977); and E. Miller (ed.), *The Agrarian History of England and Wales, III: 1348–1500* (Cambridge: Cambridge University Press, 1991).

Much of the best work on the fifteenth-century economy is to be found in studies of particular regions or individual estates. The following studies are selected to represent different parts of England: M. Bailey, *A Marginal Economy: East Anglian Breckland in the Later Middle Ages* (Cambridge: Cambridge University Press, 1989); C. Dyer, *Lords and Peasants in a Changing Society: The Estates of the Bishopric of Worcester, 680–1540* (Cambridge: Cambridge University Press, 1980); J. Hatcher, *Rural Economy and Society in the Duchy of Cornwall, 1300–1500* (Cambridge: Cambridge University Press, 1970); B. F. Harvey, *Westminster Abbey and its Estates in the Middle Ages* (Oxford: Oxford University Press, 1977); and A. J. Pollard, *North-Eastern England during the Wars of the Roses* (Oxford: Oxford University Press, 1990).

For discussion of England's overseas trade in this period, the following titles are particularly useful: J. H. Munro, *Wool, Cloth and Gold: The Struggle for Bullion in Anglo-Burgundian Trade, 1340–1478* (Toronto: University of Toronto Press, 1972); and E. Power and M. M. Postan (eds), *Studies in English Trade in the Fifteenth Century* (London: Routledge and Kegan Paul, 1933, reissued 1966). Though old, this volume has not been replaced as a survey of fifteenth-century overseas trade.

4. THE ORIGINS OF THE WARS OF THE ROSES

Valuable selections from the main primary sources relevant to the origins of the Wars of the Roses can be found in: A. R. Myers (ed.), *English Historical Documents, 1307–1485* (London: Eyre and Spottiswoode, 1969); B. Wilkinson, *Constitutional History of England in the Fifteenth Century* (London: Longman, 1964); J. R. Lander, *The Wars of the Roses* (London: Secker and Warburg, 1965). The most important contemporary narrative of the 1450s, albeit firmly pro-Yorkist, is: J. S. Davies (ed.), *An English*

Chronicle of the Reigns of Richard II, Henry IV, Henry V and Henry VI (London: Camden Society, 1856). The early Tudor, and indirectly Lancastrian, perspective can be found in: H. Ellis (ed.), *Three Books of Polydore Vergil's English History* (London: Camden Society, 1844). Informative newsletters, and evidence of the lawlessness of the times, frequently appear in: J. Gairdner (ed.), *The Paston Letters* (Gloucester: Alan Sutton, 1983).

Among recent secondary works containing much of importance on the origins of the Wars of the Roses, K. B. McFarlane, 'The Wars of the Roses', *Proceedings of the British Academy*, L(1964) reprinted in *England in the Fifteenth Century* (London: Hambledon Press, 1981), pp. 231–61; and R. L. Storey, *The End of the House of Lancaster* (originally published 1966; 2nd edn, Gloucester: Alan Sutton, 1986), have now achieved the status of modern classics in the field. The best textbook on the political history of later medieval England, containing helpful discussion of both long-term trends and the more immediate issues at stake in the wars, is M. Keen, *England in the Later Middle Ages* (London: Methuen, 1973).

Specific, and stimulating, coverage of the origins of the wars is provided by C. Ross, *The Wars of the Roses* (London: Thames and Hudson, 1976) and A. J. Pollard, *The Wars of the Roses* (London: Macmillan, 1988). R. A. Griffiths, *The Reign of King Henry VI* (London: Ernest Benn, 1981) is exhaustive on politics, government and society 1422–61; B. P. Wolffe, *Henry VI* (London: Eyre Methuen, 1981), working independently on the same subject at the same time, is less comprehensive in coverage but more provocative in interpretation. Lively thumb-nail sketches of a number of leading participants in the Wars of the Roses are contained in M. Hicks, *Who's Who in Later Medieval England* (London: Shepheard-Walwyn, 1991).

Specialist books and articles of particular value for the origins of the Wars of the Roses include: M. Aston, 'Richard II and the Wars of the Roses', in C. M. Barron and F. R. H. Du Boulay (eds), *The Reign of Richard II* (London: Athlone Press, 1971), pp. 280–317; R. A. Griffiths, 'Duke Richard of York's Intentions in 1450 and the Origins of the Wars of the Roses' and 'The Sense of Dynasty in the Reign of Henry VI', in *King and Country: England and Wales in the Fifteenth Century* (London: Hambledon Press, 1991), pp. 83–101, 277–304; P. A. Johnson, *Duke Richard of York, 1411–1460* (Oxford: Clarendon Press, 1988); M. K. Jones, 'Somerset, York and the Wars of the Roses', *EHR*, XIV (1989), 285–307; P-A. Lee, 'Reflections of Power: Margaret of Anjou and the Dark Side of Queenship', *Renaissance Quarterly*, XXXIX(1986), 183–217; A. J. Pollard, *North-Eastern England during the Wars of the Roses* (Oxford: Clarendon Press, 1990).

5. PERSONALITIES AND POLITICS

Christine Carpenter, *Locality and Polity: A Study of Warwickshire Landed Society, 1401–1499* (Cambridge: Cambridge University Press, 1992);

Michael Hicks, 'Idealism in Late Medieval English Politics', in M. Hicks, *Richard III and his Rivals: Magnates and their Motives in the Wars of the Roses* (London: Hambledon Press, 1991), Ch. 2, pp. 41–60; Philippa C. Maddern, *Violence and Social Order: East Anglia 1422–1442* (Oxford: Clarendon Press, 1992) and 'Honour among the Pastons: Gender and Integrity in Fifteenth-century English Provincial Society', *Journal of Medieval History*, XIV (1988), 357–71; E. Powell, 'Law and Justice', in R. Horrox (ed.), *Fifteenth-century Attitudes: Perceptions of Society in Late Medieval England* (Cambridge: Cambridge University Press, 1994), Ch. 2, pp. 29–41; and Colin Richmond, *The Paston Family in the Fifteenth Century: The First Phase* (Cambridge: Cambridge University Press, 1990).

6. IDEAS, PRINCIPLES AND POLITICS

Political historians have, in recent years, become much more interested in political ideas and principles. The historiographical background to this development is discussed in E. Powell, *Kingship, Law and Society: Criminal Justice in the Reign of Henry V* (Oxford: Oxford University Press, 1989), pp. 1–9, and C. Carpenter, *Locality and Polity: a Study of Warwickshire Landed Society, 1401–99* (Cambridge: Cambridge University Press, 1992), pp. 1–9. In both these works, there is a sustained attempt to draw on the evidence of political ideas and assumptions to provide a framework for the analysis of politics: Powell focuses on the themes of law and justice; Carpenter looks at the attitudes of landowners, especially the gentry, to a broader range of issues, including crime, lineage, lordship and governance. My own forthcoming book, *The Rule of England in the Time of Henry VI* (Cambridge: Cambridge University Press), will explore the effect of contemporary ideas about government on the politics of the 1430s, 1440s and 1450s. Other full-length studies of fifteenth-century national politics which draw attention to ideological features include R. Horrox, *Richard III: A Study of Service* (Cambridge: Cambridge University Press, 1989) and G. L. Harriss (ed.), *Henry V: the Practice of Kingship* (Oxford: Oxford University Press, 1985). In addition, a number of articles discuss the role of particular codes of ideas in specific episodes during the period: M. K. Jones, 'Somerset, York and the Wars of the Roses', *EHR*, CIV (1984), 285–307, and D. A. L. Morgan, 'From a Death to a View: Louis Robessart, Johan Huizinga, and the Political Significance of Chivalry', in S. Anglo (ed.), *Chivalry and the Renaissance* (Woodbridge: Boydell, 1990), pp. 93–106, look at chivalric influences; M. Hicks, 'Idealism in Late Medieval English Politics', in M. Hicks, *Richard III and His Rivals* (London: Hambledon, 1991), pp. 41–59, explores the roles of chivalry, piety and loyalty; J. L. Watts, '*De Consulatu Stiliconis*: Texts and Politics in the Reign of Henry VI', *Journal of Medieval History*, XVI (1990), 251–66, considers the possible impact of a particular text on Richard of York. Finally, D. Starkey, 'Which Age of Reform?', in D. Starkey and C. Coleman (eds), *Revolution Reassessed* (Oxford: Oxford University Press, 1986), pp. 13–27, explores the relationship between the ideas of Sir John

Fortescue, the language of common weal and the reformist activities of kings and magnates during the period of the Wars.

A brief introduction to Quentin Skinner's views on how political ideas ought to be approached by historians appears in Q. Skinner, *The Foundations of Modern Political Thought*, 2 vols (Cambridge: Cambridge University Press, 1978), I, pp. ix–xv. The points made in the text about the political impact of publicly-expressed ideas are mostly drawn from Skinner's article 'The Principles and Practice of Opposition: The Case of Bolingbroke *vs* Walpole', in N. McKendrick (ed.), *Historical Perspectives: Studies in English Thought and Society* (London: Europa, 1974), pp. 93–128. A very good short treatment of later medieval political thinking on the issues covered in my chapter is J. Dunbabin, 'Government', in J. H. Burns (ed.), *Cambridge History of Medieval Political Thought* (Cambridge: Cambridge University Press, 1988), ch. 16, though see also S. B. Chrimes, *English Constitutional Ideas in the Fifteenth Century* (Cambridge: Cambridge University Press, 1936), ch. 1. For useful comment on Fortescue, see Chrimes, *Constitutional Ideas*, ch. 4; J. H. Burns, *Lordship, Kingship and Empire: The Idea of Monarchy, 1400–1525* (Oxford: Oxford University Press, 1992), pp. 58–70; C. A. J. Skeel, 'The Influence of the Writings of Sir John Fortescue', *TRHS*, 3rd ser., x (1916), 77–114. Additionally, David Starkey has some interesting things to say about Fortescue and other theorists of the period in his chapter called 'England', in R. Porter and M. Teich, *The Renaissance in National Context* (Cambridge: Cambridge University Press, 1992), ch. 8.

Not many of the primary sources for the ideas of this period are available in modern English translation, although a new edition of *The Governance of England* is currently in preparation (ed. S. C. Lockwood; publ. Cambridge University Press) and several of the tracts and manifestoes mentioned in the text appear in B. Wilkinson, *The Constitutional History of England in the Fifteenth Century* (London: Longmans, 1964), chs 2 and 3. For editions of the originals, see C. Plummer (ed.), *The Governance of England ... by Sir John Fortescue, knight* (Oxford: Oxford University Press, 1885); M. Kekewich (ed.), *John Vale's Book* (forthcoming, Richard III and Yorkist History Trust) for many of the manifestoes; and, for the 'Somnium Vigilantis', J. P. Gilson, 'A Defence of the Proscription of the Yorkists in 1459', *EHR*, xxvi (1911), 512–25.

7. THE CHURCH AND THE WARS OF THE ROSES

For bibliographies of the considerable recent primary and secondary literature on the Church in the fifteenth century, with major overviews, see (e.g.) R. N. Swanson, *Church and Society in Late Medieval England* (revised edn, Oxford: Oxford University Press, 1992); R. N. Swanson, *Catholic England* (Manchester: Manchester University Press, 1993); E. Duffy, *The Stripping of the Altars* (New Haven and London: Yale University Press, 1992); P. Heath, 'Between Reform and Reformation', *JEcc.H*, 41

(1990), 647–78; P. Heath, *Church and Realm, 1272–1461* (London: Collins, 1988); R. Hutton, *The Rise and Fall of Merry England* (Oxford: Oxford Unversity Press, 1994); M. M. Harvey, *England, Rome and the Papacy 1417–1464* (Manchester: Manchester University Press, 1993). The International Medieval Bibliography project and the Royal Historical Society both intend exhaustive CD-Rom and printed bibliographies in the near future.

8. THE WARS OF THE ROSES IN EUROPEAN CONTEXT

There is little direct discussion of the theme of this chapter in other works. The best introduction to the question of how to characterise relations between princes, of the various forms of political entities, of to what extent and in what circumstances it is useful to talk about 'states', is in Bernard Guenée, *States and Rulers in later Medieval Europe* (Eng. transl.; Oxford: Blackwell, 1985). I have also found useful E. J. Hobsbawm, *Nations and Nationalism since 1780* (Cambridge: Cambridge University Press, Canto edn, 1991).

For the most part events have to be pieced together from the standard accounts, listed in the notes to my chapter. The international context does get unusual prominence in John Gillingham (ed.), *Richard III: A Medieval Kingship* (London: Collins and Brown, 1993), especially the essays by the editor, by Michael K. Jones, and by Alexander Grant. The Franco-Burgundian context is best studied in Richard Vaughan, *Valois Burgundy* (London: Allen Lane, 1977), and in Emmanuel le Roy Ladurie, *The French Royal State, 1460–1610* (Eng. transl.; Oxford: Blackwell, 1994). A counter to the tendency to see 'Burgundy' from a French angle is provided by Walter Prevenier and Wim Blockmans, *The Burgundian Netherlands* (Eng. transl.; Cambridge: Cambridge University Press, 1986). The pioneering and detailed articles by C. A. J. Armstrong, collected as *England, France and Burgundy in the Fifteenth Century* (London: Hambledon Press, 1983), are invaluable. David Potter, *War and Government in the French Provinces: Picardy, 1470–1560* (Cambridge: Cambridge University Press, 1993) deals at length with the Franco-Netherlands border. For naval aspects, see Colin Richmond, 'English Naval Power in the Fifteenth Century', *History*, 52 (1967), 1–15, and the early chapters of David Loades *The Tudor Navy* (Aldershot: Scolar Press, 1992). Philippe de Commynes, *Memoirs: The Reign of Louis XI* (Eng. transl., and ed., Michael Jones, London, 1972; Harmondsworth: Penguin Classics, 1992), provides an insider's view of diplomacy.

9. THE VISUAL CULTURE OF FIFTEENTH-CENTURY ENGLAND

The work which I have found either useful or stimulating or both is cited in the footnotes. General surveys of fifteenth-century English culture seem to be rare. E. F. Jacob, *The Fifteenth Century, 1399–1485* (Oxford: Oxford University Press, 1961), chapter XIV, 'The Peaceful Arts', is still a good starting point, even if one of its sub-headings, 'Pattershall and Ockwell', is a little off-putting until one realises Tattershall and Ockwells are the houses meant. I have always thought J. R. Lander, *Conflict and Stability in Fifteenth-Century England* (London: Hutchinson, 1966), chapter 6, 'Education and the Arts', to be that book's best chapter. The many books of Colin Platt on the art, architecture and archaeology of the English later Middle Ages are informative. Richard Morris, *Churches in the Landscape* (London: Dent, 1989), is original and rewarding. There are good introductory essays in Nigel Saul (ed.), *Age of Chivalry: Art and Society in Late Medieval England* (London: Collins and Brown, 1992); this is a 'History Today Book': it serves to remind us that *History Today* is the first journal to turn to for recent scholarship on aspects of late Medieval England. The cultural conference held annually at Harlaxton in Lincolnshire has produced two volumes on the fifteenth century: Daniel William (ed.), *England in the Fifteenth Century: Proceedings of the 1986 Harlaxton Conference* (Woodbridge: Boydell and Brewer, 1987) and Nicholas Rogers (ed.), *England in the Fourteenth Century: Harlaxton Medieval Studies III* (Stanford: Paul Watkins Publishing, 1993). On specific topics, Francis Cheetham, *English Medieval Alabasters* (London: Phaidon, 1984), and Richard Marks, *Stained Glass in England during the Middle Ages* (London: Routledge, 1993), are to be highly recommended.

Mr Brian Spencer's remarkable work on pilgrim badges needs also to be mentioned: *King Henry of Windsor and the London Pilgrim* (The Museum of London, 1978); *Medieval Pilgrim Badges from Norfolk* (Norfolk Museums Service, 1980); *Pilgrim Souvenirs and Secular Badges. Salisbury Museum Medieval Catalogue, Part 2* (Salisbury, 1990).

Notes and References

The place of publication is London unless otherwise stated.

1. INTRODUCTION *A. J. Pollard*

1. W. C. Sellar and R. J. Yeatman, *1066 and All That*, 2nd edn (1975), p. 54; M. E. Aston, 'Richard II and the Wars of the Roses', in F. R. H. Du Boulay and C. M. Barron (eds), *The Reign of Richard II* (1971), pp. 282–3.

2. A. J. Pollard, *The Wars of the Roses* (1988), pp. 74–85.

3. W. Lamont, *The Tudors and Stuarts* (1976), pp. 14–15.

4. A. Goodman, *The Wars of the Roses: Military Activity and English Society, 1452–97* (1981); C. D. Ross, *The Wars of the Roses* (1976), pp. 109–50; H. Summerson, *Medieval Carlisle*, 2 vols (Cumberland and Westmorland Antiquarian and Archaeological Society, Extra Series, XXV, 1993), vol. II, pp. 446–8.

5. See also R. A. Griffiths, 'The Sense of Dynasty in the Reign of Henry VI', in C. D. Ross (ed.), *Patronage, Pedigree and Power in Later Medieval England* (Gloucester, 1979), pp. 23–5; and R. B. Pugh, *Henry V and the Southampton Plot* (Gloucester, 1988), pp. 134–5, who argues that 'there can be little doubt that he had long regarded himself the rightful king of England'.

6. W. E. Hampton, 'The White Rose under the First Tudors, Part 3. Richard De La Pole, "The king's Dreaded Enemy" ', *The Ricardian*, VII 99 (December 1987), 525–40.

7. See, for instance, the discussions in R. E. Horrox, *Richard III: a Study of Service* (Cambridge, 1989), pp. 89–104, 327–8; A. J. Pollard, *Richard III and the Princes in the Tower* (Stroud, 1991), pp. 83–5, 97–9, 103–6; C. D. Ross, *Edward IV* (1974), pp. 424–5.

8. K. B. McFarlane, 'The Wars of the Roses', *Proceedings of the British Academy*, L (1964), 95–6.

9. Pollard, *Wars of Roses*, 49–50, summarises the more negative assessment; W. M. Ormrod, *The Reign of Edward III* (Newhaven, 1990) accentuates the positive.

10. See, for instance, P. R. Coss, 'Bastard Feudalism Revised', *PP*, 125 (November 1989), 27–64; G. L. Harriss, 'Political Society and the Growth of Government in Late-medieval England', *PP*, 138 (February 1993), 28–57; R. W. Kaeuper, *War, Justice and Public Order: England and*

France in the Later Middle Ages (Oxford, 1988), esp. pp. 267–8; J. R. Lander, *The Limitations of English Monarchy in the Later Middle Ages* (Toronto, 1989).

11. Coss, 'Bastard Feudalism', 30–54; S. Walker, *The Lancastrian Affinity, 1361–1399* (Oxford, 1990).

12. A. J. Pollard, *North-Eastern England During the Wars of the Roses* (Oxford, 1990), 121–43, 323–4; Horrox, *Richard III*, 39–61; P. A. Johnson, *Duke Richard of York, 1411–1460* (Oxford, 1988), pp. 15–21.

13. M. A. Hicks, 'Lord Hastings' Indentured Retainers?', in *Richard III and His Rivals: Magnates and their Motives in the Wars of the Roses* (1991), pp. 229–47; Pollard, *North-Eastern England*, 125; T. B. Pugh, 'The Magnates, Knights and Gentry', in S. B. Chrimes et al. (eds), *Fifteenth-Century England* (Manchester, 1974), pp. 101–5.

14. M. A. Hicks, 'Bastard Feudalism', in *Richard III and His Rivals*, 1–40; R. E. Horrox, 'Local and National Politics in Fifteenth-Century England', *Journal of Medieval History*, 18 (1992), 391–2.

15. See the Bibliography.

16. Harriss, 'Political Society', 32.

17. Coss, 'Bastard Feudalism', 57.

18. For County Communities in the fourteenth century see J. R. Maddicott, 'The County Community and the making of Public Opinion in Fourteenth-Century England', *TRHS*, 5th series, XXVIII (1978); 'Parliament and the Constituencies, 1272–1377', in R. Davies and J. H. Denton (eds), *The English Parliament in the Middle Ages* (Manchester, 1981). For the fifteenth century see R. Virgoe, 'Aspects of the County Community in the Fifteenth Century', in M. A. Hicks (ed.), *Profit, Piety and the Professions in Later Medieval England* (Gloucester, 1990), pp. 1–13.

19. See, for example, E. Acheson, *A Gentry Community: Leicestershire in the Fifteenth Century, c. 1422–c. 1485* (Cambridge, 1992); S. J. Payling, *Political Society in Lancastrian England: the Greater Gentry of Nottinghamshire* (Oxford, 1991). For a recent refutation of the concept of 'county community', published after this passage was written, see C. Carpenter, 'Gentry and Community in Medieval England', *Journal of British Studies*, 33 (October 1994), 340–80.

20. C. Carpenter, *Locality and Polity: A Study of Warwickshire Landed Society, 1401–1499* (Oxford, 1992), pp. 399–486; R. A. Griffiths, *The Reign of King Henry VI* (1981), pp. 584–92; M. Cherry, 'The Courtenay Earls of Devon: The Formation and Disintegration of a Later Medieval Aristocratic Affinity', *Southern History*, 1 (1979), 71–97, and 'The Struggle for Power in Mid-Fifteenth Century Devonshire', in R. A. Griffiths (ed.), *Patronage, the Crown and the Provinces in Later Medieval England* (Gloucester, 1981), pp. 123–44.

21. Pollard, *North-Eastern England*, 125–43.

22. Ibid., 245–84; A. J. Pollard, *John Talbot and the War in France* (1983), pp. 131–3; S. J. Payling, 'The Ampthill Dispute: a Study in Aristocratic Lawlessness and the Breakdown of Lancastrian Government', *EHR*, CIV (1989), 881–907.

23. C. Given-Wilson, *The Royal Household and the King's Affinity: Service, Politics and Finance in England, 1360–1413* (Newhaven, 1986); A. J. Pollard, 'The Parliamentary Class of 1399', *The Ricardian*, IX 123 (1973), 502–3.

24. H. Castor, 'The Duchy of Lancaster and the Rule of East Anglia, 1399–1440', forthcoming in R. Archer (ed.), *Politics, Society and Religion: Essays in Later Medieval History* (Stroud); Pollard, *North-Eastern England*, 249–54; Griffiths, *Reign of Henry VI*, 574–77, and Cherry, 'Struggle for Power'. Dr Castor offers a more favourable interpretation of Suffolk's career than most historians.

25. Griffiths, *Reign of Henry VI*, 443–54; G. L. Harriss, *Cardinal Beaufort: A Study of Lancastrian Ascendancy and Decline* (Oxford, 1988), pp. 292–305.

26. E. Powell, *Kingship, Law and Society: Criminal Justice in the Reign of Henry VI* (Oxford, 1989), pp. 1–6, and 'After "After McFarlane": The Poverty of Patronage and the Case for Constitutional History', in D. J. Clayton et al. (eds), *Trade, Devotion and Governance* (Stroud, 1994), pp. 1–16.

27. Carpenter, *Locality and Polity*, 5–9.

28. M. A. Hicks, 'Idealism in late-medieval English politics', *Richard III and his Rivals*, 41–60; M. K. Jones, 'Somerset, York, and the Wars of the Roses', *EHR*, CIV (1984), 285–307; and D. A. L. Morgan, 'From a Death to a View; Louis Robessart, Johan Huizinga and the Political Significance of Chivalry', in S. Anglo (ed.), *Chivalry and the Renaissance* (Woodbridge, 1990).

29. I am grateful to Dr Jones for allowing me to draw upon his ideas in this and the following paragraph.

30. M. A. Hicks, 'Edward IV, the Duke of Somerset and Lancastrian Loyalism in the North', *Northern History*, XX (1984), 23–37; Pollard, *North-Eastern England*, 298–300. For a thoughtful discussion of the ritualised nature of violence see P. C. Maddern, *Violence and Social Order: East Anglia, 1422–1442* (Oxford, 1992).

31. See P. F. C. Field, *The Life and Times of Sir Thomas Malory* (Woodbridge, 1994), passim.

32. R. A. Griffiths and R. S. Thomas, *The Making of the Tudor Dynasty* (Gloucester, 1985), pp. 47–73; G. Williams, *Recovery, Reorientation and Reformation: Wales, c. 1415–1642* (Oxford, 1987), pp. 185–242.

33. S. G. Ellis, *Tudor Ireland: Crown, Community and the Conflict of Cultures, 1470–1603* (1985), pp. 53–84; A. Cosgrove (ed.), *A New History of Ireland*, vol. II, *Medieval Ireland, 1169–1534* (Oxford, 1986), pp. 557–69, 591–619, 638–47. See also p. 673 for Irish involvement in the last Yorkist plot of 1524–5.

34. For an excellent exploration of the international scene as it affected England in the 1490s, see I. Arthurson, *The Perkin Warbeck Conspiracy, 1491–1499* (Stroud, 1994).

35. Ross, *Wars of the Roses*, 176.

36. See C. L. Kingsford, 'Social Life and the Wars of the Roses', in *Prejudice and Promise in Fifteenth-century England* (Oxford, 1925), pp. 48–77; J. R. Lander, 'The Wars of the Roses', in *Crown and Nobility, 1450–1509* (1976), pp. 57–73; Ross, *Wars of the Roses*, 151–76.

2. THE SOURCES   *M. A. Hicks*

1. C. A. J. Armstrong, 'Politics and the Battle of St Albans, 1455', *England, France and Burgundy in the Fifteenth Century* (1981), 1. This paragraph is based on ibid., 1–72.

2. M. K. Jones, 'Somerset, York and the Wars of the Roses', *EHR*, CIV (1989).

3. J. A. F. Thomson, '"The Arrivall of Edward IV": The Development of the Text', *Speculum*, XLVI (1971), 84–93, esp. 91–2; *Arrivall*, 13–14, 31, 38.

4. *Warkworth*, 18–19; 'John Benet's Chronicle, 1400–62', ed. G. L. and M. A. Harriss, *Camden Miscellany*, XXIV (1972), 233; C. L. Kingsford, *English Historical Literature in the Fifteenth Century* (Oxford, 1913), pp. 377–8; C. D. Ross, 'Some "Servants and Lovers" of Richard III in his Youth', *The Ricardian* IV (1976), 2–4; W. H. Dunham, *Lord Hastings' Indentured Retainers* (Transactions of Connecticut Academy of Arts and Sciences, XXXIX, 1955), 25; C. F. Richmond, 'Fauconberg's Kentish Rising of May 1471', *EHR*, LXXXV (1970), 683–6; PRO, KB 9/41/38.

5. P. J. Foss, *The Field of Redemore* (Leeds, 1990), pp. 18–20 and pl. 1. For what follows, see M. Bennett, *The Battle of Bosworth* (Gloucester, 1985); C. F. Richmond, 'The Battle of Bosworth', *History Today*, 35 (1985); C. D. Ross, *Richard III* (1981), pp. 217–20; and sources there cited.

6. A. Goodman and A. Mackay, 'A Castilian Report on English Affairs, 1486', *EHR*, LXXXVIII (1973), 92–9.

7. As suggested by C. F. Richmond, '1485 and All That', in P. W. Hammond (ed.), *Richard III: Loyalty, Lordship and Law* (Gloucester, 1985), p. 179.

8. A. Grant, 'Foreign Affairs under Richard III', in J. Gillingham (ed.), *Richard III: A Medieval Kingship* (1993), pp. 127–30.

9. Armstrong, 'St Albans', 1.

10. As suggested by A. Hanham, *Richard III and his Earlier Historians, 1483–1535* (Oxford, 1975), p. 135.

11. *Crowland*, 78–101; H. A. Kelly, 'The Last Chroniclers of Crowland', *The Ricardian*, VII (1985), 142–77.

12. M. A. Hicks, *Richard III: The Man Behind the Myth* (1991), p. 79.

13. *Polydore Vergil*, 167. Dr M. K. Jones has identified points even earlier for which Vergil is a primary source. For Gregory, see A. Gransden, *Historical Writing in England*, II, c. *1307–the Early Sixteenth Century* (1986), pp. 230–1.

14. M. A. Hicks, *Richard III and his Rivals* (1991), ch. 23. For what follows about Warkworth, see J. R. Lander, *Crown and Nobility, 1450–1509* (1976), p. 253.

15. Hanham, *Richard III*, 104–7; but see Hicks, *Man*, 153.

16. R. Lovatt, 'John Blacman Revisited: A Collector of Apocryphal Anecdotes', in A. J. Pollard (ed.), *Property and Politics: Essays in Later Medieval English History* (Gloucester, 1984).

17. K. B. McFarlane, *England in the Fifteenth Century* (1981), pp. 209–10; Lander, *Crown and Nobility*, 110n.; C. F. Richmond, '1483: The Year of

Decision', in Gillingham, *Richard III*, 40; see also A. R. Myers, *Crown, Household and Parliament in 15th-Century England* (London, 1985), ch. 12.

18. For what follows, see A. J. Pollard, 'North, South and Richard III', *The Ricardian*, 74 (1982), 384–9.

19. J. G. Nichols (ed.), 'Chronicle of the Rebellion in Lincolnshire, 1470' (Camden Miscellany, I, 1847). For the next sentence, see Thomson, 'Arrivall', 84, 86, 91–3.

20. Hicks, *Man*, 84–5, 146 ff. 151.

21. E.g. B. P. Wolffe, 'Hastings Reinterred', *EHR*, XCI (1976), 813–24; C. H. D. Coleman, 'The Execution of Hastings: A Neglected Source', *BIHR*, LIII (1980).

22. M. A. Hicks, *False, Fleeting, Perjur'd Clarence* (rev. edn, Bangor, 1992), ch. 3; J. Gairdner (ed.), *The Paston Letters*, 6 vols (1906), II, pp. 297; C. L. Kingsford (ed.), *Stonor Letters and Papers, 1290–1483*, 2 vols (Camden, third series, XXIX, XXX, 1919), II, p. 161.

23. B. P. Wolffe, *The Crown Lands, 1471–1536* (1971), p. 102.

24. E.g. Ross, *Richard III*, 75; Hicks, *Man*, 91, 99, 104 etc.

25. W. H. Dunham (ed.), *The Fane Fragment of the 1461 Lords Journal* (New Haven, Conn., 1935).

26. Lander, *Crown and Nobility*, 138, 139n. For what follows, see Hicks, *Clarence*, 108–10.

27. E. g. M. A. Hicks, 'The 1468 Statute of Livery', *HR* LXIV (1991); Lander, *Crown and Nobility*, ch. 9; R. A. Griffiths, *King and Country* (1991), ch. 21; Hicks, *Rivals*, chs 8, 13; Hicks, *Clarence*, ch. 4.

28. Lander, *Crown and Nobility*, Ch. 5; B. P. Wolffe, 'Acts of Resumption in the Lancastrian Parliaments, 1399–1456', *EHR*, LXXIII (1958); Hicks, *Rivals*, ch. 3.

29. N. Pronay and J. Taylor (eds), *Parliamentary Texts of the Later Middle Ages* (Oxford, 1980), p. 188.

30. E.g. G. L. Harriss, 'Fictitious Loans', *EcHR*, 2nd ser. VII (1955); 'Preference at the Medieval Exchequer', *BIHR*, XXX (1957); 'Marmaduke Lumley and the Exchequer Crisis of 1446–9', in J. G. Rowe (ed.), *Aspects of Late Medieval Government and Society* (Toronto, 1986); L. Clark, 'The Benefits and Burdens of Office: Henry Bourgchier (1408–83), Viscount Bourgchier and Earl of Essex, and the Treasureship of the Exchequer', in M. A. Hicks (ed.), *Profit, Piety and the Professions* (Gloucester, 1990); B. P. Wolffe, 'The Management of English Royal Estates under the Yorkist Kings', *EHR*, LXXI (1956).

31. E.g. Hicks, *Clarence*, 136–7.

32. Griffiths, *King and Country*, ch. 19.

33. R. E. Horrox, 'Financial Memoranda of the Reign of Edward V', *Camden Miscellany*, XXIX (Camden 4th ser., XXXIV, 1987).

34. R. E. Horrox, *Richard III: A Study of Service* (Cambridge, 1989); I. Arthurson and N. Kingwell, 'The Proclamation of Henry Tudor as King of England, 3 November 1483', *HR*, LXIII (1990); J. A. F. Thomson, 'Bishop Lionel Wydeville and Richard III', *BIHR*, LXIX (1986).

35. E.g. R. Benson and H. Hatcher, *Old and New Sarum, 1443–1702* (London, 1843); *VCH, Yorks. East Riding*, I (1969), p. 345. For what follows, see L. Attreed, *York House Books, 1460–90*, 2 vols (Gloucester, 1991).

36. Kingsford (ed.), *Stonor Letters*; A. Hanham (ed.), *The Cely Letters* (EETS, CCLXXIII, 1975); C. F. Richmond, *The Paston Family in the Fifteenth Century: The First Phase* (Cambridge, 1990). For what follows, see Kingsford, *Stonor Letters*, II, 159–61.

37. A. Hanham, *The Celys and their World* (1985); J. W. Kirby, 'A Fifteenth Century Family: the Plumptons of Plumpton, and their Lawyers, 1461–1515', *Northern History*, XXV (1989); C. F. Richmond, 'Landlord and Tenant: The Paston Evidence', in J. Kermode (ed.), *Enterprise and Individuals in the Fifteenth Century* (Gloucester, 1991). For what follows, see esp. Richmond, *Paston Family: First Phase*.

38. E.g. J. S. Davies (ed.), *The Troponell Cartulary*, 2 vols (Devizes, 1908); T. B. Pugh (ed.), *Marcher Lordships of South Wales, 1415–1536* (Cardiff, 1963) [accounts]; A. Crawford (ed.), *Household Books of John Howard, Duke of Norfolk* (London, 1992).

39. S. Payling, 'The Widening Franchise: Parliamentary Elections in Lancastrian Nottinghamshire', in D. Williams (ed.), *England in the Fifteenth Century* (Woodbridge, 1987), pp. 178–85.

40. R. L. Storey, *The End of the House of Lancaster* (rev. edn, Gloucester, 1986), p. 127.

41. E.g. C. E. Moreton, *The Townshends and their World* (Oxford, 1992); P. Maddern, *Violence and the Social Order* (Oxford, 1992).

42. E.g. M. C. Carpenter, *Locality and Polity: A Study of Warwickshire Landed Society, 1401–1499* (Cambridge, 1992); I. Rowney, 'Government and Patronage in Staffordshire, 1439–1459', *Midland History*, VIII (1983).

43. C. E. Moreton, 'A Local Dispute and the Politics of 1483: Roger Townshend, Earl Rivers and the Duke of Gloucester', *The Ricardian*, 107 (1989).

3. THE ECONOMIC CONTEXT   *R. H. Britnell*

1. 'These be the Comodytes of Englond', in J. Fortescue, *The Works*, ed. T. Fortescue (1869), p. 552; J. Fortescue, *The Governance of England*, ed. C. Plummer (Oxford, 1885), pp. 113–15.

2. H. P. Brown and S. V. Hopkins, *A Perspective of Wages and Prices* (1981), p. 22; C. Dyer, *Standards of Living in the Later Middle Ages* (Cambridge, 1989), pp. 158–60.

3. A. Dyer, *Decline and Growth in English Towns, 1400–1640* (1991), p. 33.

4. R. H. Britnell, *Growth and Decline in Colchester, 1300–1525* (Cambridge, 1986), p. 247.

5. R. H. Britnell, *The Commercialisation of English Society, 1000–1500* (Cambridge, 1993), p. 195; E. M. Carus-Wilson, 'Evidences of Economic Growth on some Fifteenth-Century Manors', *EcHR*, 2nd ser., XII (1959), 191–7; E. M. Carus-Wilson, 'The Textile Industry before 1550', in *VCH, Wiltshire*, IV, pp. 128–38; J. N. Hare, 'The Wiltshire Rising of 1450: Political and Economic Discontent in Mid Fifteenth Century England', *Southern History*, IV (1982), 18–19.

6. Local variations in crop production are discussed by contributors to E. Miller (ed.), *The Agrarian History of England and Wales, III: 1348–1500* (Cambridge, 1991), especially in chapters 2 and 3.

7. A. Watkins, 'Cattle Grazing in the Forest of Arden in the Later Middle Ages', *Agricultural History Review*, XXXVII (1989), 13; C. Dyer, 'A Small Landowner in the Fifteenth Century', *Midland History*, I (1972), 6–7.

8. A. Hanham, *The Celys and Their World: An English Merchant Family of the Fifteenth Century* (Cambridge, 1985), pp. 111–12; E. Power, 'The Wool Trade in the Fifteenth Century', in E. Power and M. M. Postan (eds), *Studies in English Trade in the Fifteenth Century* (1933), p. 49.

9. M. Bailey, 'The Rabbit and the Medieval East Anglian Economy', *Agricultural History Review*, XXXVI (1988), 1–20; C. Richmond, *John Hopton: A Fifteenth-Century Suffolk Gentleman* (Cambridge, 1981), pp. 39–40.

10. M. Bailey, *A Marginal Economy: East Anglian Breckland in the Later Middle Ages* (Cambridge, 1989), p. 311; Britnell, *Growth and Decline*, 204; R. Faith, 'Berkshire: Fourteenth and Fifteenth Centuries', in P. D. A. Harvey (ed.), *The Peasant Land Market in Medieval England* (Oxford, 1984), p. 157; P. J. P. Goldberg, *Women, Work and Life Cycle in a Medieval Economy: Women in York and Yorkshire, c. 1300–1520* (Oxford, 1992), p. 299; D. G. Shaw, *The Creation of a Community: The City of Wells in the Middle Ages* (Oxford, 1993), pp. 151–2; E. B. DeWindt, *Land and People in Holywell-cum-Needingworth: Structures of Tenure and Patterns of Social Organization in an East Midlands Village, 1252–1457* (Toronto, 1971), pp. 178–9.

11. F. G. Davenport, *The Economic Development of a Norfolk Manor, 1086–1565* (Cambridge, 1906), pp. 78, 104–5; A. J. Pollard, 'Estate Management in the Later Middle Ages: The Talbots and Whitchurch, 1383–1525', *EcHR*, XXV (1972), 559; L. R. Poos, A *Rural Society after the Black Death: Essex 1350–1525* (Cambridge, 1991), pp. 49–50, 91–106. For a general survey of the changing population of the late Middle Ages, see J. Hatcher, *Plague, Population and the English Economy, 1348–1530* (1977).

12. C. Dyer, *Lords and Peasants in a Changing Society: The Estates of the Bishopric of Worcester, 680–1540* (Cambridge, 1980), p. 287; B. F. Harvey, *Westminster Abbey and its Estates in the Middle Ages* (Oxford, 1977), p. 270.

13. R. S. Gottfried, *Bury St Edmunds and the Urban Crisis: 1290–1539* (Princeton, 1982), p. 55; M. Mate, 'The Occupation of the Land: Kent and Sussex', in Miller, *Agrarian History*, III, 127–8; L. R. Poos, 'The Rural Population of Essex in the Later Middle Ages', *EcHR*, 2nd ser., XXXVIII (1985), 522–3, 525.

14. R. S. Gottfried, *Epidemic Disease in Fifteenth-Century England: The Medical Response and the Demographic Consequences* (Leicester, 1978), pp. 47–9; B. Harvey, *Living and Dying in England, 1100–1540: The Monastic Experience* (Oxford, 1993), pp. 122, 127–9, 143; J. Hatcher, 'Mortality in the Fifteenth Century: Some New Evidence', *EcHR*, 2nd ser., XXXIX (1986), 28–9.

15. A. J. Pollard, 'The North-Eastern Economy and the Agrarian Crisis of 1438–40', *Northern History*, 25 (1989), 93–4; A. J. Pollard, *North-Eastern England during the Wars of the Roses* (Oxford, 1990), pp. 49–52.

16. Britnell, *Growth and Decline*, 182, 202; Dyer, *Lords and Tenants*, 222–5; Gottfried, *Epidemic Disease*, 98–9.

17. J. Day, *The Medieval Market Economy* (Oxford, 1987), pp. 44–5, 47; P. Spufford, *Money and its Use in Medieval Europe* (Cambridge, 1988), pp. 356–62.

18. 3 Edward IV cc. 2–4; A. Luders et al. (eds), *Statutes of the Realm (1101–1713)* (Record Commission, 11 vols, 1808–28), II, pp. 395–8; J. H. Munro, *Wool, Cloth and Gold: The Struggle for Bullion in Anglo-Burgundian Trade, 1340–1478* (Toronto, 1972), pp. 159–61; Appendix B, in Power and Postan, *Studies*, 402–4; J. H. Ramsay, *Lancaster and York*, 2 vols (Oxford, 1892), II, pp. 311–13; Spufford, *Money*, 360, 362.

19. M. M. Postan, 'The Economic and Political Relations of England and the Hanse from 1400 to 1475', in Power and Postan, *Studies*, 127–31, 402–3.

20. Munro, *Wool, Cloth and Gold*, 136–8, 141, 146.

21. H. L. Gray, 'English Foreign Trade from 1446 to 1482', in Power and Postan, *Studies*, 28–9; M. K. James, *Studies in the Medieval Wine Trade*, ed. E. M. Veale (Oxford, 1971), pp. 52–3.

22. C. L. Kingsford, *Prejudice and Promise in Fifteenth-Century England* (Oxford, 1925), pp. 48–67.

23. J. R. Lander, *The Wars of the Roses* (Gloucester, 1990), p. 83; Pollard, *North-Eastern England*, 280.

24. Rochester Bridge Trust, bridge accounts 1449–50, 1450–1; Durham University Library, Dean and Chapter Muniments, cell accounts; C. Ross, *The Wars of the Roses: A Concise History* (1976), p. 163. I am grateful to Mr A. J. Piper for making available to me his notes on the Durham cells.

25. Bailey, *Marginal Economy*, 290; Dyer, *Lords and Peasants*, 151, 189; M. Mate, 'Pastoral Farming in South-East England in the Fifteenth Century', *EcHR*, 2nd ser., XL (1987), 527; S. M. Wright, *The Derbyshire Gentry in the Fifteenth Century* (Derbyshire Record Society, VIII, Chesterfield, 1983), pp. 19–20.

26. PRO, SC 6/941/3; R. H. Britnell, 'The Pastons and their Norfolk', *Agricultural History Review*, XXXVI (1988), 32–44.

27. A. J. Piper, *The Durham Monks at Jarrow*, Jarrow Lecture 1986 (Durham, 1986), pp. 11–12.

28. D. Moss, 'The Economic Development of a Middlesex Village', *Agricultural History Review*, XXVIII (1980), 110.

29. Bailey, *Marginal Economy*, 294–5; R. B. Dobson, *Durham Priory, 1400–1450* (Cambridge, 1973), p. 277; Wright, *Derbyshire Gentry*, 19, 155 (n. 39).

30. Dyer, 'Small Landowner', 6–8; P. A. Johnson, *Duke Richard of York, 1411–1460* (Oxford, 1988), p. 24; Watkins, 'Cattle Grazing', 18–19, 24.

31. C. Carpenter, *Locality and Polity: A Study of Warwickshire Landed Society, 1401–1499* (Cambridge, 1992), pp. 172–3.

32. Dobson, *Durham Priory*, 270–1, 273, 285–9; Pollard, 'North-Eastern Economy', 94, 98.

33. J. M. W. Bean, *The Estates of the Percy Family, 1416–1537* (Oxford, 1958), pp. 29–30; I. S. W. Blanchard, 'Economic Change in Derbyshire in the Late Middle Ages, 1272–1540' (University of London Ph.D. thesis,

1967), pp. 89, 94, 97–9, 214–5; Pollard, *North-Eastern England*, 50–2; Pollard, 'North-Eastern Economy', 94–7, 101.

34. Bailey, *Marginal Economy*, 266–9; F. R. H. Du Boulay, *The Lordship of Canterbury: An Essay on Medieval Society* (1966), p. 225; Dyer, *Lords and Peasants*, 188; J. Hatcher, *Rural Economy and Society in the Duchy of Cornwall, 1300–1500* (Cambridge, 1970), pp. 151–4, 157–9, 262–3; Mate, 'Pastoral Farming', 525, 531.

35. Blanchard, 'Economic Change', 94–7, 212–17, 220.

36. J. N. Hare, 'Lords and Tenants in Wiltshire, c.1380–c.1520' (University of London Ph.D. thesis, 1975), pp. 159–61, 166; J. N. Hare, 'Durrington: A Chalkland Village in the Later Middle Ages', *Wiltshire Archaeological Magazine*, 74–5 (1981), 141.

37. Johnson, *Duke Richard*, 23–4; C. Rawcliffe, *The Staffords, Earls of Stafford and Dukes of Buckingham, 1394–1521* (Cambridge, 1978), pp. 47–8, 114; G. Williams, *Recovery, Reorientation and Reformation: Wales, c.1415–1642* (Oxford, 1987), p. 178.

38. Dyer, *Lords and Peasants*, 165–71; Johnson, *Duke Richard*, 25.

39. Pollard, 'Estate Management', 562–3.

40. Dyer, *Lords and Peasants*, 184, 189; C. Dyer, 'A Redistribution of Incomes in Fifteenth-Century England?', in R. H. Hilton (ed.), *Peasants, Knights and Heretics: Studies in Medieval English Social History* (Cambridge, 1976), pp. 203–5; M. Mate, 'Tenant Farming and Tenant Farmers', in Miller, *Agrarian History*, III, 685–7.

41. Blanchard, 'Economic Change', 220, 236–7; Hare, 'Lords and Tenants in Wiltshire', 166, 194; M. K. McIntosh, *Autonomy and Community: The Royal Manor of Havering, 1200–1500* (Cambridge, 1986), pp. 221–3, 226–7.

42. E. Acheson, *A Gentry Community: Leicestershire in the Fifteenth Century, c.1422–c.1485* (Cambridge, 1992), pp. 64–7; Blanchard, 'Economic Change', 99–112, 223–4; Carpenter, *Locality and Polity*, 155, 185–7.

43. Rawcliffe, *The Staffords*, 110.

44. B. P. Wolffe, *The Royal Demesne in English History: The Crown Estate in the Governance of the Realm from the Conquest to 1509* (1971), pp. 117–23.

45. This argument is particularly associated with K. B. McFarlane, *The Nobility of Later Medieval England* (Oxford, 1973), pp. 179–86.

46. A. J. Pollard, *The Wars of the Roses* (1988), p. 54.

47. Rawcliffe, *The Staffords*, 110, 115.

48. R. I. Jack (ed.), *The Grey of Ruthin Valor of 1467–8* (Sydney, 1965).

49. Britnell, 'Pastons', 140; M. Mate, 'The Economic and Social Roots of Medieval Popular Rebellion: Sussex in 1450–1451', *EcHR*, XLV (1992), 672.

50. Dyer, *Standards of Living*, 92–4.

51. John Lydgate, *The Fall of Princes*, II, lines 869–72; H. Bergen (ed.), *Lydgate's Fall of Princes*, 4 vols (EETS, extra series, CXXI-CXXIV, 1924–7), I, p. 223.

52. *English Chronicle*, 64–5.

53. R. A. Griffiths, 'Local Rivalries and National Politics: The Percies, the Nevilles and the Duke of Exeter', reprinted in R. A. Griffiths, *King and Country: England and Wales in the Fifteenth Century* (1991), p. 331;

Hare, 'Wiltshire Rising', 16–19; I. M. W. Harvey, *Jack Cade's Rebellion of 1450* (Oxford, 1991), p. 17; R. H. Hilton, *The English Peasantry in the Later Middle Ages* (Oxford, 1975), pp. 71–2; Johnson, *Duke Richard*, 109n; Mate, 'Economic and Social Roots', 661–75; Poos, *Rural Society*, 260–1.

54. *Rot Parl*, V, 464; *Warkworth*, 46.

55. Pollard, *Wars of the Roses*, 55; Pollard, 'North-Eastern Economy', 104–5; M. M. Postan, 'The Fifteenth Century', *EcHR*, IX (1939), 166; T. B. Pugh and C. D. Ross, 'The English Baronage and the Income Tax of 1436', *BIHR*, XXVI (1953), 1–2.

56. R. A. Griffiths, *The Reign of King Henry VI: The Exercise of Royal Authority, 1422–1461* (1981), pp. 582–3; Pollard, *North-Eastern England*, 254; Pollard, 'North-Eastern Economy', 104–5.

57. V. J. Scattergood, *Politics and Poetry in the Fifteenth Century* (1971), pp. 161, 183; Wolffe, *Royal Demesne*, 106–12.

58. Wolffe, *Royal Demesne*, 91; H. L. Gray, 'English Foreign Trade from 1446 to 1482', in Power and Postan, *Studies*, 18 (with corrected arithmetic), 20; H. L. Gray, 'Tables of Enrolled Customs and Subsidy Accounts, 1399 to 1482', in Power and Postan, *Studies*, 326.

59. G. L. Harriss, *Cardinal Beaufort: A Study of Lancastrian Ascendancy and Decline* (Oxford, 1988), pp. 284–8; J. H. Munro, 'Monetary Contraction and Industrial Change in the Late-Medieval Low Countries, 1335–1500', in N. J. Mayhew (ed.), *Coinage in the Low Countries (880–1500)* (BAR International Series, 54, Oxford, 1979), p. 151.

60. In 1421 these were about £15,067 from royal demesne and other non-parliamentary sources, and about £15,800 from the Duchy of Lancaster: Wolffe, *Royal Demesne*, 91; G. L. Harriss, 'Financial Policy', in G. L. Harriss (ed.), *Henry V: The Practice of Kingship* (Oxford, 1985), p. 169.

61. C. Ross, *Edward IV* (1974), p. 373.

62. Ramsay, *Lancaster and York*, I, 321; II, 267.

63. Griffiths, *Reign of Henry VI*, 384; K. B. McFarlane, *Lancastrian Kings and Lollard Knights* (Oxford, 1972), p. 95.

64. A 'fifteenth and tenth' in the fifteenth century was a fixed levy on each town and village in the kingdom. Methods of assessing individual taxpayers varied locally.

65. Griffiths, *Reign of Henry VI*, 378–9.

66. *English Chronicle*, 64–5, 87; *Warkworth*, 69–71; E. B. Fryde and N. Fryde, 'Peasant Rebellion and Peasant Discontents', in Miller, *Agrarian History*, 800–1.

67. Harriss, *Cardinal Beaufort*, 332–43; Johnson, *Duke Richard*, 56–62.

68. Harriss, *Cardinal Beaufort*, 288–91, 316.

69. Griffiths, *Reign of Henry VI*, 329–46; S. J. Payling, *Political Society in Lancastrian England: The Greater Gentry of Nottingham* (Oxford, 1991), pp. 142–56.

70. Griffiths, *Reign of Henry VI*, 320–2; Harvey, *Jack Cade's Rebellion*, 43, 187, 191.

4. THE ORIGINS OF THE WARS OF THE ROSES   *Keith Dockray*

1. W. Denton, *England in the Fifteenth Century* (1888), p. 114.
2. C. A. J. Armstrong, 'Politics and the Battle of St Albans, 1455', *BIHR*, XXXIII (1960), 7.
3. A. Goodman, *The Wars of the Roses* (1981), p. 8.
4. J. Stevenson (ed.), *Letters and Papers Illustrative of the Wars of the English in France*, II (R S, 1864), p. 770.
5. A. J. Pollard, *The Wars of the Roses* (1988), p. 19.
6. B. Wilkinson, *Constitutional History of England in the Fifteenth Century* (1964), p. 50 (for the Neville judgements and Jean de Waurin); *EHD*, 281–2 (for the *English Chronicle*); B. P. Wolffe, *Henry VI* (1981), p. 19 (for Whetehamstede's *Register*).
7. *EHD*, 269–70 (York's 1452 manifesto); J. Gairdner (ed.), *The Paston Letters*, 6 vols (1904), II, pp. 290–2 (Norfolk's 1453 petition); Wilkinson, *Constitutional History*, 134–6 (1460 manifesto); *Polydore Vergil*, 93.
8. *EHD*, 526 (Fortescue), 281–2 (*English Chronicle*); Wilkinson, *Constitutional History*, 134–6 (1460 manifesto).
9. Ibid., 82–6 (Cade's manifesto), 50 (Gascoigne), 131 (Whetehamstede's *Register*); *EHD*, 282 (*English Chronicle*).
10. *EHD*, 274–5 (Hardyng's *Chronicle* and *English Chronicle*); Wilkinson, *Constitutional History*, 134–6 (1460 manifesto); C. Plummer (ed.), *The Governance of England* (Oxford, 1885), pp. 128–9 (Fortescue); Gairdner, *Paston Letters*, I, 103–4 (York's 1452 accusations), II, 290–2 (Norfolk's 1453 petition); *Polydore Vergil*, 87, 94.
11. J. R. Lander, *The Wars of the Roses* (1965), pp. 63–4 (allegations against Oldhall); Wilkinson, *Constitutional History*, pp. 114 (*Annales* on Young), 128 (Chancery memorandum), 131 (Whetehamstede's *Register*); *EHD*, 269–70 (York's 1452 manifesto), 264, 282 (*English Chronicle* on Cade and Margaret of Anjou).
12. *Polydore Vergil*, 86, 94; M. E. Aston, 'Richard II and the Wars of the Roses', in C. M. Barron and F. R. H. Du Boulay (eds), *The Reign of Richard II* (1973), pp. 282–3 (Sir Thomas Smith), 286–7 (17th-century verdicts); W. Stubbs, *The Constitutional History of England* (Oxford, 1878), III, p. 5; A. L. Rowse, *Bosworth Field and the Wars of the Roses* (1966).
13. D. Hume, *The History of England* (1834), III, pp. 307–8; Plummer, *Governance*, pp. 15–16; C. L. Kingsford, *Prejudice and Promise in Fifteenth Century England* (Oxford, 1925), pp. 75–6; M. M. Postan, 'The Fifteenth Century', *EcHR*, IX (1939), reprinted in *Essays in Medieval Agriculture and Economy* (Cambridge, 1973), p. 48; C. D. Ross and T. B. Pugh, 'The English Baronage and the Income Tax of 1436', *BIHR*, XXVI (1953), 1–2.
14. K. B. McFarlane, 'The Wars of the Roses', Raleigh Lecture on History, *Proceedings of the British Academy*, L (1964), reprinted in *England in the Fifteenth Century* (1981), especially pp. 238–40. This volume of McFarlane's collected essays also includes 'Parliament and Bastard Feudalism', originally published in *TRHS*, 4th ser., XXVI (1944), and 'Bastard Feudalism', *BIHR*, XX (1945). See also McFarlane's *The Nobility of Later Medieval England* (edited and published posthumously, Oxford, 1973).

15. R. L. Storey, *The End of the House of Lancaster* (2nd edn, Gloucester, 1986), especially pp. 27–8.

16. M. Keen, *England in the Later Middle Ages* (1973), especially pp. 449–51; R. A. Griffiths, 'Local Rivalries and National Politics: the Percies, the Nevilles and the Duke of Exeter, 1452–55', *Speculum*, XLIII (1968), reprinted in *King and Country: England and Wales in the Fifteenth Century* (1991), pp. 321–64; M. Cherry, 'The Struggle for Power in Mid-Fifteenth-Century Devonshire', in R. A. Griffiths (ed.), *Patronage, the Crown and the Provinces in Later Medieval England* (Gloucester, 1981), pp. 123–44; S. J. Payling, 'The Ampthill Dispute: a Study in Aristocratic Lawlessness and the Breakdown of Lancastrian Government', *EHR*, CIV (1989), 881–907.

17. P. R. Coss, 'Bastard Feudalism Revised', *PP*, CXXV (1988), 27–64; M. Hicks, 'Bastard Feudalism: Society and Politics in Fifteenth-Century England', *Richard III and his Rivals: Magnates and their Motives in the Wars of the Roses* (1991), pp. 1–40; D. Crouch, D. A. Carpenter and P. R. Coss, 'Debate: Bastard Feudalism Revised', *PP*, CXXXI (1991), 165–203.

18. Keen, *Later Middle Ages*, 451; C. Ross, *The Wars of the Roses* (1976), especially pp. 37–42; Pollard, *Wars*, 65; Storey, *Lancaster*, x; see also Storey's 'Bastard Feudalism Revisited', *Bulletin of the Manorial Society of Great Britain*, III (1983), 7–15.

19. Keen, *Later Middle Ages*, 454–6; Wolffe, *Henry VI*, especially 133–4.

20. M. K. Jones, 'Somerset, York and the Wars of the Roses', *EHR*, XIV (1989), 285–307.

21. J. R. Lander, 'Introduction: aspects of fifteenth-century studies', in *Crown and Nobility 1450–1509* (1976), p. 19; Pollard, *Wars*, 55–6; G. L. Harriss, 'Political Society and the Growth of Government in Late Medieval England', *PP*, CXXXVIII (1993), 40.

22. M. Levine, *Tudor Dynastic Problems 1460–1571* (1973), p. 15; R. A. Griffiths, 'The Sense of Dynasty in the Reign of Henry VI', in C. Ross (ed.), *Patronage, Pedigree and Power in Later Medieval England* (Gloucester, 1979), pp. 13–36; Pollard, *Wars*, 45, 65–6.

23. Wolffe, *Henry VI*, 25–83; R. A. Griffiths, *The Reign of Henry VI* (1981), pp. 11–228.

24. Lander, *Wars*, 39–41; see also R. Lovatt, 'A Collector of Apocryphal Anecdotes: John Blacman Revisited', in A. J. Pollard (ed.), *Property and Politics: Essays in Later Medieval English History* (1984), pp. 172–97.

25. *Polydore Vergil*, 70; J. W. McKenna, 'Piety and Propaganda: the Cult of Henry VI', in B. Rowland (ed.), *Chaucer and Middle English Studies in Honour of R. H. Robbins* (Kent, Ohio, 1974), pp. 72–88.

26. B. P. Wolffe, 'The Personal Rule of Henry VI', in S. B. Chrimes, C. D. Ross and R. A. Griffiths (eds), *Fifteenth-century England 1399–1509* (Manchester, 1972), pp. 29–48, and Wolffe, *Henry VI*, 19.

27. Griffiths, *Reign of Henry VI*, 11–228.

28. Wilkinson, *Constitutional History*, 82–6; see also I. M. W. Harvey, *Jack Cade's Rebellion of 1450* (Oxford, 1991).

29. Storey, *Lancaster*, 34–5 (remarks of 1442, 1447 and 1450 on Henry VI); J. Blackman, *Henry the Sixth* (Cambridge, 1919), p. 38; A. Gransden,

Historical Writing in England, II, c. 1307 to the Early Sixteenth Century (1982), p. 384 (Whetehamstede's *Register*).

30. Patricia-Anne Lee, 'Reflections of Power: Margaret of Anjou and the Dark Side of Queenship', *Renaissance Quarterly*, XXXIX (1986), 183–217; *EHD*, 272–3 (newsletter of January 1454).

31. C. Rawcliffe, 'Richard Duke of York, the King's "obeisant liegeman": a New Source for the Protectorates of 1454 and 1455', *HR*, LX (1987), 232–9.

32. A. J. Pollard, 'Percies, Nevilles and the Wars of the Roses', *History Today*, XLIII (September 1993), 42–8.

33. T. B. Pugh, 'Richard, Duke of York, and the Rebellion of Henry Holand, Duke of Exeter, in May 1454', *HR*, LXIII (1990), 248–64 (especially 261, for John Benet's *Chronicle* on York's 1st Protectorate); R. A. Griffiths, 'The King's Council and the First Protectorate of the Duke of York, 1450–1454', *EHR*, XCIX (1984), 67–82, reprinted in *King and Country*, 305–20.

34. Storey, *Lancaster*, p. 159.

35. K. R. Dockray, 'Japan and England in the Fifteenth Century: The Onin War and the Wars of the Roses', in Ross, *Patronage, Pedigree and Power*, 143–70 (especially p. 151, for similar sentiments on the origins of the Wars of the Roses).

5. PERSONALITIES AND POLITICS   *Rosemary Horrox*

1. HMC Rutland MSS, I, 4.

2. Curt F. Buhler (ed.), *The Dicts and Sayings of the Philosophers* (EETS original series, CCXI, 1941 for 1939), p. 6.

3. *Warkworth*, 4. The spelling of all quotations has been modernised, except for words which have changed their meaning, which have been left, italicised, in the original spelling.

4. R. F. Green, *Poets and Princepleasers: Literature and the English Court in the Late Middle Ages* (Toronto, 1980), p. 13.

5. *PL*, II, 282.

6. HMC Rutland MSS, I, 8; *Rot Parl*, VI, 328.

7. M. James, *Society, Politics and Culture: Studies in Early Modern England* (Cambridge, 1986), pp. 24–5; B. R. McRee, 'Religious Gilds and Regulation of Behavior in Late Medieval Towns', in J. Rosenthal and C. Richmond (eds), *People, Politics and Community in the Later Middle Ages* (Gloucester, 1987), p. 113.

8. C. Monro (ed.), *Letters of Queen Margaret of Anjou and Bishop Beckington and others* (Camden Soc., old series, LXXXVI, 1863), p. 79.

9. *PL*, II, 448; Thomas Malory, *Works*, ed. E. Vinaver (Oxford, 2nd edn, 1971), p. 61.

10. *PL*, II, 98.

11. Monro, *Letters*, 108: A. J. Pollard, 'St Cuthbert and the Hog: Richard III and the County Palatine of Durham, 1471–85', in

R. A. Griffiths and J. Sherborne (eds), *Kings and Nobles in the Later Middle Ages* (Gloucester, 1986), p. 120.

12. *PL*, I, 80–1.

13. *Ibid*, II, 258–9.

14. HMC Rutland, I, 2–6; IV, 188.

15. E. Dudley, *The Tree of Commonwealth*, ed. D. M. Brodie (Cambridge, 1948), pp. 36–7.

16. Essex Record Office, D/DQ 14/124/3/15.

17. Monro, *Letters*, 34. *Gentilnesse* was behaviour appropriate to someone of gentle birth.

18. *Warkworth*, 46–51.

19. Francis Bacon, Essay LVI, *Of Judicature*: 'let them [the judges] be lions, but yet lions under the throne; being circumspect that they do not check or oppose any points of sovereignty'.

20. P. A. Johnson, *Duke Richard of York, 1411–1460* (Oxford, 1988), p. 214.

21. *Arrivall*, 12.

22. Edward Hall, *The Union of the Two Noble Families of Lancaster and York* (1550; facsimile reprint, Menston, 1970), fo. 99.

23. *Arrivall*, 12.

24. R. Horrox, *Richard III: A Study of Service* (Cambridge, 1989), p. 167; I. Arthurson, 'The Rising of 1497: a Revolt of the Peasantry?', in Rosenthal and Richmond, *People, Politics and Community*, 7.

25. *VCH, Worcestershire*, IV, 342; *PL*, II, 456.

26. *PL*, I, 267.

27. BL, Harleian Charter 58.F. 49.

6. IDEAS, PRINCIPLES AND POLITICS   *John L. Watts*

1. R. Virgoe, 'The Death of William de la Pole, Duke of Suffolk', *BJRL*, XLVII (1964–5), 499, 501.

2. Quotations from J. R. Green, *A Short History of the English People*, 4 vols (1892–3), II, p. 561, and A. J. Pollard, *The Wars of the Roses* (1988), p. 40.

3. See e.g. J. R. Lander, *Crown and Nobility, 1450–1509* (1976), pp. 16–28; C. D. Ross, *The Wars of the Roses* (1976), pp. 37–42, 164–6; A. Goodman, *The Wars of the Roses* (1981), pp. 1–3. B. Wilkinson, *Constitutional History of England in the Fifteenth Century* (1964), chs i and ii, has been almost alone in arguing for a real conflict of principle between Yorkists and Lancastrians, at least up to 1469.

4. M. K. Jones, 'Somerset, York and the Wars of the Roses', *EHR*, CIV (1989), 285–307; R. E. Horrox, *Richard III: A Study of Service* (Cambridge, 1989), pp. 324–8 and generally.

5. C. Carpenter, *Locality and Polity: a Study of Warwickshire Landed Society, 1401–99* (Cambridge, 1992), pp. 6–9 and generally.

6. For an account which does seek to relate the idea of the 'common weal' to the politics of the period, see D. Starkey, 'Which Age of

Reform?', in D. Starkey and C. Coleman (eds), *Revolution Reassessed* (Oxford, 1986), pp. 13–27. In addition, G. L. Harriss shows how the ideals of '*bone governance*' (good government) may have influenced the policies of Henry V and their success, in *Henry V: The Practice of Kingship* (Oxford, 1985), chs 1 and 7. Finally, Horrox, *Richard III*, is rather more than a 'study of service': the themes of 'continuity' and stability – the latter a key element in the 'common weal' – are also accorded an important role in determining Richard's political fortunes.

7. *Polydore Vergil*, 84–95; D. Hay, *The Anglica Historia of Polydore Vergil* (Camden, 3rd ser., LXXIV, 1950), p. 13.

8. C. Plummer (ed.), *The Governance of England ... by Sir John Fortescue, knight* (Oxford, 1885), pp. 128–9.

9. See especially A. B. Ferguson, *The Articulate Citizen and the English Renaissance* (Durham, North Carolina, 1965), pp. 29–30, 39–40; and J. P. Genet, 'Ecclesiastics and Political Theory in Late Medieval England: the End of a Monopoly', in R. B. Dobson (ed.), *The Church, Patronage and Politics in the Fifteenth Century* (Gloucester, 1984), pp. 35–6. Quotation from N. Machiavelli, *The Prince*, ed. and tr. G. Bull, 3rd edn (Harmondsworth, 1981), p. 90.

10. J. R. Lander, *Conflict and Stability in Fifteenth-Century England* (1969), p. 189.

11. BL, Add MS 48031A, fo. 126r; B. Tierney, 'Bracton on Government', *Speculum*, XXXVIII (1963), 299–305.

12. W. Stubbs, *The Constitutional History of England*, 3 vols (Oxford, 1875–8), II, pp. 623–4, III, pp. 233–7.

13. The importance of loyalty and piety (as well as chivalry and ideas of good government) in motivating the acts of individuals is discussed in M. Hicks, 'Idealism in Late Medieval English Politics', in M. Hicks, *Richard III and His Rivals* (1991), pp. 41–59.

14. This comment appears in Q. R. D. Skinner, 'The Principles and Practice of Opposition: the Case of Bolingbroke vs. Walpole', in N. McKendrick (ed.), *Historical Perspectives: Studies in English Thought and Society in Honour of J. H. Plumb* (1974), pp. 93–128, p. 128.

15. This interpretation will be developed further in 'Polemic and Politics in the 1450s', in M. Kekewich (ed.), *John Vale's Book*, to be published by the Richard III and Yorkist History Trust.

16. Horrox, *Richard III*, esp. chs 2, 5, 6 and the 'Conclusion'.

17. J. P. Genet (ed.), *Four English Political Tracts of the Later Middle Ages* (Camden, 4th ser., XVIII, 1977), p. 189; F. J. Furnivall (ed.), *Hoccleve's Works, iii. The Regement of Princes* (EETS, extra ser., LXXII, 1897), l. 2885.

18. Plummer, *Governance*, 127.

19. *Rot Parl*, v, 35.

20. For a classic statement, see A. P. D'Entreves (ed), *Aquinas: Selected Political Writings* (Oxford, 1959), pp. 2–7.

21. Plummer, *Governance*, p. 127. (The phrase was normally applied to the pope in respect of the Church, of course).

22. This issue of how royal power should be characterised is explored more fully in my forthcoming book, *The Rule of England in the Time of Henry VI*. For a good short introduction to the conventional view, see

A. L. Brown, *The Governance of Late Medieval England, 1272–1461* (1989), ch. 1, esp. pp. 12–17.

23. *EHD* 186.

24. Note that, as David Starkey has pointed out, the term 'common weal' was not widely used until the later 1450s, although the concept it embodied was much older ('Which Age of Reform?' 19–21).

25. This version of the manifesto, taken from BL Add.MS 48031(A), fo. 139, is slightly different from the printed edition in I. M. W. Harvey, *Jack Cade's Rebellion of 1450* (Oxford, 1991), p. 189.

26. S. B. Chrimes, *English Constitutional Ideas in the Fifteenth Century* (Cambridge, 1936), p. 173.

27. J. Gairdner (ed.), *The Paston Letter*, 6 vols (1906), I, p. 97.

28. The last charge was made by the Yorkists against Buckingham, Shrewsbury, Beaumont and co. in 1460: see *English Chronicle*, 88. Similar accusations were made against the Yorkists when they were in possession of Henry VI between Northampton and St Albans II.

29. These occasions were the confrontations at Dartford (1452) and Ludford Bridge (1459), when no battles took place, at St Albans (1455 and 1461) and at Northampton (1460). Since the battles of 1460–1 form part of a civil war in which central authority had effectively collapsed and dynastic claims had begun to play a part in politics, they do not quite fit the model. It is worth noting that all five occasions fell in the reign of the 'inane' Henry VI, when the idea of confronting the acknowledged king may have seemed less outrageous.

30. Gairdner, *Paston Letters*, III, 44.

31. K. B. McFarlane, 'The Wars of the Roses', in his *England in the Fifteenth Century* (Oxford, 1981), Ch. xii, pp. 255–6. See Carpenter, *Locality and Polity*, Ch. 15, for the view that Henry VII was less effective at restoring order than has usually been thought.

32. J. P. Gilson, 'A Defence of the Proscription of the Yorkists in 1459', *EHR*, xxvi (1911), 512–25.

33. This is a central theme of my forthcoming book: see n. 22, above.

34. Even Fortescue, who set out to justify the Lancastrian claim to the throne, conceded the principle of hereditary right as the basis for royal power. To defeat the Yorkist claim, he added two riders. The first was that owing to the nature of the royal inheritance, which involved the exercise of authority over men, it could never be held by a woman. The second was that because it could never be *held* by a woman, it could not be *transmitted* by a woman either, so that Edward of York, whose claim ran through Philippa, daughter of Lionel of Clarence, could not be king. There is no reason to assume that others necessarily thought as Fortescue did and there was no clear law on the subject. See Chrimes, *Constitutional Ideas*, 10–13.

35. Although Fortescue had taken an active part in the succession debate, the *Governance* is plainly unconcerned about the dynastic title of the king. Its advice – in some texts offered to Henry VI, in some to Edward IV – is intended to aid the *de facto* king in assuring his throne and fulfilling his obligations to the community.

36. Fortescue's work raises many more issues than can be considered here. A fuller version of my views appears in my article, '"A Newe Ffundacion of is Crowne": Monarchy in the Age of Henry VII', in the forthcoming proceedings of the July 1993 Harlaxton colloquium on Henry VII. C. A. J. Skeel, 'The Influence of the Writings of Sir John Fortescue', *TRHS*, 3rd ser., x (1916), 83–91, shows some of the ways in which Fortescue's ideas may have influenced Yorkist and Tudor policy. Other useful material on Fortescue appears in the Bibliography.

7. THE CHURCH AND THE WARS OF THE ROSES   *Richard G. Davies*

1. See Bibliography for important contextual works and guides to recent writings. I have minimised references to manuscript sources in this chapter, but wish to thank the Borthwick Institute, York, for access to its manuscripts and microfilms.

2. R. L. Storey, 'Episcopal King-makers in the Fifteenth-century', in R. B. Dobson (ed.), *The Church, Politics and Patronage in the Fifteenth Century* (Gloucester, 1984), pp. 82–98, and cf. the important comments of P. Heath, *Church and Realm, 1272–1461* (1988), pp. 338–9.

3. F. R. H. Du Boulay (ed.), *Registrum Thome Bourgchier* (Canterbury and York Soc., 1957), pp. xxxii–vi, 102–7; cf. Heath, *Church and Realm,* 345–8: 'The Lancastrian dynasty's fall was neither impeded nor accelerated by the clergy and their interests'.

4. C. A. J. Armstrong, 'The Inauguration Ceremonies of the Yorkist Kings and their Title to the Throne', *TRHS*, 4th ser., 5 (1948), 51–73; J. W. McKenna, 'The Coronation Oil of the Yorkist Kings', *EHR*, 82 (1967), 102–4; A. F. Sutton and P. W. Hammond (eds), *The Coronation of Richard III* (Gloucester, 1983), pp. 1–9. If Cardinal Bourgchier was indeed 'reluctant' to crown Richard III in 1483 (Mancini, 122) – and indeed he personally had much recently to be reluctant about, shamefaced being the more exact word – he showed it at most by turning down a free lunch for the first and only time in his life, and even then only by pleading elderly fatigue, and by 'retiring' forthwith to his home at Knole in Kent, a gesture made less compelling by the fact that he had been largely 'retired' there for several years already; see Du Boulay, *Reg. Bourgchier,* 530–57, for his recent itinerary.

5. C. S. L Davies, 'Bishop John Morton, the Holy See and the Accession of Henry VII', *EHR* LII (1987), 2–30, esp. 14–15. For the significant hypothesis that Henry VII was inspired by continental examples during his exile to renew the religious authority and initiative of kingship, see A. Goodman, 'Henry VII and Christian Renewal', in K. Robbins (ed.), *Religion and Humanism* (Oxford, 1981), pp. 115–25.

6. R. Lovatt, 'A Collector of Apocryphal Anecdotes: John Blacman Revisited', in A. J. Pollard (ed.), *Property and Politics* (Gloucester, 1984), pp. 172–97; and 'John Blacman: Biographer of Henry VI', in R. H. C. Davis and J. M. Wallace-Hadrill (eds), *The Writing of History in the Middle Ages* (Oxford, 1981), pp. 415–44.

7. R. N. Swanson, *Universities, Academics and the Great Schism* (Cambridge, 1979), esp. pp. 109–12 (Nicholas Fakenham); see also M. Harvey, *Solutions to the Schism: A Study of some English Attitudes, 1378 to 1409* (St Ottilien, 1983).

8. A. B. Emden, *Biographical Dictionary of the University of Oxford to 1500* (Oxford, 1957), III, p. 1756, for John Bale's list of his works.

9. R. L. Storey, 'The Universities during the Wars of the Roses', in D. Williams (ed.), *England in the Fifteenth Century* (Woodbridge, 1987), pp. 315–28; and 'University and Government, 1430–1500', in J. I. Catto and R. Evans (eds), *History of the University of Oxford, II: Late Medieval Oxford* (Oxford, 1992), pp. 719–38.

10. Gregory, 158. Ive had his compensation after the change of dynasty, receiving the mastership of Whittington hospital, the most fashionable pulpit in London.

11. C. A. J. Armstrong, 'Inauguration Ceremonies', 55–6 (Neville); for the problem over three eminent 'Dr Goddards' at this time, see M. A. Hicks, *Clarence* (rev. edn, Bangor, 1992), p. 137; for Shaa, see Mancini, pp. 94, 128–9 and refs, and *Great Chronicle*, 231–2.

12. *Warkworth*, 12. The chronicler was well-liked by William Grey, bishop of Ely, who was in sanctuary at this time as Edward IV's chancellor, and had been with him at least once in London in this crisis-year (Cambridge UL: Reg. William Grey (Ely) fo. 92).

13. S. B. Chrimes, *English Constitutional Ideas in the Fifteenth Century* (Cambridge, 1936), pp. 167–91. Cf. Mancini, p. 83 for Gloucester's development of much the same theme before a nervous royal council. Russell's 'laborious' style is criticised by Pronay and Cox (*Crowland*, 88) who perhaps have a low boredom threshold. The bishop's itinerary from his register (Lincoln DRO), if sometimes difficult to establish, suggests a chancellor with an unusual degree of opportunity to spend time in his diocese.

14. J. M. George Jnr, 'The English Episcopate and the Crown, 1437–1450' (Columbia University Ph.D. thesis, 1976), is excellent; cf. L. R. Betcherman, 'The Making of Bishops in the Lancastrian Period', *Speculum*, 41 (1966), 413–8; J. T. Rosenthal, 'The Training of an Elite Group: English Bishops in the Fifteenth Century', *Transactions of the American Philosophical Society*, n.s., 60, part 5 (1970), esp. p. 49; R. G. Davies, 'The Attendance of the Episcopate in English Parliaments, 1376–1461', *Proceedings of the American Philosophical Society*, 129, part 1 (1985), 48–9, 66–8.

15. R. A. Griffiths, 'The King's Council and the First Protectorate of the Duke of York, 1450–1454', *EHR*, 99 (1984), 318, with some uncharacteristic and unjustified spleen towards the bishops' pleas of diocesan conscience: at least four had a sound record to plead.

16. E. g. T. Wright (ed.), *Political Poems and Songs*, II (RS, 1861), pp. 232–4; *Rot Parl*, V, 216–7; T. Gascoigne, *Loci e Libro Veritatum*, pp. 193–4.

17. R. J. Knecht, 'The Episcopate and the Wars of the Roses', *University of Birmingham Historical Journal*, 6 (1957–8), 117; R. G. Davies, 'The Episcopate and the Readeption of Henry VI' (forthcoming). Cf.

R. M. Haines, 'Aspects of the Episcopate of John Carpenter, Bishop of Worcester, 1444–1476', *JEccH*, 19 (1968), 11–40; and 'The Practice and Problems of a fifteenth-century English Bishop: the Episcopate of William Gray', *Mediaeval Studies*, 34 (1972), pp. 435–45. The Canterbury and York Society has published few episcopal registers from this period: some are very fine.

18. G. I. Keir, 'The Ecclesiastical career of George Neville, 1432–1476' (University of Oxford B. Litt. thesis, 1970), is superb; see also Emden, *Oxford*, II, pp. 1347–9; R. B. Dobson, 'Richard III and the Church of York', in R. A. Griffiths and J. Sherborne (eds), *Kings and Nobles in the Later Middle Ages* (Gloucester, 1986), pp. 133–5.

19. *Warkworth*, 24–6. Borthwick Institute, York: Reg. G. Neville, vol. II, leaves some doubt whether, for all his early death, his health really was ruined by imprisonment. In 1475, for example, (fo. 8r–v) he travelled from Bisham to Westminster in June and thence to Calais in August and September, back to Westminster, to Bisham for Christmas, then back to Westminster once more. His putative appearance in Gloucester in May 1474 requires a second opinion.

20. R. J. Knecht, 'Episcopate', 109–31.

21. See Du Boulay *Reg. Bourgchier*, vii–xxiii; C. L. Scofield, *Edward the Fourth*, 2 vols (1923), I, p. 23, naturally saw through him.

22. A. J. Pollard, *North-East England during the Wars of the Roses* (Oxford, 1990), pp. 146–9, 267–8, 294–7, 329–31; and, 'St Cuthbert and the Hog', in *Kings and Nobles*, 114–5; Knecht, 'Episcopate', 115–6.

23. There is no good modern biography, but C. S. L. Davies, 'Bishop John Morton', is excellent for the period in hand.

24. Knecht, 'Episcopate', covers most of what follows.

25. Cambridge, Corpus Christi College Ms. 170, p. 216 (no. 167).

26. J. H. Parry and A. T. Bannister (eds), *Registrum Johannis Stanbury* (Canterbury and York Soc., 1919), pp. 55–7.

27. J. le Neve, *Fasti Ecclesiae Anglicanae, 1300–1541, XI: Welsh Dioceses*, ed. B. Jones (1965), pp. 38–9, 55; Emden, *Oxford*, I, pp. 191, 557.

28. Cambridge, Corpus Christi College Ms. 170, pp. 229–33 (nos. 184, 185, 187). None the less, Chedworth remained active in his last years. That he was at Oxford throughout the period of the Lincolnshire rebellion is interesting but unremarkable, because he was often there for long stays. His register (Lincoln DRO) shows that he did make a trip from Oxford to London and back in August 1470 and was in London constantly (apart from a Christmas trip home) from October 1470 to July 1471, possibly under a cloud in the last weeks.

29. A. B. Hinds (ed.), *Calendar of State Papers Milan* (1912), pp. 164–5, 169.

30. E. E. Barker (ed.), *Reg. T. Rotherham (York)*, I (Canterbury and York Soc., 1976), p. 73.

31. D. Hay, *Polydore Vergil* (Oxford, 1952), pp. 79–168.

32. A. R. Myers, 'The Captivity of a Royal Witch', *BJRL*, 24 (1940), 263–84, and 26, 82–100 (Joan of Navarre); R. A. Griffiths, 'The Trial of Eleanor Cobham', *BJRL*, 51 (1969), pp. 381–99; I. M. W. Harvey, *Jack Cade's Rebellion of 1450* (Oxford, 1991), p. 98.

33. *Rot Parl*, VI, p. 241.

34. Hicks, *Clarence*, 133–40.

35. J. M. Thielmann, 'Political Canonization and Political Symbolism in Medieval England', *Journal of British Studies*, 29 (1990), 241–66; J. R. Bray, 'Concepts of Sainthood in Fourteenth-century England', *BJRL*, 66(ii) (1984), esp. pp. 51–65.

36. P. McNiven, 'Rebellion, Sedition and the Legend of Richard II's Survival in the Reigns of Henry IV and Henry V', *BJRL*, 76 (1994), 93–117, esp. pp. 111–12, 115.

37. J. W. McKenna, 'Popular Canonization and Political Propaganda: the Cult of Archbishop Scrope', *Speculum*, 45 (1970), 608–23.

38. J. W. McKenna, 'Piety and Propaganda: the Cult of Henry VI', in B. Rowland (ed.), *Chaucer and Middle English Studies* (1974), pp. 72–88.

39. Dobson, 'Richard III and the Church of York', 130–1.

40. A. Payne, 'The Salisbury Roll of Arms of c.1463', in D. Williams (ed.), *England in the Fifteenth Century* (Woodbridge, 1987), p. 187 n. 3, lists the various accounts.

41. Scofield, *Edward IV*, I, 268–9; II, 167–8.

42. *Rot Parl*, V, pp. 182–3.

43. G. L. and M. A. Harriss (eds), 'John Benet's Chronicle for the Year 1400 to 1462', in *Camden Miscellany*, XXIX (Camden, 1972), p. 201; Gregory, 193.

44. P. A. Johnson, *Duke Richard of York* (Oxford, 1988), pp. 110–12.

45. C. A. J. Armstrong, 'Politics and the Battle of St Albans, 1455', *BIHR*, 33 (1960), 23, 28.

46. V. Davis, *William Waynflete* (Woodbridge, 1994); and 'William Waynflete and the Wars of the Roses', *Southern History*, 11 (1989), 1–22. Dr Davis's view of her bishop is very different.

47. *English Chronicle*, 77 (actually taken from the *Brut* at this point); Davis, 'William Waynflete', 3; J. Gairdner (ed.), *Paston Letters*, 6 vols (1904), III, p. 127 (no. 366, John Bocking to Sir John Fastolf, 15 March 1458) – 'my lord of Canterbury takith grete peyne up on hym daily'.

48. *Rot Parl*, V, 281; Du Bouley, *Reg. Bourgchier*, 78–93; *English Chronicle*, 94.

49. For detail of what follows, H. T. Riley (ed.), *Registrum Abbatiae Johannis Whethamstede Abbati Monasterii Sancti Albani*, 2 vols (RS, 1872–3), I, pp. 372–3; J. Gairdner (ed.), *Three Fifteenth-century Chronicles* (Camden Society, New Series, XXVIII, 1880), p. 153; Knecht, 'Episcopate', 112 and n. 25; Scofield, *Edward IV*, I, pp. 87–8; R. A. Griffiths, *The Reign of Henry VI* (1981), pp. 863–9.

50. G. E. Caspary, 'The Deposition of Richard II and the Canon Law', in S. Kuttner and J. J. Ryan (eds), *Proceedings of the Second International Congress of Medieval Canon Law* (Washington DC, 1965), pp. 189–201.

51. C. Head, 'Pope Pius II and the Wars of the Roses', *Archivum Historiae Pontificiae*, 8 (1970), 139–78; M. Harvey, *England, Rome and the Papacy, 1417–64* (Manchester, 1993), pp. 193–206.

52. Hicks, *Clarence*, 44–5. Archbishop Neville was, of course, at the centre of the intrigue. Less predictably, Bishop Thomas Kemp of

London, the late cardinal's nephew, lent personal support, as to much else in the Readeption period to come (Guildhall Library, London: Reg. T. Kemp fos. 117v–8v).

53. *Rot Parl*, VI, 100–1; *Crowland*, 133.

54. *Crowland*, 174–5.

55. *Rot Parl*, VI, 240; *Crowland*, 168–71, 'even though that lay court was not empowered to determine on it ... nevertheless it presumed to do so and did so on account of the great fear'. See M. O'Regan, 'The Precontract and its Effect on the Succession in 1483', and A. Sutton, 'Richard III's 'tytylle and right': A New Discovery', in J. Petrie (ed.), *Richard III: Crown and People* (Gloucester, 1985), pp. 54–5, 59–60.

56. A. Goodman, *John of Gaunt* (1992), pp. 73–4; L. C. Hector and B. F. Harvey (eds), *Westminster Chronicle* (Oxford, 1982), pp. 310–13, 324–7 (Tresilian).

57. J. S. Roskell, 'Sir William Oldhall', in his *Parliament and Politics in Medieval England*, II (1981), p. 192.

58. R. A. Griffiths, 'Local Rivalries and National Politics', *Speculum*, 43 (1968), 620 and n. 158; T. B. Pugh, 'Richard, Duke of York, and the Rebellion of Henry Holand, Duke of Exeter, in May 1454', *HR*, 63 (1990), 256.

59. Scofield, *Edward IV*, I, 541. A. L. Bannister (ed.), *Reg. T. Milling (Hereford)* (Canterbury and York Soc., 1920), esp. p. 33, tracks the abbot's continuing service and affection.

60. *Warkworth*, 20; Reg. W. Grey, fo. 82v; Knecht, 'Episcopate', 117–8; see also Davies, 'Episcopate and Readeption'.

61. *Arrivall*, 22.

62. Scofield, *Edward IV*, I, 587–8; *Warkworth*, 18–19, 'whiche uppone trust of the kynges pardone yeven in the same chirche the saturday, abode their stille, where thei myght have gone and savyd ther lyves'; *Arrivall*, 30–1, 'he gave [many of the rebels] his fre pardon, albe it there ne was, ne had nat at any tyme bene grauntyd, any fraunchise to that place for ony offenders agaynst ther prince ... ', but thereafter executed other offenders whom he had *not* pardoned.

63. The best summary is in R. E. Horrox, *Richard III: A Study of Service* (Cambridge, 1989), pp. 116–7; Mancini, 88–9; *Great Chronicle*, 231; *Crowland*, 158–9.

64. J. A. F. Thomson, 'Bishop Lionel Woodville and Richard III', *BIHR*, 59 (1986), 1305; see also, Storey, 'University and Government', 116–7; R. C. Hairsine, 'Oxford University and the Life and Legend of Richard III', in Petrie, *Richard III*, 315–16; R. E. Horrox and P. W. Hammond (eds), *BL Harley 433* (Gloucester, 1980) II, pp. 59, 92, 177, III, pp. 1, 123–4; *Calendar of Patent Rolls, 1476–85*; p. 387.

65. P. I. Kaufman, 'Henry VII and Sanctuary', *Church History*, 53 (1984), 469 and n. 16; C. H. Williams, 'The Rebellion of Humphrey Stafford in 1486', *EHR*, 43 (1928), 181–9.

66. H. C. Maxwell-Lyte (ed.), *Reg. Robert Stillington* (Somerset Rec. Soc., 52, 1937), pp. xi–xii; W. E. Hampton, 'The Later Career of Robert Stillington', in Petrie, *Richard III*, 161–5.

67. Succinct rehearsals are to be found in Storey, 'University and Government', 738–40; Hairsine, 'Oxford University', 320–3; and Maxwell-Lyte, *Reg. Stillington*, xii–xiii.

68. Kaufman, 'Henry VII and Sanctuary', 465–76; R. J. Rodes, *Lay Authority and Reformation in the English Church* (Notre Dame, 1982), pp. 32–3.

69. J. A. F. Thomson, '"The Well of Grace": Englishmen and Rome in the Fifteenth Century', in R. B. Dobson (ed.), *Church, Politics and Patronage* (Gloucester, 1984), pp. 99–114.

70. F. R. H. Du Boulay, 'The Fifteenth Century', in C. H. Lawrence (ed.), *The English Church and the Papacy in the Middle Ages* (London, 1965), pp. 195–242; Harvey, *England, Rome and the Papacy*; J. A. F. Thomson, *Popes and Princes, 1417–1517* (1980); Heath, *Church and Realm*, 293–6, 305–8; Swanson, *Church and Society*, 11–16; W. E. Lunt, *Financial Relations of the Papacy with England, 1327–1534* (Cambridge Ma., 1962), pp. 133–52; A. N. E. D. Schofield, 'England and the Council of Basel', *Annuarium Historiae Conciliorum*, 5(i) (1973), pp. 1–117.

71. Harvey, *England, Rome and the Papacy*, 171–206; Lunt, *Financial Relations*, 133–53. See also A. McHardy, 'Clerical Taxation in Fifteenth-century England: the Clergy as Agents of the Crown', in Dobson, *Church, Politics and Patronage*, 168–92, and Heath, *Church and Realm*, 303–5, 336–7, for illustrations of the thin, but consistent, grants of taxation to both the rival dynasties.

72. Head, 'Pius II', passim; Harvey, *England, Rome and the Papacy*, 193–206.

73. Storey, 'University and Government', 721–34.

74. du Boulay, *Reg. Bourgchier*, xxii; Cambridge, Corpus Christi College, Ms. 170 (Letterbook of N. Collys), pp. 217, 219, 220.

8. THE WARS OF THE ROSES IN EUROPEAN CONTEXT   *C. S. L. Davies*

1. Bernard Guenée, *States and Rulers in later Medieval Europe* (Eng. transl., Oxford, 1985), pp. 108–9.

2. Richard Vaughan, *Valois Burgundy* (1975), pp. 102–3.

3. David Potter, *War and Government in the French Provinces: Picardy, 1470–1560* (Cambridge, 1993), p. 19.

4. K. B. McFarlane, 'The Wars of the Roses', *Proceedings of the British Academy*, L (1964), repr. in his *England in the Fifteenth Century: Collected Essays* (Oxford, 1981), pp. 254, 256–7; Simon Walker shows that, far from joining his other lord, Clarence, as McFarlane implied, Vernon kept out of the way at Derby; 'Autorité des Magnats et Pouvoir de la "Gentry"', in P. Contamine (ed.), *L'état et les Aristocracies* (Paris, 1989), pp. 189, 202.

5. M. G. A. Vale, *Charles VII* (1974), pp. 157–8; S. H. Cuttler, *The Law of Treason in later Medieval France* (Cambridge, 1981), pp. 210–11.

6. G. L. Harriss, 'The Struggle for Calais', *EHR*, 75 (1960), 30–53; Caroline M. Barron, 'London and the Crown, 1451–61', in

J. R. L. Highfield and Robin Jeffs (eds), *The Crown and the Local Communities* (1981), pp. 88–109; J. L. Bolton, 'The City and the Crown, 1456–61', *London Journal*, 12 (1986), 11–24.

7. Ralph A. Griffiths, *The Reign of Henry VI* (1981), pp. 814–15 (letter from Charles VII to James II).

8. Ibid., pp. 815, 846 n. 262; Bertram Wolffe, *Henry VI* (1981), pp. 314–15.

9. Cora L. Scofield, *Edward IV*, 2 vols (1923), 1, pp. 162, 179–80, 188.

10. Vale, *Charles VII*, 171; Vaughan, *Valois Burgundy*, 53.

11. Scofield, *Edward IV*, 1, 159–60.

12. Margaret Harvey, *England, Rome, and the Papacy, 1417–1464* (Manchester, 1993), pp. 193–213. See also R. G. Davies, above pp. 157–9.

13. Charles Ross, *Edward IV* (1974), pp. 105–6, 359–65, 377–8. See also R. H. Britnell, above pp. 44–6.

14. Scofield, *Edward IV*, 65, 96; Richard Vaughan, *Charles the Bold* (1973), p. 61.

15. Christine Weightman, *Margaret of York: Duchess of Burgundy* (Gloucester, 1989); Mark Ballard, 'Anglo-Burgundian Relations, 1464–72' (University of Oxford, D.Phil. thesis, 1992).

16. T. H. Lloyd, *England and the German Hanse, 1157–1611* (Cambridge, 1991), pp. 200–3.

17. The first recorded meeting between Warwick and Charles appears to have been in 1466, although they had certainly exchanged gifts in 1457; the suggestion that their enmity dated from 1460 relates to Charles's close dealings with Somerset when Somerset was trying to wrest Calais from Warwick; Scofield, *Edward IV*, I, 65, 96. For Rouen, ibid., I, 424–5, and Paul Murray Kendall, *Warwick the Kingmaker* (1957), pp. 201–5.

18. J. Calmette and G. Périnelle, *Louis XI et l'Angleterre, 1461–83* (Paris, 1930), p. 124; Scofield, *Edward IV*, 1, pp. 556–7, 560–3.

19. Ross, *Edward IV*, 160; Vaughan, *Charles the Bold*, 71.

20. Lloyd, *England and the Hanse*, 207–17, authoritatively challenges the usual view of a sell-out by Edward IV.

21. For Flemish and other soldiers, see P. W. Hammond, *The Battles of Barnet and Tewkesbury* (Gloucester, 1990), p. 141. A detailed study of London in 1470–1 is badly needed.

22. Thomas Basin, quoted by P. Contamine, *Des Pouvoirs en France, 1300–1500* (Paris, 1992), pp. 81–2.

23. See the story of Commynes persuading Louis to grant a pension of 2,000 crowns to Lord Hastings; Commynes had dealt with Hastings when he served Charles, who had paid him 1,000 crowns. Hastings distinguished himself by refusing to give Louis a receipt, although he had provided one for Charles. See Philippe de Commynes, *Memoirs*, ed. and transl. Michael Jones (Harmondsworth, 1972), pp. 359–61, and the comment by D. A. L. Morgan in David Starkey (ed.), *The English Court from the Wars of the Roses to the Civil War* (1987), p. 61.

24. Vaughan, *Charles the Bold*, pp. 346–51; Ross, *Edward IV*, 224–31; Contamine, *Pouvoirs*, pp. 87–98.

25. M. A. Hicks, *False, Fleeting, Perjur'd Clarence* (Gloucester, 1980), pp. 130–4; Weightman; *Margaret of Burgundy*, pp. 105–18, 127–30.

26. Scofield, *Edward IV*, II, p. 185; Weightman, *Margaret of Burgundy*, p. 109.

27. Ralph A. Griffiths and Roger S. Thomas, *The Making of the Tudor Dynasty* (Gloucester, 1985), pp. 75–88.

28. C. S. L. Davies, 'Richard III, Brittany, and Henry Tudor, 1483–1485', *Nottingham Medieval Studies*, 37 (1993), 1–18.

29. See the remarks of the Chancellor of France to the States-General in 1484, and other French opinions, quoted by C. A. J. Armstrong in his introduction to Mancini, 22–4.

30. Griffiths and Thomas, *Making of the Tudor Dynasty*, pp. 117–31; A. V. Antonovics, 'Henry VII, King of England, "By the Grace of Charles VIII of France"', in Ralph A. Griffiths and James Sherborne (eds), *Kings and Nobles in the Later Middle Ages: a Tribute to Charles Ross* (Gloucester and New York, 1986), pp. 169–84. Chastellain had made a similar claim for Philip of Burgundy after Towton; Scofield, *Edward IV*, 1, p. 160. The usual estimate is that the invading force was about 4,000 men, the great majority French or Scots; see, for instance, Alexander Grant, 'Foreign Affairs under Richard III', John Gillingham (ed.), *Richard III: A Medieval Kingship* (1993), pp. 127–30. However, seven ships would total about 500 tons, enough to transport about 700 soldiers; even if the fleet were larger than this, and if no horses were shipped, it seems unlikely that the force could have been much over 1,000 men, of which about 500 would be English exiles. Seven ships were sent to England in 1485 to transport a promised force of 1,000 archers to Brittany; see Davies, 'Richard III, Brittany and Henry Tudor', 111. I am grateful to Dr Anne Curry for her advice, based on her 'Military Organisation in Lancastrian Normandy, 1422–1450' (CNAA/Teesside Polytechnic Ph.D. thesis, 1985).

31. Michael Bennett, *Lambert Simnel and the Battle of Stoke* (Gloucester, 1987).

32. Weightman, *Margaret of York*, 169–81. For the argument that Margeret may have been involved as early as 1491, see Mark Ballard and C. S. L. Davies, 'Étienne Fryon: Burgundian Agent, English Royal Secretary, and "Principal Counsellor" to Perkin Warbeck', *HR*, 62 (1989), 245–59. See also I. Arthurson, *The Perkin Warbeck Conspiracy, 1491–99* (Stroud, 1994).

33. David Dunlop, 'The "Masked Comedian"; Perkin Warbeck's Adventures in Scotland from 1495 to 1497', *Scottish Historical Review*, 70 (1991), 97–128.

34. S. B. Chrimes, *Henry VII* (1972), pp. 92–4.

35. R. B. Wernham, *Before the Armada* (1966), pp. 32–7; J. D. Mackie, *The Earlier Tudors* (Oxford, 1952), pp. 81–111; Chrimes, *Henry VII*, pp. 277–82.

36. The possible emergence of a 'German' political system, with the King of France no more powerful than the Emperor, normally discounted, implicitly at least, by historians of France, is considered by Emmanuel le Roy Ladurie, *The French Royal State, 1460–1610* (Eng. transl. Oxford, 1994), pp. 60–3.

37. Alexander Grant, 'Foreign Affairs', 114–15, 130–1, argues that the shift in the balance made English threats problematic, and explains Edward IV's calling off of the 1475 invasion.

38. Ranald Nicholson, *Scotland the Later Middle Ages* (Edinburgh, 1974), pp. 347–8.

39. *Ibid.*, pp. 393–4; A. J. Pollard, *North-Eastern England during the Wars of the Roses* (Oxford, 1990), p. 223.

40. Nicholson, *Scotland*, 394–406; Pollard, *North-Eastern England*, 223–30.

41. Nicholson, *Scotland*, pp. 472–8; Pollard, *North-Eastern England*, 231–2. 'Great Britain' appears in the Treaty of Edinburgh of 1474, an unusual usage in the fifteenth century ('Britain' was normally used in a historical context rather than in reference to present-day reality), though it was to be common among advocates of political union in the sixteenth century.

42. Nicholson, *Scotland*, 489–517; Pollard, *North-Eastern England*, 235–44; Norman Macdougall, *James III: a Political Study* (Edinburgh, 1982), pp. 140–83; 208–14.

43. Nicholson, *Scotland*, 518–19; Macdougall, *James III*, 215–17.

44. Nicholson, *Scotland*, 549–55; Norman Macdougall, *James IV* (Edinburgh, 1989), pp 112–46; Pollard, *North-Eastern England*, 393–6; Dunlop, 'Masked Comedian'.

45. Anthony Goodman and David Morgan, 'The Yorkist Claim to the Throne of Castile', *Journal of Medieval History*, 11 (1985), 61–9.

46. In contrast to Pius II in 1460–1, Pope Innocent VIII in 1485 looked to French support in Italian politics; and this at least partly explains his marked favour to Henry VII after Bosworth. See C. S. L. Davies, 'Bishop John Morton, the Holy See, and the Accession of Henry VII', *EHR*, 102 (1987), 1–30.

9. THE VISUAL CULTURE OF FIFTEENTH-CENTURY ENGLAND
Colin Richmond

1. Neil Ker, *Medieval Manuscripts in British Libraries*, III (Oxford, 1983), pp. 165–6. Compare the donor folios 2v–3r in Fitzwilliam Museum MS 34, a missal made in England at the same date for Richard (d. 1479) and Elizabeth Fitzwilliam, 'stiff and even coarse in execution', according to M. R. James, *Catalogue of Fitzwilliam Museum Manuscripts* (Cambridge, 1895), I, p. 88.

2. Janet Backhouse, 'Founders of the Royal Library: Edward IV and Henry VII as Collectors of Illuminated Manuscripts'; Jenny Stratford, 'The Manuscripts of John, Duke of Bedford: Library and Chapel'; Nicholas Rogers, 'Fitzwilliam Museum MS 3–1979: A Bury St Edmunds Book of Hours and the Origins of the Bury Style'; and Pamela Tudor-Craig, 'The Hours of Edward V and William Lord Hastings: British Library Additional Manuscript 54782', all in David Williams (ed.),

England in the Fifteenth Century: Proceedings of the 1986 Harlaxton Symposium (Woodbridge, 1987).

3. The frontispiece of the Ghent Register is described by Wim Blockmans, 'The Devotion of a Lonely Duchess', in Thomas Kren (ed.), *Margaret of York, Simon Marmion, and the Visions of Tondal* (The J. Paul Getty Museum, Malibu, California, 1992), pp. 37–9, and is illustrated at figure 8. I have not found the two frontispieces compared before; comparison might readily be made: the Luton Register is in the Luton Museum and the Ghent Register is in the Royal Library at Windsor. The frontispiece of the Luton Guild Register is illustrated in A. J. Pollard, *Richard III and the Princes in the Tower* (Stroud, 1991), p. 94, which is where I first came upon it.

4. I am deeply grateful to Mr John Lunn of Dunstable for taking me to Luton Museum to show me the two registers and for discussing them with me. Both deserves to be far more widely known.

5. Thomas Kipping, draper of London, who was a founder member of the Luton guild, owned and imported manuscripts. Mr Lunn believes that it was Thomas Kipping who was responsible for getting the frontispiece of the Luton Register illuminated in the highest-class workshop of the Netherlands. For Kipping, see Kathleen L. Scott (ed.), *The Mirroure of the Worlde: Bodley 283* (Roxburghe Club, 1980), ch. III. That is a reference I owe to the kindness of Mr Lunn. The next I owe to that of Dr Philip Morgan: Kathleen L. Scott, *The Caxton Master and his Patrons* (Cambridge Bibliographical Society Monograph, No. 8, 1976).

6. Malcolm Vale, 'Cardinal Henry Beaufort and the "Albergati" Portrait', *EHR*, cv (1990), 338–54.

7. Colin Thompson and Lorne Campbell, *Hugo van der Goes and the Trinity Panels in Edinburgh* (National Gallery of Scotland, 1974); K. B. McFarlane, *Hans Memling* (Oxford, 1971).

8. For all but the Withypoll altarpiece, which is in Bristol Museum and Art Gallery, see Christa Grössinger, *North-European Panel Paintings: A Catalogue of Netherlandish and German Paintings before 1600 in English Churches and Colleges* (1992). Ms Grössinger has also written an article on the Sherborne altarpiece: 'The Raising of Lazarus: a French Primitive in Sherborne, Dorset', *Journal of the British Archaeological Association*, cxxxii (1979), 91–101. For the royal chantry chapel at All Hallows, see *The Parish of All Hallows Barking* (Survey of London, XII, Part I, 1929), pp. 9–17. For Paul Withypoll, see G. C. Moore Smith, *The Family of Withypoll* (Walthamstow Antiquarian Society, Official Publication No. 34, 1936), pp. 13–23.

9. M. Davies, *Early Netherlandish School* (National Gallery Catalogues, 1968), p. 55; Anne Sutton, 'Christian Colborne, Painter of Germany and London, died 1486', *Journal of the British Archaeological Association*, 135 (1982), 56.

10. Gilbert Thurlow, *The Medieval Painted Retables in Norwich Cathedral* (Norwich, n.d.), p. 2; Pamela Tudor-Craig, *Richard III* (National Portrait Gallery, 1973), pp. 19–20.

11. William Dugdale, *The Antiquities of Warwickshire* (Coventry, 1730), I, pp. 446–7. A good idea of John Brentwood's Doom, which no longer

exists, may be had from that over the chancel arch in St Thomas's church, Salisbury, although the latter dates from thirty or forty years later.

12. Tudor-Craig, *Richard III*, 20–1.

13. P. Tudor-Craig, 'Painting in Medieval England', in Nigel Saul (ed.), *Age of Chivalry* (1992), p. 116.

14. Mention ought to be made of the late fifteenth-century donor priest at Romsey; he is all that survives of a wall painting from a chantry of St George. And of the early fifteenth-century crucifixion, which I have not seen, in the refectory of the Charterhouse at Coventry; there is, apparently, an inscription of 1415: N. Pevsner and Alexandra Wedgwood, *The Buildings of England: Warwickshire* (1966), *sub* Cheylesmore.

15. One of the striking exceptions is what remains of the rood screen at Binham Priory, Norfolk. The screen, as the guide book by Donald Insall tells us, 'was painted over at the Reformation with black-letter texts from the Tyndale and Coverdale translations of the Bible, but the original saints are now showing through'. It is a somewhat startling, even moving, sight, and would have pleased Leonardo da Vinci, who said that pictures were more powerful than words.

16. The first authority is G. R. Owst, 'Some Books and Book-Owners of Fifteenth-Century St Albans', *Transactions of the St Albans and Hertfordshire Architectural and Archaeological Society* (1928) pp. 194–5. The second is Arthur Hind, *An Introduction to a History of Woodcut*, vol. II (New York, 1935, reprinted 1963), p. 707.

17. Richard Field, *Fifteenth-Century Woodcuts* (Metropolitan Museum of Art, New York, 1977), introduction.

18. Susan Foister, 'Paintings and Other Works of Art in Sixteenth-Century English Inventories', *The Burlington Magazine*, CXXIII (1981), p. 276; Malcolm Underwood, 'Politics and Piety in the Household of Lady Margaret Beaufort', *JEccH*, 38 (1987), p. 49.

19. Lynda Rollason, 'English Alabasters in the Fifteenth Century', in Williams, *England in the Fifteenth Century*, 245–54.

20. S. E. Rigold and E. Clive Rouse, 'Piccotts End: A Probable Medieval Guest House and its Wall Paintings', *Hertfordshire Archaeology*, III (1973), 78–89.

21. I am grateful for the help of Brian Spencer. To find the picture in the museum I needed it: the picture, as Mr Spencer says, 'is exhibited very obscurely at the back of a cubbyhole in which we display two or three bits of medieval furniture'. For the house, see *Parish of Hackney, Part I: Brooke House* (Survey of London, XXVIII, 1960).

22. E. Clive Rouse, 'Elizabethan Wall Paintings at Little Moreton Hall', *National Trust Studies 1980* (1979), 113–18; *Proceedings of the Suffolk Institute of Archaeology*, XXIII (1939), 181–2; XXIX (1963), 345–7.

23. M. Hicks, *Richard III and His Rivals* (1991), pp. 107–10.

24. James M. Clark, *The Dance of Death in the Middle Ages and the Renaissance* (1950).

25. *Religions et traditions populaires* (Musée national des arts et traditions populaires, Paris, 1979); Lenz Kriss-Rettenbeck, *Bilden und Zeichen religiösen Volksglaubens* (Munich, 1963); Larch S. Garrad, *A Present from …*

Holiday Souvenirs of the British Isles (Newton Abbot, 1976); for the description of the shrines of St Chad in 1445 I am grateful to Mr Douglas Johnson: I have quoted his transcription of the eighteenth-century transcription in Shrewsbury Public Library, MS 2, ff. 92 and 94.

26. E. K. Chambers, *English Literature at the Close of the Middle Ages* (Oxford, 1945), pp. 125–6.

27. Sleaford Trinity Guild Accounts: BL Additional MS 28533, fs 2, 3v; Rev. David McRoberts, 'The Fetternear Banner', *Innes Review*, 7 (1956), 69–86; Shrewsbury Weavers: National Library of Wales, Castle Hill MSS, no. 2637; Norwich Almanack: BL Egerton MS 2724; Cameron Lewis (ed.), *The Commonplace Book of Robert Reynes of Acle. An Edition of Tanner MS 407* (Garland Medieval Texts, Number I, New York and London, 1980), pp. 169 and 295.

28. Bertram Wolffe, *Henry VI* (1981), ch. 8; cf. A. H. R. Martindale, 'The Early History of the Choir of Eton College Chapel', *Archaeologia*, CIII (1971), 179–98; Nikolaus Pevsner, *The Englishness of English Art* (1956), p. 187.

29. Charles Ross, *Richard III* (1981), p. 132; N. Pevsner, *The Buildings of England. London I. The Cities of London and Westminster* (1957), p. 348; W. H. St John Hope, *Windsor Castle*, vol. I (1913), plates XX and XXI; Andrew Hamilton, *Nottingham's Royal Castle* (Nottingham, n.d.), p. 15; A. D. K. Hawkyard, 'Thornbury Castle', *Transactions of the Bristol and Gloucestershire Archaeological Society*, XCV (1977), 51–8. None the less, Henry VII's particular brand of pretentiousness is disclosed by an examination of his indenture with Canterbury Cathedral Priory for the prayers of the monks; the indenture is dated 20 November 1504, has an illuminated first page very like work done for John Islip, abbot of Westminster, who is a party to the indenture, and is bound in wooden boards covered in blue velvet, decorated with brass portcullises and roses, with two handsome clasps which are still functioning. I wish to thank the staff of the Cathedral Archives for finding the indenture for me during a busy Cricket Week; its call number is DCC/Ch.Ant. W48a. I first came upon it in Sally Rousham, *Canterbury: The Story of a Cathedral* (Canterbury, 1975), p. 4, fig. 3. It should be written about.

30. N. Pevsner, *The Buildings of England. North-West and South Norfolk* (1962), p. 308; Pevsner, *English Art*, 81 and 83.

31. N. Pevsner, *The Buildings of England. Cambridgeshire* (second edn, 1970), p. 367; Pevsner, *English Art*, 81.

32. Christopher Wilson, *The Shrines of St William of York* (Yorkshire Museum, 1977); *Painted Glass from Leicester* (Leicester Museums, 1962); Francis Cheetham, *English Medieval Alabasters* (Oxford, 1984), pp. 28–30, figs 17 and 33; Henry A. Hudson, *The Medieval Woodwork of Manchester Cathedral* (Manchester, 1924); J. C. D. Smith, *Church Woodcarvings: A West Country Study* (Newton Abbot, 1969); N. Pevsner, *The Buildings of England: Berkshire* (1966), p. 274; *The Buildings of England: Cheshire* (1971), p. 66.

33. Phillip Lindley, '"Una Grande Opera al mio Re": Gilt-Bronze Effigies in England from the Middle Ages to the Renaissance', *Journal of the British Archaeological Association*, CXLIII (1990), 112–30; Carol Galvin

and Phillip Lindley, 'Pietro Torrigiano's Tomb for Dean Yonge', *Church Monuments*, III (1988), pp. 42–60.

34. PRO, PCC, Probate 11/19, f. 223 (28 Ayloffe).

35. *St Marks: The Lord Mayor's Chapel Bristol* (Bristol, 1979), pp. 18–19.

36. Christopher Woodforde, *The Norwich School of Glass-Painting in the Fifteenth Century* (Oxford, 1950), pp. 165–6. Other unusual English glass, depicting the life of St Helen, is to be found in Ashton-under-Lyne parish church, Lancashire: Henrietta Reddish, 'The St Helen Window, Ashton-under-Lyne: a Reconstruction', *Journal of Stained Glass*, XVIII (1986–7), 150–61.

37. It is illustrated in *Frühe Zeichnungen. L'Art Ancien S. A. Zürich. Katalog 54* (Zurich, n.d.), no. 3.

38. N. Pevsner (ed.), *The Buildings of England. Lincolnshire* (1964); Rev. R. W. M. Lewis, p. 300; *Walberswick Churchwardens' Accounts AD 1450–1499* (Ashford, 1947), p. vii; Helmingham: L. F. Salzman, *Building in England down to 1540: A Documentary History* (Oxford, 1952), Appendix B, no. 97; Thornham: PRO, Early Chancery Proceedings, C1/76/30.

39. Richard G. Davies, 'Lollardy and Locality', *TRHS*, 6th Ser., 1 (1991), 191–212.

40. J. Carnwath, 'The Churchwardens' Accounts of St Mary the Virgin, Thame (Oxon.) to 1524, (University of Manchester, M. Phil. thesis, 1992).

41. Jean Corke and others (eds), *Suffolk Churches* (Suffolk Historic Churches Trust, 1976), p. 16.

42. Norwich Record Office, NCC, Register 13 Brosyard.

43. 'The Library of John Blacman and Contemporary Carthusian Spirituality', *JEccH*, 43 (1992), pp. 195–230.

44. W. J. Loftie (ed.), *Ye Oldest Diarie of Englysshe Travell: being the hitherto unpublished narrative of the pilgrimage of Sir Richard Torkington to Jerusalem in 1517* (1884), cf. E. M. Blackie (ed.), *The Pilgrimage of Robert Langton* (Cambridge, Mass., 1924).

45. P. Heath, 'Between Reform and Reformation', *JEccH*, 41 (1990), 678.

46. Was William Pecock's the only original mind in fifteenth-century England? The measure of distance between him and, say, John Carpenter, clever and innovative after a fashion but an Establishment man through and through, is instructive, as is what the Establishment did to him. See, Margaret Aston, *Faith and Fire: Popular and Unpopular Religion, 1350–1600* (1993), pp. 87–93, esp. p. 93.

47. Peter Lewis, *Later Medieval France: The Polity* (1968), pp. 17–18.

48. The extremes are marked in the life of his father. In 1456 at Coventry Richard Woodville, Lord Rivers, watched the tableaux and pageants with Queen Margaret of Anjou and drank a glass of rosewater, which cost the mayor two shillings. Thirteen years later, his own daughter having become queen, he was beheaded on Gosford Green at Coventry: did he, or anyone else, remember the days of wine and rosewater? See M. D. Harris (ed.), *The Coventry Leet Book*, Part II (EETS, 1908), pp. 292, 346.

49. A. Gransden *Historical Writing in England, II, c. 1307 – the Early Sixteenth Century* (1986), Appendix A.

50. For Jan Długosz, see Harold B. Segel, *Renaissance Culture in Poland: The Rise of Humanism, 1470–1543* (Ithaca, 1989), p. 120; Henryk Samsonowicz (ed.), *Polska Jana Długosz* (Warsaw, 1984), *passim.* Jan wrote his twelve-volume *Annales seu cronicae incliti regni Poloniae* between 1455 and 1480.

Notes on Contributors

R. H. BRITNELL is Reader in History at the University of Durham. He has written extensively on the economic history of medieval England and is author of *Growth and Decline in Colchester, 1300–1640* (1986) and *The Commercialisation of English Society, 1000–1500* (1993). He is now preparing a general history of England between 1471 and 1529.

C. S. L. DAVIES is Fellow and Tutor of Wadham College and Lecturer in History at Oxford University. He is author of *Peace, Print and Protestantism, 1450–1558*, in the Paladin History of England (1977 and many reprints), and of several articles on Tudor social and political history. In recent years he has moved back to working on international aspects of late fifteenth-century history with a special interest in the Tudor rebellion of 1485.

RICHARD G. DAVIES is a Senior Lecturer in History at the University of Manchester. He has written extensively about relations between church and state in later medieval England, the episcopate and heresy in that period. He is co-editor of *The English Parliament in the Later Middle Ages* (1981) and *Trade, Devotion and Governance* (1994).

KEITH DOCKRAY recently took early retirement from his post as Senior Lecturer in Medieval and Early Modern History at the University of Huddersfield. He studied at the University of Bristol in the 1960s and undertook postgraduate research under the supervision of Charles Ross. Now back in Bristol as a freelance teacher and writer, he is the author of *Richard III: A Reader in History* (1988) and a range of articles on fifteenth-century England.

M. A. HICKS is Professor of History at King Alfred's College, Winchester. Many of his shorter pieces on fifteenth-century English political history have been brought together and published as *Richard III and His Rivals: Magnates and their Motives in the Wars of the Roses* (1991). He is the author of *False, Fleeting, Perjur'd Clarence* (1980) and *Richard III: The Man behind the Myth* (1991). His *Bastard Feudalism* has recently been published and he is currently working on a major study of Warwick the Kingmaker.

ROSEMARY HORROX is Fellow of Fitzwilliam College, Cambridge. She is author of many works on the political and social history of fifteenth-

251

century England including *Richard III: A Study of Service,* and most recently is editor of a collection of essays, *Fifteenth-Century Attitudes: Perceptions of Society in Late-medieval England,* for Cambridge University Press.

A. J. POLLARD is Professor of History at the University of Teesside. His field is the economic, social and political history of fifteenth-century England, especially the north. He is the author of *The Wars of the Roses* (1988) in the Macmillan British History in Perspective series and a detailed regional study, *North-Eastern England during the Wars of the Roses* (1990). He is currently writing the final volume in a new four-volume history of medieval England.

COLIN RICHMOND is Professor of History at the University of Keele. His interests lie in late-medieval social, cultural and political history. He is author of *John Hopton: A Suffolk Gentleman in the Fifteenth Century* (1981), and *The Paston Family in the Fifteenth Century: The First Phase* (1990). The second of his three-volume study of the Pastons is soon to be published.

JOHN L. WATTS is a lecturer in medieval history at the University of Wales, Aberystwyth. His first book, *The Rule of England in the Time of Henry VI,* is to be published at the same time as this volume. He is primarily interested in the interplay of ideas, politics and political structures in fourteenth- and fifteenth-century England.

Index

Wolffe, B. P., 32, 35, 78, 82–3,
   198
Woodcuts, 1923
Woodhouse, John, 20
Woodville, Anthony, lord Scales
   and earl Rivers, 17, 28, 40,
   152, 208
   Elizabeth, *see under* Elizabeth,
      queen of England
   family of, 58
   Lionel, bishop of Salisbury, 35,
      142, 152, 154
   Margaret, 202–3
   Richard, lord Rivers, 249
Worcester, bishopric of, 47, 53–4
   cathedral, 194, 200
   earl of, *see under* Tiptoft

Worcestershire, 52
Worcester, William, 27, 136, 209
Worsley, William, dean of St
   Paul's, 195
Wressle, 58
Wymondham, 90

York, 36, 57, 145, 154
   dukes of, *see under* Richard
   archbishop of, *see under*, Neville;
      Rotherham; Scrope
   minster, 144, 146, 198, 200
Yorkshire, 10, 11, 22, 66
Young, Thomas, 71

Zeeland, 165, 173

South East Essex College
of Arts & Technology
Camarvon Road Southend-on-Sea Essex SS2 6LS
Tel: (01702) 220400 Fax: (01702) 432320 Minicom: (01702) 220642